CREATIVE TEACHING:

ENGLISH IN THE EARLY YEARS AND PRIMARY CLASSROOM

Also available:

Creative Teaching: Science in the Early Years and Primary Classroom
Ann Oliver
1-84312-259-6

Creative Teaching: History in the Primary Classroom
Rosie Turner-Bisset
1-84312-115-8

CREATIVE TEACHING:
ENGLISH IN THE EARLY YEARS AND PRIMARY CLASSROOM

Chris Horner and Vicki Ryf

Routledge
Taylor & Francis Group

LONDON AND NEW YORK

First published 2007 by Routledge
2 Park Square, Milton Park, Abingdon, Oxon OX14 4RN

Simultaneously published in the USA and Canada
by Routledge
270 Madison Ave, New York, NY 10016

Reprinted 2008

Routledge is an imprint of the Taylor & Francis Group, an informa business

© 2007 Chris Horner and Vicki Ryf

Typeset by Refincatch Ltd, Bungay, Suffolk
Printed and bound in Great Britain by The Cromwell Press, Trowbridge, Wiltshire

British Library Cataloguing in Publication Data
A catalogue record for this book is available from the British Library

Library of Congress Cataloging in Publication Data
A catalog record for this book has been requested

ISBN10: 1 84312 260 X
ISBN13: 978 184312 260 9

Dedication

For Heidi and Florence

Contents

Acknowledgements

We would like to thank everyone who helped us to complete this book and, in particular, the creative input from Anna, Charlie, John, Frank, Giselle, James, Karma, Lucy, Paul and Zachary.

The authors and publisher gratefully acknowledge permission to publish copyright material as follows:

Penguin Group Children's Division (Puffin): 'Patterns on the beach' from *Five Furry Teddy Bears* by Linda Hammond (1990).

Mrs M. Harrison, for 'Alone in the Grange' by Gregory Harrison, from his *Night of the Wild Horses*, 1971, Oxford University Press.

Every effort has been made to obtain permission to use copyright material. The publisher would be happy to add any acknowledgement for any material for which permission has not been forthcoming in any future printing.

Introduction

In this introduction we set out what we mean by creativity and specifically what we mean by creativity in English. We also consider why there is a renewal of interest in the creative curriculum at this time and why a creative approach is important for learners and teachers.

What is creativity?

A useful starting point for defining creativity is *All Our Futures: Creativity, Culture and Education,* a report by the National Advisory Committee on Creative and Cultural Education (NACCCE 1999).

- Creativity involves thinking and behaving *imaginatively*.
- Second, overall this imaginative activity is *purposeful:* that is, it is directed to achieving an objective.
- Third, these processes must generate something *original*.
- Fourth, the outcome must be of *value* in relation to the objective.

The ideas that we present in this book provide practical examples of what these features look like in relation to the teaching of English, both within literacy lessons and through other areas of the curriculum.

As teachers we can encourage children to use their *imagination* by planning open-ended activities that recognise and build on their early language and literacy experiences; that enable them to question what is presented, make links with previous knowledge and respond in different ways. Creative English teaching allows children to interpret material or tasks in ways that the author or teacher had perhaps not envisaged. For example, appreciation or enjoyment of a poem might be expressed through art, dance or music. One child's interpretation may be very different to another's and by allowing children to explore a range of possibilities they may arrive at a deeper understanding.

1

In a creative environment, children engage in *purposeful* activities. The texts they encounter are relevant and challenging. The stories that children tell, the dramas they perform, the books that they write, the information they research and present have a wider audience than the teacher, although in some instances the audience may be the creator of the text itself. Creative teachers do not just share the learning objective with the children but may involve them in formulating it. The creative teacher recognises that incidental but equally important learning may have taken place outside the confines of the learning objective and will involve the children in self- and peer-assessment.

What do we mean by *originality* when considering the work that children produce in English? If children are encouraged to express their ideas and feelings and move beyond formulaic responses that are either 'right' or 'wrong', then they may demonstrate ideas that are *new to them*. They are behaving creatively.

As teachers we need to encourage children to critically evaluate the responses that they make, the work that they produce in relation to what they set out to achieve. An activity, response, artefact or solution is of *value* if it reflects worthwhile endeavour. It is important that children, however young, have the opportunity to discuss what it is they and other people value. Both what is produced and the effort that it entailed in relation to the individual child are important.

More recently, *Learning to Learn: Progression in Key Aspects of Learning* (DfES 2004b) set out some indicators of creative thinking, an important aspect of learning and one that runs through this book. These indicators reflect important features of both the early years and primary curriculum and are relevant to our focus on creativity in English. For these reasons we include them below:

Some indicators of creative thinking

Children may demonstrate that they can:

- generate imaginative ideas in response to stimuli;
- discover and make connections through play and experimentation;
- explore and experiment with resources and materials;
- ask 'why', 'how', 'what if' or unusual questions;
- try alternatives or different approaches;
- look at and think about things differently and from other points of view;
- respond to ideas, tasks and problems in surprising ways;
- apply imaginative thinking to achieve an objective;
- make connections and see relationships;
- reflect critically on ideas, actions and outcomes.

Throughout the age phase chapters we suggest how you might promote a creative learning environment and provide practical examples of activities that provide children with the opportunities to engage in creative thinking. Not all of these indicators will be evident in their response to any one activity but the establishment of a creative learning culture will ensure that children are willing to take risks in a supportive environment.

Why the interest in creativity now?

This book has been written eight years after the implementation of the National Literacy and Numeracy Strategies (1998) in Primary schools with their formidable list of objectives. While some teachers have worked imaginatively within the frameworks, others have felt disempowered by their prescriptive nature and have moved away from or not experienced a creative, cross-curricular approach, where children work collaboratively in an inclusive environment.

The introduction in 2003 of *Excellence and Enjoyment: A Strategy for Primary Schools* (DfES) signalled a change in government strategy which recognised the growing body of research from academics on the sterility of the standards curriculum and its effect on children's enjoyment of school and the deprofessionalisation felt by many teachers (for example see Pollard and Triggs 2000; Willis 2002; Hartley-Brewer 2001; Troman 2000). Coupled with this were the growing concerns voiced by a significant number of respected children's authors on the narrowness of the National Literacy Strategy and the damage it was inflicting on children's reading and writing for pleasure. Not only was NACCCE (1999) instrumental in raising the profile of creativity, Ofsted (2003) were also reporting on creative practice in schools which was evidenced where there were links between curriculum subjects and areas of learning and a focused engagement with the individual pupil.

Excellence and Enjoyment specifically invites teachers to take ownership of the curriculum and be creative and innovative in how they teach. It emphasises through its professional development materials *Excellence and Enjoyment: Learning and Teaching in the Primary Years* (DfES 2004a) three major themes:

- planning and assessment for learning
- creating a learning culture
- understanding how learning develops.

These themes underpin an approach to learning that puts the child at the heart of the curriculum and enables the teacher to be creative and imaginative in facilitating learning. Our understanding of how children learn and creating a learning culture are reflected in the overview to each section as well as in the age phase chapters themselves. In this book we promote the importance of talk, collaborative ways of working, interactive teaching and learning and inclusion of all learners through differentiation and scaffolding.

However, it is in this introductory chapter that we consider some of the generic issues relating to Assessment for Learning (AfL) across the age phases that inform the inclusive pedagogy that we believe encourages and supports the creative teaching and learning that we promote throughout this book.

Planning and assessment for learning

Assessment for learning (also known as formative assessment) is central to our philosophy of education. The key factors that permeate the practice that we describe are taken from Black and William (1998). These key factors are identified in *Excellence and Enjoyment: Learning and Teaching in the Primary Years: Planning and Assessment for Learning.*

- providing effective feedback to children

- actively involving children in their own learning

- adjusting teaching to take account of the results of assessment

- recognising the profound influence assessment has on the motivation and self-esteem of children, both of which are crucial to learning

- considering the need for chidren to be able to assess themselves and to understand how to improve.

(DfES 2004a:11)

The feedback that we give children should be part of a dialogue. It should reflect a genuine interest in the individual child's efforts and provide confirmation of what is good and discussion of areas that might be improved upon. It is not about providing external rewards or comparing one child's work with another. Although we believe that children should be aware of learning objectives and how they might be met, creative teaching and learning acknowledges that valuable learning may occur that is not planned for and that this needs to be recognised and valued.

Creative teachers provide opportunities for children to be involved in deciding what it is they need to learn. The KWFL grids that are discussed in later chapters are one way of encouraging children to reflect on what they already know (K) and decide what they want to find out (W). Setting individual targets in consultation with the children is another way of involving them in their learning. Providing some degree of autonomy on their preferred ways of working and some choice on how to present their work also encourages a creative approach to learning.

Listening and responding to what a child says, asking open questions that we don't know the answer to and discussing work with the child are important ways of enabling us to understand what stage of learning the child is at and to modify the curriculum to meet their individual needs.

A major emphasis in each chapter is the importance we place on valuing children's culture outside the school rather than seeing it as a negative influence. We stress the importance of building on the experiences the children bring to school and developing home–school partnerships to ensure that parents' and carers' knowledge about their children contributes to our assessment of them. By valuing the culture of the community, we convey our belief that children's learning does not stop at the school gates, but is seen as relevant to their lives. Creative teaching means planning activities that are stimulating, challenging and inspiring and that accommodate different learning styles, so that children have the internal motivation to learn and produce something of value. By knowing what the individual child is capable of we can plan suitable activities to consolidate their learning or move them on. If children's efforts to achieve are praised they will grow in confidence.

Many of the examples of practice that we describe involve children in self-assessment and peer assessment. This might be through discussion with the teacher, or in the form of a video of a drama activity or responding to a partner's story. This means providing an ethos where children are encouraged to take risks and to realise we all learn from our mistakes. We need to model not only how to provide positive feedback but how to give and receive constructive criticism so that learning is taken forward.

What does the future hold?

The wider educational context

Schools are in the midst of major changes. There is a range of new initiatives, some of which have already been implemented, others firmly on the agenda. The introduction of *Every Child Matters* (2004) is already having a major impact on how schools operate. Its aim is to close the gap between advantaged and disadvantaged children from birth to 19. The recognition that parents, carers and community members can help to promote high educational standards has long been on the agenda, but there is a renewed emphasis on encouraging voluntary and community sector initiatives both within and outside school hours and seeing the role of other adults as crucial to children's progress. However, we need to ensure that creativity and enjoyment retain a central focus, as changes to the workforce develop over the next three or four years.

Throughout this book we actively promote building and developing home, school and community partnerships throughout the early years and primary stages and provide practical examples of how this might be achieved. Our belief is that in a partnership we learn from each other and that in order for a partnership to grow and develop and encompass new initiatives, there must be a shared understanding of what education is for and how this is best achieved. If we hope to encourage children to be creative thinkers, able to adapt to the changing world and workplace, we must translate the aims of *Excellence and Enjoyment* through creative teaching.

The extended schools' prospectus Extended Schools: Access to Opportunities and Services for All is another initiative that must be implemented by 2010. The extended school will provide access to childcare from 8 am to 6 pm, offering before- and after-school activities, parenting support, family learning opportunities, wider access for ICT, sports and arts facilities. It promotes the use of voluntary organisations in offering activities such as drama, dance, visits to galleries and theatre.

Many of the activities that we suggest draw on the performance arts as a way of developing a response to texts and providing a stimulus for writing. It is to be hoped that increased exposure to the creative arts will reinforce a cross-curricular and more creative approach to learning.

There are many other initiatives (for example SureStart Community Centres, the National Literacy Trust, Creative Partnerships) that may change the way the curriculum develops and influence how language and literacy are learnt within the school environment and beyond. As creative teachers we need to reflect on developments and make informed judgements based on our understanding of how children learn.

An overview of the book

This book is divided into three parts:

- Fiction
- Non-fiction
- Poetry

Within each part we supply a short introduction outlining the generic principles relating to these broad areas and then provide a separate chapter on teaching Early Years, key stage 1 and key stage 2. This structure is designed to provide a coherent approach to teaching children in the Foundation and Primary stages.

Central to each chapter is the integrated nature of speaking and listening, reading and writing, the central nature of play as a vehicle for learning, the importance of building on home literacy and a collaborative approach to learning in an inclusive environment. Throughout there are examples of creative activities, case studies of activities in action in the classroom showing existing good practice, opportunities for drama, ICT and cross-curricular work.

As the reader, you are encouraged to reflect on your own experience and consider how you might develop your own creative practice through a series of activities. Engaging in such activities helps you to activate prior knowledge and experience, evaluate your own and others' practice.

We hope that, by sharing practical examples to underpin the Foundation stage curriculum and Primary curriculum, this book will help and inspire Early Years and Primary student teachers and teachers to implement a more creative English curriculum; that it will help student teachers and teachers to reflect on and develop their creative practice and provide a classroom where children can take risks, enjoy and experiment with language and discover and pursue their interests and talents.

References

Black, P. and William, D. (1998) *Inside the Black Box: Raising Standards through Classroom Assessment.* Kings College London, Department of Education and Professional Studies (now available from NFERNelson).

Creative Partnerships website; www.creativepartnerships.com

DfES (2003) *Excellence and Enjoyment: A Strategy for Primary Schools.* London: HMSO.

DfES (2004a) *Excellence and Enjoyment: Learning and Teaching in the Primary Years.* London: HMSO.

DfES (2004b) *Learning to Learn: Progression in Key Aspects of Learning.* London: HMSO.

Hartley-Brewer, E. (2001) *Learning to Trust and Trusting to Learn: How Schools Can Affect Children's Mental Health.* London: Institute for Public Policy Research.

National Advisory Committee on Creative and Cultural Education (NACCCE 1999) *All Our Futures: Creativity, Culture and Education.* London: DfEE/DCMS.

Office for Standards in Education (2003) *Expecting the Unexpected: Developing Creativity in Primary and Secondary Schools,* Ofsted e-publication.

Pollard, A. and Triggs, P., with Broadfoot, P., McNess, E. and Osborn, M. (2000) *What Pupils Say: Changing Policy and Practice in Primary Education.* London: Continuum.

Troman, G. (2000) 'Teacher stress in the low-trust society', *British Journal of Sociology of Education,* 21 (3), 331–53.

Willis, P. (2002) *Stressed at Seven? A Survey into the Scandal of Sats for Seven Year Olds.* London: Liberal Democratic Party.

Useful websites

www.everychildmatters.gov.uk
provides current information on the government's approach to the well-being of children and young people from birth to nineteen. Every Child Matters will have a major impact on education over the next ten years and many of the initiatives underpin the approach to learning advocated throughout this book, not least preschool learning, the involvement of parents and carers, personalised learning and extended schools.

www.literacytrust.org.uk

presents easily accessible information on the National Literacy Trust's commitment to building a literate nation. There are free e-mail newsletters. The Early Years section provides information on preschool children's reading and useful resources for parents and professionals, reinforcing the value placed on home–school partnerships throughout this book. The Primary section includes government approaches, research, statistics and initiatives, also reading and resources.

PART 1

Creativity and fiction: An overview

The most valuable attitude we can help children adopt – the one that, among other things, helps them to read and write with most fluency and effectiveness and enjoyment – is one I can best categorise by the word playful.

(Philip Pullman, *The Guardian*, 22 January 2005)

At the start of the 21st century, much in our lives is ordered, framed and regulated by mass information and technology. The emphasis on the scientific, the provable, the measurable has not, however, dimmed our passion for reading stories and telling stories. Indeed the growth in technology has enabled us to *expand* our experience of, and interaction with, fiction through an ever-increasing range of media. We can now watch DVDs of feature films on a laptop on the train, in a cafe or indeed almost anywhere; text messages can be sent to our mobile phones giving us daily updates on our favourite soap operas; short films and radio plays can be downloaded from the internet as podcasts and played on our MP3s again and again; digital cameras record stories from our daily lives; publishing that first novel has never been easier or more instant than on the World Wide Web and Richard and Judy's Book Club has caused a publishing phenomenon. Our insatiable appetite for fiction seems to be boundless.

What is fiction?

Fiction is shared through a variety of media and permeates all aspects of our lives. We tell stories all the time. 'Did you watch *EastEnders* last night?'; 'Did you hear the one about the . . .?'; 'You'll never guess what happened to me on the way to work this morning . . .'. We tell stories to define who we are, how we feel and to make sense of the world around us. These stories allow us to share experiences with others and in doing so, they help to frame our community, our culture, race and gender and identity. Fiction is essentially the embellishment of these stories, designed and spoken or written or read to entertain an audience, the reader.

Fact or fiction?

The stories we tell and write and show are rarely total fabrication. The characters are familiar, the places well known, the problems and resolutions often commonplace. Similarly we rarely provide a completely factual account when relating events. In the telling we embellish our stories with details to capture and sustain the interest of the audience and to make our lives more fascinating. This process sometimes takes us away from the mundane truth. The distinction between fact and fiction is thus not easy to define and this is particularly evident in the classroom where fictional stories are frequently a mixture of the familiar and the fantastic.

Story elements and structure

Vladimir Propp's research into Russian folk tales at the beginning of the last century demonstrates the similarities in structural elements and themes or 'morphemes' between stories (Propp 1928). In other words, there are only so many stories that can be told.

Understanding the common elements that most stories have is helpful in supporting children's response to fictional texts as well as supporting their attempts to construct their own. In order to foster creativity and innovation in telling stories, it is vital to first understand how basic stories work. Common elements of a simple story will include:

- structure – including a beginning, middle and end
- characters – usually with human characteristics and emotions
- setting – real or imaginary places where the story happens
- events – exposition, problem, resolution.

These elements form a basic pattern which can be copied, adapted, extended and subverted enabling creative interpretation and interaction with the telling, reading or writing of fictional texts. The most common or basic pattern consists of:

Opening > something happens > dilemma > something goes wrong > climax > events to sort it out > resolution > end (DfES 2001)

Genre: Different types of fictional stories

The basic structure of narrative stories outlined above is of course adapted, subverted, inverted and fine-tuned according to the type of story to be told. The 'author' or teller of the tales adapts their language and syntactic choices to tell a certain type of story – the genre. Experienced tellers, readers and writers recognise the differences between broad text types.

> Lizzie French jumped involuntarily as the church door clanged noisily behind a latecomer. Had he come? She had almost given up hope, but now, heart-in-mouth, she turned.
>
> (www.lizfielding.com/tips.html)

It is probably quite evident to you which genre is suggested by this opening sentence taken from Liz Fielding's website offering helpful hints to the budding romantic authors of the world. Although the Primary Strategy offers a very straightforward view of genre in *Grammar for Writing* (DfEE 2000a) and the importance of text types, it is important to consider that most texts present a range of features and elements from different types of stories.

The reader

Once the story leaves the teller, it will be interpreted in different ways by the audience who bring their own values and experiences with them. The story then becomes theirs to remember, to retell, to improve upon. This idea that there is no text unless there is a reader is an important tenet in 'reader response theory' which has gained in popularity since the 1970s. In 'Unity Identity Text Self', Norman Holland opens his article by stressing the importance of the reader in creating meaning from text:

> My title has big words but my essay aims into the white spaces between those big words. Those spaces suggest to me the mysterious openness and receptivity of literature. Somehow, all kinds of people from different eras and cultures can achieve and re-achieve a single literary work, replenishing it by infinitely various additions of subjective to objective.
>
> (Holland 1975)

We believe that this view of the power of the reader in making meaning is an important premise when considering a creative approach to teaching English, as children may be creative in their interpretation of the material that is presented to them as well as creative producers of texts.

Teaching fiction creatively

The creative elements of telling and responding to fictional stories are compelling and yet the teaching of reading stories and writing stories is sometimes consigned to closed comprehension questions on an uninspiring text or worse, a decontextualised excerpt from a text. The Standard Assessment Tests (SATs) at the end of key stage 1 (KS1) and KS2 reinforce this impoverished view of reading in the comprehension reading booklets and it is important that the creative practitioner understands the need for children to gain a deeper understanding of the text by a more active involvement with the content.

In Chapter 1, we discuss the importance of building upon children's love of stories from babyhood and the value of creating a classroom environment where children can inhabit the stories they read literally through their dynamic role play. This continues into Chapter 2 where we stress the value of generating real purposes and audiences for children's stories and stress the value of bookmaking, in particular. In Chapter 3 we look at children's popular films as texts and consider ways of extending children's confidence in reflecting on meaning.

Telling stories

It is important to understand the centrality of the oral tradition in all cultures and to recognise the repertoire of stories children bring to school. As teachers we will hear children telling stories in the playground, to their friends, over dinner. We share with them well-known stories that have been passed down through the years and adapted to reflect different cultures.

We often want to share our stories. When we tell our stories we begin to elaborate and embellish our tales to make them more interesting to the listener. The structure of our stories is informed by the tales we hear, see and read. These structures can be as simple as a nursery rhyme or as complex as a multi-layered novel containing time shifts and flashbacks. If we are to promote creativity in telling stories we must establish a classroom ethos where children and adults can tell and listen to each other's stories.

There are many important reasons for telling stories to children of all ages as well as supporting them to tell their own:

- The telling of stories to and fro helps to establish and maintain a supportive and interactive classroom community of listening and telling.
- The children and adults in the setting will build up a shared repertoire of stories from a range of cultural and linguistic traditions representative of the class and brought in from the wider community.
- Highlighting storytelling emphasises the value and diversity of oral language.
- Storytelling and sharing enables the class to make sense of the world through a range of diverse cultural perspectives.

- The immediate and unstructured nature of oral stories allows them to be used and adapted to challenge stereotypes.
- Opportunities to tell stories enable us all to build on our home experiences and thus help us to see each other as individuals.
- Telling and listening to stories can support children's ability to read and write fiction through familiarity with structure, characters and linguistic conventions.
- Storytelling can unite and develop all areas of the curriculum (e.g. stories in maths to introduce a new concept).
- Storytelling can allow us the opportunity to try on new voices and registers and thereby extend our ability to manipulate spoken language including the use of standard English.
- Preparing and telling stories helps to develop presentational aspects of talk and the ability to consider and adapt according to the needs of the audience.

Reading and responding to fiction

Far beyond the analysis of synthetic phonics or the decoding of alphabetic systems, reading fiction is essentially about being taken on a journey. As adults, we read our novels on the beach, in the bath, on the train, tube or bus in order to be transported, sometimes literally, to another world where we are welcomed and enticed into other people's lives, adventures, hopes and dreams.

When teaching children to read fiction, we need to understand how important these journeys are and that understanding the meaning of the text and applying it to our own lives and experiences is the key. Throughout the following chapters, we have reinforced the importance of play and drama to explore the themes and issues raised in the stories from hot-seating Max in *Where The Wild Things Are* in the Early Years to try to find out why he is so angry with everyone to exploring themes of alienation in fairy tales though improvisation towards the end of KS2.

A wide-ranging, challenging and creative reading curriculum encourages children to become involved with texts, to respond personally and imaginatively and to explore worlds beyond their immediate experience.

(PNS 2005a: 5)

Writing and constructing stories

Planning, constructing and presenting fiction can be developed in a number of ways in the creative classroom, including storywriting, filmmaking, play-script writing, and animation. Stories are very rarely constructed in isolation by one person and are never conceived, written and published in one 20-minute slot during a literacy hour. Making stories in the classroom takes time, collegiality, security and inspiration – just like in real life. The three-year-old in the nursery needs time to play through their ideas, time to talk and time to record or tell their story to a scribe. The child at 7 will need to know that if they share their ideas with the class or group, no one will laugh and that they can expect others to help them enhance their work. The child in Y5 needs to know what to do, where to go when she gets stuck half-way through her film.

Writing stories down or recording them on film enables them to be read and shared again and again with an audience. It is important that children understand the purpose of the writing beyond the teacher's need to mark it. Central to this book is the belief that children's stories are worth recording and therefore must be recognised and celebrated and, most importantly, shared with their intended audience. No one writes in a vacuum. All writing has a purpose and an audience that dictate the form and type of writing needed.

The creative classroom environment

Classrooms of all shapes and sizes from the nursery to Y6 can be transformed by a love of story. The creative practitioner needs to consider:

- the range of fictional texts including children's popular cultural interests, and how they entice the readers in your class;
- the potential of multimodal stories and fiction in a variety of media including: film, interactive computer games, 'talking books';
- the organisation and lure of the book area;
- resources to support role play and drama;
- displays to celebrate and support;
- publication of children's stories.

Inclusive practices

A classroom that offers a creative environment where fictional stories are encouraged must be an inclusive classroom. All children irrespective of their race, gender, class, ability have stories to tell. Wonderful, funny, tragic, long, short, in English or Urdu, in standard English or in a West Country dialect. The creative classroom ensures that the interests and needs of all children are considered and that children are not withdrawn from classroom activities but supported within the class itself. Differences between children and their lives and experiences are welcomed and can only enhance the range of stories to be told, written, recorded or heard.

Learning styles and special educational needs

As creative teachers we want to promote an inclusive learning environment where a range of learning styles are recognised and children and adults learn with and from each other. Each chapter looks at a range of teaching and learning methods to support individual children's access to fictional texts including:

- a classroom environment where risk-taking is celebrated and innovation is admired within a safe environment;
- the use of a range of information and communication technologies to broaden the range of fiction including interactive multimodal texts;
- visual aids such as pictures, big books or interactive whiteboards and physical props such as story characters or dressing-up clothes related to themes from fiction;
- drama techniques to actively explore the meaning of texts;
- thinking time where the children are given the opportunity to reflect and consider, enabling all children to respond;
- interactive and participatory whole-class or group work including shared and guided reading;
- open-ended questions where children can contribute their ideas and be valued for their thoughts at their own level;
- emphasis on ways of recording and telling stories to suit a range of learning strengths including speaking and drawing, not just writing;
- paired work with children working with similar and mixed-ability partners to encourage discussion and pooling of ideas;
- individual independent work where children can read and write personal stories and can rehearse and practise new skills.

Gender

Much has been written on the need to enhance the writing curriculum to accommodate boys' underachievement in writing fiction (Ofsted 2003; DfES 2003). The Primary National Strategy states that the following strategies will make a difference to boys' success in writing:

- provide boys with real purposes and audiences for writing;
- ensure a wide range of texts linking with boys' interests, including visual literacies;
- ensure boys are given opportunities for oral rehearsal before writing;
- provide effective feedback to boys orally before writing. (DfES 2005)

The activities and teaching methods described in the following chapters argue that these strategies are vital for all children to make progress and to enjoy reading and writing fiction.

Bilingual pupils

Fictional stories are intrinsic to all cultures and are told and recorded in all languages. The activities discussed in the following chapters recognise the wealth of stories needing to be told from across the world and encourage the use of visual prompts and drama to explore and extend children's understanding. The study of fiction can offer a wonderful opportunity for exploring language through story.

References

DfEE (2000a) *Grammar for Writing*. London.

DfEE (2000b) *National Curriculum*. London.

DfES (2001) *NLS Writing Flier 2: Writing Narrative*. London.

DfES (2003) *Using the National Healthy School Standard to Raise Boys' Achievement*. London.

DfES (2004) *Excellence and Enjoyment: Learning and Teaching in the Primary Years*. London.

DfES (2005) *Raising Standards in Writing*. London.

Holland, N. (1975) 'Unity Identity Text Self', *PMLA*, 90 (5), 813–22.

Ofsted (2003) *Yes He Can: Schools Where Boys Write Well*, HMI 505. London.

PNS (2005a) *Raising Standards in Reading – Achieving Children's Targets*. London: DfES.

PNS (2005b) *Raising Standards in Writing – Achieving Children's Targets*. London: DfES.

Propp, V. (1928) *Morphology of the Folktale*. Leningrad.

Sendak, M. (1967) *Where the Wild Things Are*. London: The Bodley Head.

Useful websites

Download this wonderful film about Ben, a 39-year-old mongrel in need of love, to inspire classroom filmmaking: www.bbc.co.uk/dna/filmnetwork/A3819080

To download electronic copies of all NLS and PNS documents: www.standards.dfes.gov.uk/primary/publications/literacy

For some useful ideas on gender and literacy resources go to: www.literacytrust.org.uk/database/boys/Boysres.html

CHAPTER 1

Teaching fiction creatively in the Early Years

Look, there we go. It's a mouse,
'hello mousie, hello mousie what are you doing there?'

(Charlie, aged 2, playing with nutshells)

Introduction

In this chapter we will consider how to build upon children's positive home experiences of language and literacy. We will look at how to use the existing frameworks for language and literacy teaching as outlined in the *Curriculum Guidance for the Foundation Stage* (DfEE 2000) and the *National Literacy Strategy Framework for Teaching* guidance for YR (DfEE 1998) in a creative and innovative manner in order to maintain and extend young children's love of story. The emphasis in this chapter is on telling and responding to stories as it is through the development of planning and telling stories, of structuring and attuning to the language and impact of stories, that children will begin to gain an understanding of how to read, write and make stories for themselves.

Building on home literacy

Up to the age of 3 or 4, most children are encouraged by family, friends and carers to be creative users of language and literacy. Stories are the stuff of bedtime routines to help settle and secure warm and intimate relationships between parents and their children: bath-time books are squishy bestsellers for babies; buggies with three-month-old babies are rarely seen without chewed cardboard versions of Eric Carle's *The Very Hungry Caterpillar* attached; the wealth of dressing-up costumes bursting off the racks at Toys 'R' Us are all testimony to our acceptance and encouragement of young children's dynamic and participatory role within stories, within fiction.

As children enter nursery or preschool settings, they will often already know how to re-tell a simple story ('What happened to Humpty Dumpty?'), be able to comment on complex characterisation ('Why do you like La La more than Tinky Winky?'), be able to identify the key moments in a text ('. . . and then the monster ate him all up'). Indeed, stories form the basis of much of the dialogue between adults and young children in these early years: 'Once upon a time, there lived a little girl called Florence who wouldn't eat up all of her vegetables . . .'

The pleasure of stories

In order to harness these infants' love of story, the Early Years practitioner needs to ensure stories remain relevant and enjoyable. The reality of the busy school day can sometimes reinforce the idea that stories at home are fun and stories at school are not. Young children's lively and talkative interactive approach to sharing a picture book with a parent is sometimes replaced by boredom and frustration while sitting on a brown carpet reading 'very quietly' while waiting for other children to tidy up. Singing stories on an attentive grandparent's lap may be replaced by listening to a tape of a 'seen better days' fairytale on dusty headphones. Favourite and familiar storybooks are often replaced by less familiar texts you can only buy as part of school catalogues, many of which are designed to 'teach reading', not to have a genuine story. In school the texts are mainly chosen by the adult – TV programmes are limited to those 'educational' series detailed in grey educational supplements and titled 'For Schools'. Children are often read to at designated times of the day and children are expected to listen and respond 'appropriately' when asked. School and home learning arenas are, of course, very different owing to often unchallengeable child:adult ratios, resources, curriculum, etc. and yet schools and Early Years classes will benefit from looking more closely at the successful reading and writing and storytelling practices evident at home.

Popular culture

This artificial divide between home and school reading practices is often unwittingly emphasised by the teacher's attitudes towards the child's home literary experiences and passions. I remember the occasions when a little girl burst through my Reception class door pressing her much-loved stories of Barbie into my hands, pleading with me to read it to the other children or the children wanting to act out the story of the previous day's *Power Rangers* episode in the outdoor area complete with sound effects and dangerous kicks. The teacher's well trained and well intentioned instinct is, as mine often was, to challenge the appropriateness of the text offered in these situations – Barbie terrifies me in her subservient 'girliness' and the somewhat aggressive tone of the outdoor play offended my liberal sensibilities. And yet, what these examples demonstrate is the instinctive need of many children to bring their home 'literacies' into the classroom in order to give their stories status and demonstrate what they already know about often quite complex texts.

In order to foster a creative classroom, however, where children are encouraged to draw on their wide experience of stories, these texts and tales must be respected and indeed shared with other children in order that the child sees recognition of their reading practices at home. This does not mean that stereotypical portrayals should be ignored. Rather, by allowing space and time in the school day, you are affording an opportunity to open debate: 'What do *you* think Barbie does all day?'

Playing with fiction

The centrality of imaginative play in extending children as story makers is well documented: 'The children were in fact natural born storytellers who created literature as easily as I turned the pages of a book' (Paley 2005: 16).

As soon as a baby is born, stories will be heard. As soon as the child is able to speak, stories will be told. Let's have a look at Charlie, aged 2 years and 3 months, as she plays alone, unaware that her play is being recorded and observed:

> Charlie is sitting at the kitchen table, playing with some nutshells. At first she plays a game asking which hand are they in, then she puts two of them onto her fingers and pretends they are mice. She hides them under the tabletop, produces them with a flourish, talks to them and finally drops one on the floor. Part of the time, she is talking to the shells as mice, some of the time describing what her mice are doing, 'That, hand, that hand, that hand (*laughs*), da da! (*in a singing flourish*). Look, there we go, it's a mouse, hello mousie, hello mousie, (*puts them under the table top*) what are you doing there? (*One shell falls on the floor*) I just dropped mouse (*an unhappy voice*). Put mousie down there.'

It is helpful to look a little more closely at what Charlie is doing here. She is involved in what is known as solitary symbolic play (Macintyre 2001). She is giving everyday objects feelings and language. She is using simple dialogue to tell her story to herself. She is engaged with the nutshell mice. She is in the story. She is able to sustain her story even when the shell is dropped. Her ability to tell stories and to be a part of those stories allows her to be part of her environment and enables her to explore an imaginary world.

Charlie is being allowed the time and space to inhabit her make-believe world for a while. Allowing children in the classroom time to play without adult intervention to break the spell is an important stage – one which many teachers find hard to plan for and yet a vital stage in the process of independent meaning-making.

In order to extend Charlie's play to include other children and develop her ability to construct and perform stories for the enjoyment and interest of others, it is necessary to offer her the opportunity to see the power her storymaking and storytelling may have upon others.

This instinctive need to create and tell stories through play should be nurtured and enthusiastically built upon throughout the Primary school and way beyond. In the words of a past Children's Laureate, Philip Pullman:

> It's when we do this foolish, time-consuming romantic, quixotic, childlike thing called play that we are most practical, most useful, and most firmly grounded in reality, because the world itself is the most unlikely of places, and it works in the oddest of ways, and we don't make any sense of it by doing what everyone else has done before us. It's when we fool about with the stuff the world is made of that we make the most valuable discoveries, we create the most lasting beauty, we discover the most profound truths.
> (Pullman 2005)

Partnership between home and school

Since the 1980s, schools have tried to open pathways between school and home, recognising the research detailing the value of parents and carers reading with their children at home (see for example the work undertaken in Haringey by Tizzard, Schofield and Hewison, 1982). Much of the research has, however, tended to focus on a one-way communication citing the experts as school-based and attempting to introduce school reading routines into home routines. If we are to harness and maintain the child's early enthusiasm for stories, the Early Years practitioner needs to know and understand the literary experiences and preferences that each child has *at home*. Some ideas to support this more equal and dynamic partnership between home and school in the Early Years setting might include:

Home 'literacy diary'

This involves asking parents or carers to maintain a simple 'literacy diary' in their own language over a week or even over one day and share parts of the diary during a home–school introductory meeting. This can be very revealing in terms of the extensive prior experience and enjoyment many children already have. Below is a short extract from three-year-old Zachary's mum's diary of a typical day's literary experiences:

6.30 am	Milk and *Teletubbies* (lots of singing and squealing!)
7.30 am	Looked at *Bath Bunnies* in the bath (splashing and reading and blowing bubbles)
8 am	Checked e-mails – very excited by attached photo of friend's new baby dressed as a pumpkin!
9 am	Took Zac to nursery. Looked for words with Z in shop signs, adverts etc.
1 pm	Picked up Zac from nursery. He told me about a story his teacher read in class about a huge monster in the trees. We talked in Spanish.

From this brief excerpt we know a lot about Zachary's language preferences and aptitudes. We know that he enjoys watching and joining in with *Teletubbies* on television. He is familiar with handling books and sees sharing books as something fun and sociable. He is able to retell simple stories. He is bilingual and is beginning to focus on print as a form of communication. This information gives us a much fuller picture of the child as a reader and user of language. It will enable us to plan more effectively and ensure we build on his extensive knowledge.

Time for 'Stories From Home'

- Plan set times to share texts or aspects of longer texts (including computer programs, Disney DVDs etc.) from home.
- Create a display area for stories written by children at home.
- Book packs should work both ways – books to take home and books and other texts to bring into school.

Telling tales

Plan time for parents and carers to come into class and tell stories to small groups of children in their own languages on a theme: 'a funny thing happened to me on the way to school one day . . .'; 'my favourite story when I was little . . .'; 'the day a Martian came to my house . . .'.

Speaking and listening and drama: Creative approaches to telling stories in the Early Years

Valuing children's talk and planning opportunities to tell, listen and respond orally to stories should be an essential and pivotal part of all Early Years provision in order to rehearse and develop their stories: 'Children's creativity, understanding and imagination can be engaged and fostered by discussion and interaction' (DfES 2003).

Telling stories and the Early Years curriculum frameworks

The communication, language and literacy strand of the *Curriculum Guidance for the Foundation Stage* makes surprisingly little explicit reference to *telling* stories to children or indeed supporting or extending children's ability to tell stories themselves but does stress the need to give children the opportunity to 'share and enjoy a wide range of stories' (DfEE 2000: 44) and to ensure children 'listen with enjoyment and respond to stories' (DfEE 2000: 50). By the end of the Foundation stage, children should be able to 'use language to imagine and recreate roles and experiences' (DfEE 2000: 58) 'and make up their own stories' (DfEE 2000: 50).

There is more explicit reference to listening to and telling stories to develop children's reading comprehension in the YR guidance of the *National Literacy Strategy Framework for Teaching*. Children should be taught to 'notice the difference between spoken and written forms through re-telling known stories' and 'to compare told versions with what the book "says" '. It states that children should 'use knowledge of familiar texts to re-enact or re-tell to others' and to 'understand how story book language works and to use some formal elements when re-telling stories, e.g. "Once there was . . ." ' (DfEE 1998: 18).

Why *tell* stories in the Early Years setting?

The importance of telling stories cannot be overemphasised as a significant tool to develop children's understanding of the power and structure of stories as well as the social elements of creating a community of storytellers. In the Early Years setting there are further distinct reasons why telling stories needs to be an integral part of a creative provision:

- *Telling stories is the precursor to writing stories* – children can rehearse and develop the structure of story writing long before they are able to record their ideas graphically. Their ideas will not therefore be stilted by what they can record independently and the focus will be on the composition and the delivery.
- *Telling stories enables the adult to model the traditional* as well as the creative language of stories – 'once upon a time, a very long time ago indeed, there lived a "humagiantus" creature called Bill.'
- *Telling stories enables the child to be listened to* in a planned and organised environment.
- *Telling stories enables the young child to be allowed to make things up* and that's exactly what you are meant to do!

In order to encourage children to be creative story tellers, it is essential to develop a classroom environment where spoken stories are valued and shared and where both adults *and* children feel safe to share their voice without fear of ridicule. In addition to the guidance on telling stories, detailed in 'Creativity and fiction: An overview' (Part 1 of this book), this can be established through a range of simple techniques:

- Set aside a designated *storytelling time* each week.
- Seat children around the carpet where *all can see the storyteller*.
- Ensure *time to listen* to each other.

- Make a short *agreement* with the children about what they can expect when telling their story ('we all listen to each other'; 'we don't have to tell our story if the time is not right'; 'we will tell the storyteller what we liked about their story afterwards'). Remind the children of this agreement each story-telling session.

- Agree and *model positive responses* to the storyteller: 'I really enjoyed the part when you roared like a tiger. Which part did you like best, Hassan?'

- Ensure the adults and children know that they will never be forced to tell their story – *stories must want to be told!*

Children and adults telling stories

In order to build on children's enthusiasm for, and experience of, telling stories and in order to develop their success in engaging an audience with their stories, it is important to plan activities where the teacher or adult can 'scaffold' and ex-tend the child's ability to be successful and engaging storytellers. The following examples offer a range of classroom routines that can be applied to embed story-telling into everyday practice.

Special places

Developing a special area of the classroom or outside area where storytelling can especially take place (in addition to the ongoing storytelling that instinctively occurs alongside all classroom areas), can be a useful way of gathering children together and signalling the transition from 'real life' to the enchantment of the story. As when developing any imaginative classroom areas, it is important to involve the children themselves in developing the look and feel of the area so they understand how it works and are comfortable with the expectations.

Transforming an old dusty rug into a *magic carpet*, for example, a carpet imbued with magical storytelling ears indeed, takes little more than some imagi-nation, a good clean and a few scatter cushions covered in shiny or sparkly fabric. The rug could be rolled up and kept in a cupboard and brought out with grand aplomb when needed or, depending upon space, maintained as a distinct area of the classroom where children can always choose to enter with other children or adults in order to tell their story or listen to others. Alternatively, you may wish to consider:

- *a storytelling bus* made from chairs and a red 'tent' where children can be taken on a story journey with or without an accompanying adult
- *a gilded story chair* where the teller must sit before she can enthral her audience

- *a storyteller's outfit or hat* (let your and the children's imagination run wild when designing this one) which is dusted down and worn only for special tales.

Whole class or group storytelling activities

Other activities to help extend each child's ability to tell creative stories effectively to an audience:

- *telling stories with familiar repetitive refrains* to encourage children to join in (three little pigs 'I'll huff and I'll puff and I'll blow your house down'). The children will soon feel like storytellers and will be more prepared to take a risk and have a go themselves if they have had the experience of telling with you;

- *telling and retelling stories* – establishing classroom favourites that the children can mimic and elaborate upon is a helpful addition to the class repertoire of shared stories;

- *taping stories* – it is vital that diverse voices telling stories are heard in the classroom – by encouraging the adults and children access to blank tapes to record their stories, so you are extending the range of dialects, accents and languages heard; tapes and recorders can be sent home to encourage family members to record their stories. Sound effects are to be encouraged!

Children telling stories independently

When planning storytelling activities, it is essential to try to allow discrete time for children to develop and extend their unstructured solitary, paired or group play. As children play independently so they draw on their own experiences and stories heard, seen and read to create their own narratives. They are often developed for the enjoyment of the moment. At times they may be rehearsals for future stories to be told. At other times they will never be told again. The role of the adult in developing this storytelling play is to plan time, space and opportunity for the imagination to be fired and for the stories to be told.

Creative role-play areas

When developing distinct creative role-play areas where children are encouraged to play together to create wondrous and make believe worlds, it is a good idea to create an area based on a generic and yet familiar story setting where the children themselves can take their stories. Some will re-enact familiar tales, some will endlessly rework the stories, constantly improving and extending the tales as they go. When developing the area it is important to encourage input from the children from the outset. They will know what they want in their castle or tent. They will know how they want it to look. You need to help consider *how* to do it. Some themes for the development of creative role-play to particularly encourage the telling of fictional stories might include:

- The Enchanted Forest

  Trees painted by the children on large sheets of paper and cut out and stuck around the reading area with great swathes of green, brown and black twine hanging down can very easily transform a classroom reading area into a wondrous place to enact stories. Paint on some yellow eyes peeping through the trees or introduce different book characters hiding among the twine to maintain interest and to inspire development in the stories the children are making. Include a tree-trunk cupboard with displays of related storybooks. (Links with many favourite picture-book stories could include Julia Donaldson's *The Gruffalo*, Maurice Sendak's *Where the Wild Things Are*, Jez Alborough's *Where's My Teddy?*)

- Teletubbyland

  Over the hills and far away . . . Fake grass and green cushions with simple outfits of the loveable foursome borrowed or begged from older children and a portable television-video will transform your book area into a place where the children are more at home than you. Include videos or DVDs of the popular shows and introduce unusual equipment – an old-fashioned pull-along vacuum cleaner can easily be mistaken for a Noo noo!

- A Home

  A familiar setting where anything can happen and familiar narratives can be explored: ensure props reflect the homes of the children in the class and consider the cultural significance of food, utensils, books, religious artefacts, etc.

Small world play

Giving opportunities to play with small worlds (hospitals, seaside, the zoo, a fairground) offers young children the chance to inhabit and explore worlds other than their own. It enables them to manipulate the environment (setting) as well as the figures (characters) while enabling them to pursue stories and adventures that they can manipulate and control initially without adult intervention. This small world play literally encourages children to play with stories and to develop narratives that will feed their imaginations when telling or writing their own stories in more formal classroom activities.

Vivian Paley's storytelling model

Vivian Paley (American teacher and author) advocates a simple and yet enormously powerful model of classroom storytelling that can be adapted effectively in any classroom context. Her insistence on the value of listening to and recording children's stories has inspired many Early Years practitioners in the USA and across the world to put storytelling at the centre of their practice. Broadly, her model consists of the following routine:

> Over the course of a morning (perhaps weekly, perhaps more or less frequently depending upon your setting) the children are invited to dictate their stories to an adult scribe. It is essential that their words are recorded exactly without the adult editing content, vocabulary or grammar – it must be the child's own words, the child's own story. If the child is lost or unclear, the adult may question or prompt the child 'tell me more' or 'how did she feel then?' but must be led by the child's response. It must, after all, remain the child's own story. Later the same day, preferably, the children are gathered together around a stage – a clearly demarcated area of carpet or playground will do. The child who dictated the story will then be invited to stand on the stage in the middle of the other children and select the players to show the story with him or her. These will include all of the animate as well as inanimate players needed to tell the story:
>
> Once upon a time there was a little frog and he was afraid of the fox and the fox ate him up and he ran home to his mum. He went to the pond.   (Princess, aged 4)
>
> Here the child will choose a frog, a fox, a frog mum and a pond in order to tell his story. He will be able to select the part he wants to act out and the adult will help to choose the children to play the other parts. As the adult reads the story out loud in the child's original words, so the children unfold the story in their own interpretations as the remaining members of the group or class watch and partake when invited. So the child's story becomes the class's story and so the children see their stories appreciated and are inspired to tell more.

This approach is discussed with some wonderful examples of the power and impact of the children's stories in Paley's many books, including the wonderful *Walley's Stories* (Paley 1981). It is a very useful, structured approach to ensuring children's stories are heard and children are seen as storytellers. It also enables the listeners to be active participants in stories and broadens the children's view of the story world as they are guided through the imaginations of the other children.

Creative approaches to reading and responding to fiction in the Early Years

In the Early Years setting, reading for pleasure and enjoyment should be paramount. Demonstrating that learning to read is a worthwhile pursuit, that reading is 'something that I really want to do and so do my teachers' is perhaps the most important lesson of all. As a very significant adult in the children's lives, don't be afraid to pick up a book and read to yourself when the children are reading independently (keeping one eye on the children of course – Early Years educators are excellent multi-taskers!)

The important pre-reading activities related to phonemic awareness, alphabet and word recognition are, of course, vital elements in supporting young children's ability to read independently. I hope the following ideas will be read in conjunction with the plethora of practical and systematic teaching advice on these technical elements of learning to read (the National Literacy Strategy – now Primary Strategy – has produced a wealth of helpful publications related to the word- and sentence-level objectives for reading in YR). As the focus of this book is how to develop creative reading practices, however, we make no apology for focusing on activities related to the whole text in order to foster an excitement and lifelong attachment to reading fiction.

Reading and responding to fiction and the Early Years curriculum frameworks

By the end of the Foundation stage, children should 'enjoy listening to and using spoken and written language, and readily turn to it in their play and learning'. They should be able to 'sustain attentive listening, responding to what they have heard by relevant comments, questions or actions' and 'listen with enjoyment to stories' (DfEE 2000: 50) and be able to 'retell narratives in the correct sequence, drawing on language patterns of stories' (DfEE 2000: 62).

The NLS Framework for YR stresses the value of building on children's experience of reading, understanding and responding to stories. It recommends that children should be taught:

- *to use a variety of cues when reading: knowledge of the story and its context, and awareness of how it should make sense grammatically;*
- *to re-read a text to provide context cues to help read unfamiliar words;*
- *to notice the difference between spoken and written forms through re-telling known stories; to compare 'told' versions with what the book 'says';*
- *to understand how storybook language works and to use some formal elements when re-telling stories, e.g. 'Once there was . . .', 'She lived in a little . . .', 'he replied . . .';*
- *to re-read frequently a variety of familiar texts, e.g. big books, story books, taped stories with texts, poems, information books, wall stories, captions, own and other children's writing;*

- to use knowledge of familiar texts to re-enact or re-tell to others, recounting the main points in correct sequence;
- to locate and read significant parts of the text, e.g. picture captions, names of key characters, rhymes and chants, e.g. 'I'm a troll . . .', 'You can't catch me I'm the Gingerbread Man . . .', speech-bubbles, italicised, enlarged words;
- to be aware of story structures, e.g. actions/reactions, consequences, and the ways that stories are built up and concluded;
- to re-read and recite stories and rhymes with predictable and repeated patterns and experiment with similar rhyming patterns.

(DfEE 1998: 18–19)

Choice of texts

The NLS Framework guidance for YR is explicit in terms of the suggested range of fiction children should experience: 'stories with predictable structures and patterned language' (DfEE 1998: 18). It is vital, however, that we do not limit children's repertoire of texts to only the teacher's choice and that additionally we continue to build upon the out-of-school interests of the children themselves.

In order to encourage a passion for reading and for sharing stories in the Early Years classroom, it is the *quality* of the texts that is the key (Meek 1988). If children are to learn that reading is stimulating, enjoyable and exciting, then the stories must also be so. Although traditionally, stories have mainly been read from books, it is important to ensure that a breadth of texts is available including electronic texts, films and computer games as well as books and magazines.

Reading areas

Displaying children's books in a warm and comfortable area where children can sit snuggled among cushions with soothing music playing in the background can support the notion of reading stories as something wonderful and can help reproduce the powerful experience of reading at home. It is additionally important to display books in all areas of provision around the classroom to encourage the links between stories and all curriculum areas: *Come Away From the Water, Shirley* with the water tray, *The House That Jack Built* with the large wooden bricks, *Old Mother Hubbard* in the cooking area, and so on.

Reading to children

It is the role of the Early Years educator to ensure children have the opportunity to experience the excitement and satisfaction of being taken on this journey by reading stories to them as well as having them read stories to you. Reading to children has formed the mainstay of excellent Early Years reading practice for many years. Reading to children at the end of each session and indeed at intervals throughout the day is a time when all come together to share a story and yet I make no apology for considering again the very important pedagogical purposes of this vital element of the school day.

Reading stories to children can begin to recreate the safe and comfortable, warm and loving home reading environment. It is a time when the whole class can share stories together without any need to distinguish or exclude because of prior experience. The children are allowed to sit back and enjoy the story and the pictures without having to be or do anything. They can experience the excitement of being taken on a journey far beyond their independent reading ability and can therefore extend and develop their experience of story. They can listen to the sounds of words and phrases which will inform their own repertoire of book language when they come to read or write stories themselves. The reader and listeners are forming a 'community of readers' where all involved will share a common repertoire of tales to draw upon to help them describe and reference their world, their feelings and their stories. The range of stories to be read is endless: new tales, old favourites, stories from the children's home, stories from other cultures, other times. Indeed the broader the range the more exciting the story times will be. It is important too that the children are also encouraged to choose the stories to be read so it is not only the adults' reading preferences that pervade.

Response to texts

Reading is not, however, on the surface a creative and active process. The writer has been involved in the creative process of developing a story, of selecting a word or phrase and evoking atmosphere and character. And yet if we are to engage young children in reading, we must develop ways of actively involving the reader in order to allow them the opportunity to construct meaning from the writer's text. The reader must make sense of the work and must therefore be encouraged to find links and develop pathways into the text itself. The creative essence of reading is, therefore, the ability to make the text one's own – to make these connections and enable the reader to empathise with the characters and ultimately to care about what happens next. 'To learn to read a book, as distinct from simply recognising the words on the page, a young reader has to become both the teller (picking up the author's view and voice) and the told (the recipient of the story, the interpreter)' (Meek 1988: 10). Consider how the following activities can enhance the child's interaction with the texts and thereby their enjoyment:

Reading the pictures
When sharing a book or other text with a young child, the primary consideration should be mutual enjoyment. Reading the pictures together as well as the words

will enable you to begin a dialogue about the text behind the words – the real meaning is often hidden in the illustrations as it is here that the depth of meaning can be explored beyond the sometimes brief written text evident in books for younger children. Much interesting textual analysis has been done on the relationship between texts and images in children's picture books (see Lewis 2001 for example). Stories such as John Burningham's *Come Away From the Water, Shirley*, Eileen Browne's *Handa's Surprise* and Pat Hutchin's *Rosie's Walk* demonstrate how superficially simple stories have a lot more going on besides. Allowing time to inspect the pictures and to talk about the 'subtext' (Can you see anything else happening in the picture? How do you think she is feeling? How does she look?) will enable the child to learn very important lessons about stories – how what the characters say may not be what they mean; how the writing may not always be telling us the whole truth; how the reader is a vital component of the story being read and often knows more than the characters themselves. These considerations are not just important in encouraging an enquiring and active reader, they are important in life – they form the basic groundwork in determining bias and conflict in text.

Story maps

As picture books often follow a simple narrative structure of a journey, drawing a map of the story is a useful way of working with the children to build up their ability to retell and structure the events of the story. This will help them to develop a sense of narrative and will support them in structuring their ideas when they tell and write their stories. Initially the children will be encouraged to look back at the book in order to sequence events and look for key places (settings) where the story takes place. The children can then have fun retelling the story using the map. They could alter the pathways to see if they can change the story. In David McKee's classic, for example, could the monster eat Bernard's dad rather than Bernard if he went to the sitting room first before going to the garden?

Hot-seating

This is an exciting way of bringing the character to life and thereby extending children's understanding of the character beyond the limitations of the text itself. The teacher takes on the mantle of a character from the story. This persona alteration can be signalled in different ways: the adult can introduce the character and then turn around dramatically; a special hot-seating chair can be decorated and used for the sole purpose; she/he could wear or carry an item signifying the character (Maurice's crown and fork; the caterpillar's holey leaf) – be imaginative! The children will avidly fall into the make-believe scene. Once in role the children should be encouraged to ask you questions – questions only your character would know the answer to. Initially these questions would need to be modelled by an adult (How did you know that Goldilocks slept in your bed? Why do you have a television in your tummy?) The question, answers and ensuing discussion will enable the children to explore the text way beyond a simple reading. As the children become familiar with the technique it is an indispensable routine that can be adapted to reflect on any text.

Story games

Developing simple dice-driven race games or card games based on familiar children's texts is a wonderful way to engage children in the text and enable them to ask and respond to questions. It also enables them to discuss the story with each other. Items such as 'Move back 2 spaces if you think Cinderella should go to the ball' will raise questions that you want the children to discuss in a relaxed way. Again, story games can be adapted for any story and can be developed and made by older, more experienced readers and writers at KS1 and KS2 in order to develop their textual understanding.

Story bags or storysacks

These are a wonderful resource for children to borrow and take home and share with family and friends. Each bag contains a story book and a selection of related items to extend the child's experience of the themes and ideas raised in the story. It is also about having fun and developing links between home and school literacies. The other items might include a selection from a related non-fiction text, a story tape, video or interactive CD-ROM, a character toy, a race game, a list of websites with further related ideas or stories. Once the story bags are an established part of your setting's practice, it is a good idea to encourage parents and carers to help develop further bags with texts enjoyed at home (see Neil Griffiths' *Storysacks* for further wonderful examples of how to make and use these exciting bags).

Puppets and toys

These will also help retell and rework familiar and well loved stories. Many publishers now produce toys and puppets of key characters from children's story books. Soft and cuddly Elmers, Maisie and even Wild Things come in every shape and size and are enthusiastically used by the children to help tell their stories. I remember Jason, aged 4, hunting everywhere in the reception classroom for Spot to sit on his knee before settling to read the story of *Where's Spot?* Each time Jason lifted the flap to see if Spot was there, so he would squeal with delight and share his findings only with his fluffy friend. Jason was enabled to 'read' and enjoy his story with the aid and support of this character.

Creative approaches to writing fiction in the Early Years

In the early years children are just beginning to explore the medium of writing as a form of communication. Many children are in the early stages of exploring letter shapes and patterns on the page and some are just distinguishing writing from drawing. The stories the children can act out, tell, watch and respond to are far more advanced than many children are able to write down independently. It is the challenging role of the Early Years educator to maintain the development of exciting and creative stories alongside the encouragement of independent developmental writing.

The Early Years curriculum frameworks

The Early Years curriculum frameworks make little explicit reference to story writing. The *Curriculum Guidance for the Foundation Stage* refers broadly to children being encouraged to 'attempt writing for different purposes, using features of different forms such as lists, stories and instructions' (DfEE 2000: 64).

The NLS Framework for YR states that children should 'through guided and independent writing experiment with writing in a variety of play, exploratory and role-play situations' and they should also be able to 'use experience of stories, poems and simple recounts as a basis for independent writing, e.g. re-telling, substitution, extension, and through shared composition with adults' (DfEE 1998: 19).

Collaborative writing

Writing together with another adult or child can enable the child to write a story beyond his or her independent ability. Bridging the gap between independent learning practices and 'scaffolding' children's learning with the support of a more experienced partner ensure that writing is seen not only as a solitary pursuit but rather a partnership using and sharing the expertise (Pollard 2002).

Initially the child in the early years will be recording their stories using a range of marks on the page. Through sensitive intervention with an adult, these marks may be attributed a meaning by the child who will eventually be able to tell you what his or her story says. It is important for the adult to support the child by recording the child's words beneath the child's own marks initially. The adult's writing should not overpower the child's script, however, but should be evident to allow others to read the story and to draw the child's attention to the conventions of print.

These early written stories may consist of only a few words or phrases and will be represented by letter like shapes. Figure 1.1 shows Ahmed's story. When asked to 'read' his story back to the teacher he pointed to the marks on the page and read: 'The spider climbed up a pipe. Sun came out. Spider went up the pipe again.' The story will often be told using talking, drawing and developmental writing. Our role as Early Years educators is to support this process by ensuring the tools and inspirations are freely available and that we allow time for a dialogue about the stories.

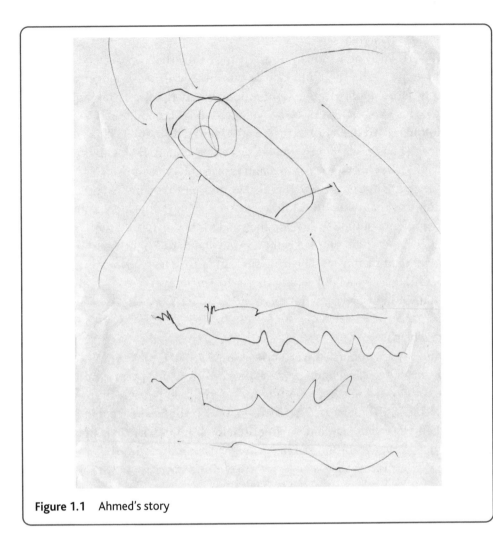

Figure 1.1 Ahmed's story

Shared storywriting

This is a wonderful opportunity to bring adults and groups of children together to help write a story that can subsequently be enjoyed by all by being made into a class or group book and displayed in the reading area. It is a time when the adult takes away the scary or difficult roles of transcribing (spelling, handwriting, punctuation) and thus enables the children to develop the themes and language of the story under the guiding structure of the experienced adult writer. In its essence, shared writing involves a large piece of paper or wipe board or interactive whiteboard where the children can all see clearly what and how the writing is progressing. The adult needs to discuss and engage all the children in the writing project by inviting their contributions, questioning and supporting their ideas by modelling and guiding the children in their story development.

Collaborations could include children and other children; older children from other classes and younger, less experienced writers; adults and children.

Adults scribing for children

This is a powerful way of demonstrating writing as an effective way to keep a story safe for others to read. The child can be encouraged to tell a longer and often linguistically more sophisticated story when somebody else is taking over the arduous task of secretary (Smith 1994). When scribing for children it is important for the adult to record the story exactly as the child tells them it. This enables the child's voice to be appreciated so their story can be valued. If you alter the vocabulary or syntax, the child's voice is lost and replaced by the adult's voice. So too is his or her attachment to the story. It is also important to retain the author's words and structures so that when the child reads back their stories they know what it says. There is plenty of time to develop the child's familiarity with the conventions of book language with an emphasis on written standard English as the child has more experience of reading and hearing stories read. Now is the time to encourage a sense of writing as a way of keeping those stories for ever – to be read by others even when they themselves are not there.

Concept keyboards

Storywriting using supportive word-processing software for example BlackCat's *Writer 2* can enable the child to write their story using preprogrammed text already stored by an adult in the setting for the children to use with picture symbols to help identify the text. These are helpful resources to enable a child to develop their story independently without being hindered by their inexperience of encoding every word. Be careful to avoid oversimplifying the storywriting process, however, as it is very easy to end up with 12 stories exactly the same.

The beginnings of creative storywriting

Writing down our stories is the way we record our ideas for others to read and enjoy – they can become more permanent than stories told and once drafted and edited they can remain unaltered (until the second edition, of course!). There is so much to have to think about when writing for the inexperienced writer: how to hold the pen, form the letters, distinguish the sounds, as well as choosing the right word, thinking of a story, setting, characters, etc. The focus for storywriting in the Early Years needs to be on developing the broad story itself: the compositional elements of the narrative as well as enabling the child to see the power and value of writing stories.

In order to develop creative storywriting practices, it is vital to inspire the young child to want to write their stories down. They need to have a story to write and they need to see the impact their story can have on others. To support and extend the compositional aspects of writing, the Early Years practitioner should consider the importance of:

Talking about writing

Encouraging creative story writing in the Early Years needs to build upon the oral work detailed at the beginning of this chapter as it is the child's experience of telling simple stories that will underpin a successful written story at this young age. Before attempting to write the story down, the child needs to be clear about what they want to say – what words they want to choose and how they want it to sound. It is important to allow plenty of talking time before expecting the story to be recorded so that the child can rehearse and hear if their story sounds right to them. It also allows them to compose without having to consider all of the other transcriptional elements of writing it down.

Play

If young children are to write innovative and unique stories, they must also be allowed to experience and explore their ideas initially through their play where they have the freedom and confidence to reorder these experiences, invent parallel worlds and create magic. Exploring the ordinary and then making the fantastical through their own self-initiated play will allow them the opportunities to take their stories as far as they can go, way beyond any predetermined story planner. Their play enables them to inhabit and rehearse other people's lives, which will inform their ability to tell stories about other characters in other settings beyond their firsthand experience. It allows them the opportunity to talk as an astronaut and make an alien a cup of tea.

Purposes and audiences for writing

Finally and perhaps most importantly, the children must be clear *why* they are writing down their stories. They need, from the very youngest and inexperienced writer, to know *who* they are writing for. In a creative classroom children's stories will not be kept inside workbooks or in a child's tray to be forgotten and eventually pushed into a plastic bag and taken home at the end of term. Like all storybooks they must be published and promoted, read and reviewed. Possible audiences for children's stories might include:

- the book corner to be enjoyed by the children in the class
- children in another class
- the school's or nursery's library
- the author of the child's favourite story (perhaps the author of the text their story is inspired by) e-mailed to their website (via the publisher)
- the book corner owl who reads all of the stories when the children have gone home and who particularly loves stories about animals (or any character developed to support the theme or the focus of the learning).

The stories the children write in their simplest form must be celebrated and shared in order to demonstrate the power and function of writing stories down. A written story is only a story when it is read and shared and discussed. Stories written on scrappy bits of paper or left unsaved on the word-processor will be lost for ever.

It is important to ensure that children understand the value of their stories and therefore making books with the children to hold their stories is so vital. The simplest book can be a piece of paper folded in half with the title of the story written on the front alongside the name of the author and illustrator, of course. Further examples and instructions for making simple books can be found in Chapter 2 'Teaching fiction creatively at key stage 1'.

Opportunities for extending experience of stories in outdoor provision

The outside area of any Early Years setting is a wonderful place to continue the development of stories in young children's play. When observing children's 'free flow' play (Bruce 1991), it is fascinating to see the complex stories the children can weave. Climbing frames become castles, tricycles become ambulances and wooden bricks become . . . well, anything they want them to become. These 'tools' aid the socio-dramatic play and enable children to rehearse and extend an amalgam of the stories they have heard, read and seen. One of the most difficult things to do as an Early Years provider is to leave these children initially to develop their stories without adult intervention or extension (unless the pirates become perilously close to the edge of the plank, of course!). Sometimes it is just as important to allow these immediate stories to grow and evolve between the players. Our role is to ensure that the resources are there to support this play: bricks, boxes, transport, dressing up, clothes, hats and, perhaps most importantly, time to enable the play to develop though never to conclude – stories have to continue tomorrow.

In addition to enabling this important independent play, it is helpful to consider other ways of utilising the outside area in order to extend children's relationship with stories:

Storytelling areas
These could be developed outside to encourage the independent telling of stories to a wider audience. I saw a wonderful example in a south London nursery school where the staff had hung old CDs from trees alongside wind chimes and coloured plastic twisters to create a very vivid place where stories could be told.

Puppet shows
The outside area is a wonderful arena for developing an arena for performing stories on warmer days. An inexpensive cardboard puppet theatre with two strategically placed benches can swiftly create a nursery amphitheatre.

Story trails

Posted around the playground using cards and props, story trails can enable small groups of children to see the relationship between a simple narrative and a physical journey. A story trail may begin with a card left in the classroom book area (themed as a pond to tie in with the nursery or class focus on 'minibeasts').

> Once upon a time there lived 3 little toy frogs: Pod, Bod and Tod. They lived together in their classroom pond next to the book area in Lark Hall Nursery. Bod grew bored living with her 2 little brothers and needed an adventure. When everyone was asleep she hopped down from the shelf and out into the playground. She left a note for anyone who wanted to follow her adventure, 'I like to climb and jump and dive, look for me outside class 5' . . .

The children would then begin the story trail looking for Bod by means of further clues from notes, pictures or artefacts aiding children onward with their journey. When the children are experienced in taking story trails, it is a great idea to encourage them to compose their own and to send other children on their own quest. This is a very useful activity to encourage links between age phases as older children in KS1 or KS2 could plan and write a story trail quest aimed at a younger audience.

Stories making the curriculum whole

Stories can form the basis of work covering the Early Learning Goals from all of the Areas of Learning identified in the *Curriculum Guidance for the Foundation Stage* (DfEE 2000). It is the creativity of the adult as well as the children that will bring the story to life and embrace the opportunities the text offers in terms of extending learning opportunities without exhausting the book itself.

Table 1.1 shows an example of the range of activities developed from one picture book. This brainstorming is a very useful starting point when considering a weekly or half-termly scheme of work and is best done with all the adults in your setting so that you can 'bounce' ideas off one another and let your imaginations run wild. These ideas offer a range of learning opportunities and should not necessarily all be used in one unit of work. Many of the suggested activities can address wider learning objectives in several areas of learning. For example, as well as addressing objectives in personal, social and emotional development, hot-seating Handa could support learning objectives in communication, language and literacy (role play to develop understanding of character and plot) as well as knowledge and understanding of the world (questions related to where she lives, how she feels, what she sees and does).

Table 1.1   Cross-curricular activities from Eileen Browne's *Handa's Surprise*

Foundation Curriculum Area of Learning	Activities	Working towards related Early Learning Goal
Personal, social and emotional development	Friendships – interviewing friends to find out what they like best: fruit, TV programme, animal, colour, etc. Hot-seating Handa	Developing awareness of views and feelings of others
Communication, language and literacy	Writing descriptive labels for fruit shop to make people want to buy your fruit – 'delicious, delectable dates'; 'yummy yams' etc.	Extend vocabulary, exploring the meaning and sounds of new words and writing captions
	Handa with her basket and her fruit and the animals laminated and with magnetic tape on the back on magnetic whiteboard to help retell story	Use language to imagine and recreate roles and experiences and retell narratives
	Animal alphabet classroom frieze starting with the animals in the book – looking at *Amazing Animals CD-ROM* for animals	Naming and sounding the letters of the alphabet
	Animated film of Handa's journey using children with masks to play characters	Retell narratives in the correct sequence, drawing on language pattern of stories
Mathematical development	Favourite fruit pictograph – collecting information from children and adults	Use developing mathematical ideas and methods to solve practical problems
	Make and play fruit snap cards (fruit and numbers to 10)	Count reliably up to 10 everyday objects; recognise numerals 1 to 9
	Make and play Handa's surprise race game drawn on to large card with dice to count spaces and instructions to read and respond to story	
Knowledge and understanding of the world	Collecting fruit from all over the world. Tasting and sorting and naming. Use blindfold to help describe and guess the fruit	Investigate objects and materials by using all their senses as appropriate

	Consider how Handa could carry the fruit next time to stop the animals eating it all up	Ask about why things happen and how things work
	Make an improved carrier to stop the animals from eating Handa's fruit next time. Try it out	Build and construct with a wide range of objects, selecting appropriate resources, and adapting their work where necessary
Physical development	Develop a 'Handa's walk' in the outside area using boxes and benches to represent the landscape	Move with confidence, imagination and in safety
Creative development	Develop a fruit market stall creative role-play area developed after a visit to a fruit stall	Use their imagination in imaginative role-play and stories
	Design and make (and eventually eat) a fruit salad and record the recipe for others to follow. Make masks of the animals to help re-enact the story, with musical instruments to help make the noises of each animal	Express and communicate their ideas, thoughts and feelings by using a widening range of materials, suitable tools, and imaginative role-play, movement, designing and making, and a variety of songs and musical instruments

These examples of work drawn from one lovely picture-book demonstrate the value of fiction to enable children to travel and explore all areas of life – all areas of the curriculum in a holistic and meaningful way. It is important to retain a love of the book for itself, however, and not to drain all the magic or excitement by over-analysing or over-reflecting. Ensure that you leave enough of the book to let the children want to go back to the story long after your scheme of work is finished.

Case Study: I-Photo stories in YR

Ann-France is the teacher in charge of a Reception Class in Leeds. The 29, predominantly bilingual, four- and five-year-olds are enjoying a half-term focus on animal stories. The children have read a range of big books in shared reading time including Mark Waddell's *Owl Babies*. They have a special box of 'Favourite Animal Stories' which is taken out by the children every day and placed on the special book table for the children to browse and share with each other through-out the day. They have made group books based on Bill Martin Jr's *Brown Bear,*

Brown Bear set on a farm ('Pink pig, pink pig what can you see? I see a yellow duck looking at me. Yellow duck, yellow duck . . .'), in a jungle ('Stripy tiger, stripy tiger . . .') and in the sea ('funny dolphin, funny dolphin') and have played extensively in their veterinary surgery role-play area.

The children are used to using story props to help them tell and retell stories independently but many were still reluctant to share these stories with a wider group. To complete the animal theme and to support the children's confidence in telling stories to other children, Ann-France wanted to involve the children in a small project that would enable them to work collaboratively in groups to create and tell a simple looped photo story – a short 'film' made from still photos with a recorded voice-over.

Four children were given a selection of favourite animal toys brought into the class over the preceding weeks. Ann-France asked the children to play with the toys and to make a little story with them. She left them to play independently for ten minutes before returning to help them shape their story.

Firstly they shared their story orally with Ann-France, who helped the children decide on four main scenes. She recorded these with the children on a simple storyboard grid (Figure 1.2).

Frame 1	Frame 2	Frame 3	Frame 4
Caption	Caption	Caption	Caption
The animals lived on a farm.	A giant teddy came.	The animals ran away. Teddy was sad.	The animals were friends. They had tea.

Figure 1.2   Storyboard

The children then set up the toys to describe each scene and took a photo using the digital camera. These were then imported by clicking 'import' on to Ann-France's laptop using *I-Photo* software. The images were displayed using the 'share' option and the children took turns to tell their part of the story, which they then recorded on to the sound-track. The children discussed a title for their film and Ann-France wrote this down on a whiteboard as well as a The End caption to top and tail the film. The 'film' was shown to the rest of the class projected on to a large whiteboard screen. The stills from the slideshow can be seen in Figure 1.3.

The Farm

A photo-story by:

Katie, Esma, Yusef and Geoff

Frame 1

Frame 2

Frame 3

Frame 4

The End

Figure 1.3   Final I-photo slide show

Developing your creative practice

In order to extend your creativity in the teaching of fiction in the Early Years, reflect on your current practice and have a go at the following activities:

- Watch some popular children's TV in order to extend your knowledge and experience of the children's current interests and inspirations (ask the children to recommend your afternoon's viewing!). Consider how you could extend links with the children's home experiences, by incorporating characters or themes from children's popular culture into your literacy and language planning.

- Consider how the outside provision of the Early Years setting you are working in is used as a resource for extending young children's creative experience of fiction. Develop your own 'story trail', building on the example given in this chapter, to encourage the children in your setting to develop story-sequencing skills, emphasising how to plan a beginning, middle and end to their story.

- Plan and develop an imaginative role-play area using some of the ideas in this chapter to support the telling of fictional stories. Ensure that you include the children's ideas and creativity into the project and that you allow time for the children to play in it!

- Select a favourite picture-book and consider how you could plan for a week's work to meet a range of Early Learning Goals across the five Areas of Learning.

Creative fiction in the Early Years: A summary

To conclude this chapter, it is helpful to summarise the key areas related to ensuring young children engage creatively with fictional stories:

- Children come to school or nursery with powerful experiences of story making and story listening already embedded from home.

- Imaginative role-play supports children's ability to construct and respond to stories.

- Reading and telling stories to children helps them to develop their own knowledge, experience and love of reading and writing stories.

- It is essential to plan time to read, listen and respond to children's stories.

- A stimulating and imaginative learning environment can inspire a story to be told.

References

Barratt-Pugh, V. and Rohl, M. (eds) (2000) *Literacy Learning in the Early Years*. Buckingham: Open University Press.

Bruce, T. (1991) *Time to Play in Early Childhood Education*. Sevenoaks: Hodder & Stoughton.

DfEE (1998) *The National Literacy Strategy: Framework for Teaching*. London: DfEE.

DfEE (2000) *Curriculum Guidance for the Foundation Stage*. London: DfEE & QCA.

DfES (2003) *Speaking, Listening, Learning: Working with Children in Key Stages 1 and 2*. London: DfES.

Gardner, P. and Grugeon, E. (2000) *The Art of Storytelling*. London: David Fulton Publishers.

Johnson, P. (1990) *A Book of One's Own*. Sevenoaks: Hodder & Stoughton.

Griffiths, N. (2001) *Storysacks*. Reading & Language Centre, University of Reading.

Lewis, D. (2001) *Reading Contemporary Picture Books: Picturing Text*. London: Routledge Falmer.

Meek, M. (1988) *How Texts Teach What Readers Learn*. Stroud: Thimble Press.

Macintyre, C. (2001) *Enhancing Learning Through Play*. London: David Fulton Publishers.

Paley, V. G. (1981) *Walley's Stories: Conversations in the Kindergarten*. Cambridge, MA: Harvard University Press.

Paley, V. G. (1997) 'Story and play: The original learning tools', a lecture delivered to Decoprim, Luxemburg reproduced at: www.script.lu/documentation/archiv/decoprim/paley.htm

Paley, V. G. (2005) *A Child's Work*. Chicago, IL: University of Chicago Press.

Pollard, A. (2002) *Reflective Teaching: Effective and Research-based Professional Practice*. London: Continuum.

Pullman, P. (2005) 'Common sense has much to learn from moonshine', *The Guardian*, 22 January.

Smith, F. (1994) *Understanding Reading: A Psycholinguistic Analysis of Reading and Learning to Read*. Hove: Lawrence Erlbaum Associates Inc.

Tizzard, J., Schofield, W. N. and Hewison, J. (1982), 'Collaboration between teachers and parents in assisting children's reading', *British Journal of Educational Psychology*, 52, 1–15.

Whitehead, M. (2004) *Supporting Language and Literacy Development in the Early Years*. Buckingham: Open University Press.

Useful websites

There are some lovely interactive games and stories with Eric Hill's ever-popular, Spot the dog:
www.funwithspot.com/house.asp?locale=UK

Young children love exploring the Teletubby website, which has some useful information and ideas for teachers and parents:
http:pbskids.org/teletubbies/parentsteachers/index.html

The children's BBC site offers some great games and explorations based on children's popular TV:
www.bbc.co.uk/cbeebies/tikkabilla/stories

A useful site to download those elusive song lyrics from:
www.kididdles.com/mouseum/lullabies.html

Some great ideas for stimulating reading activities developed by and for parents:
www.readtogether.co.uk/

Black Cat offers a range of useful interactive software for use at home or school:
www.onestopeducation.co.uk/icat/earliteracy

The British Film Institute allows you to download some fantastic free materials on the use of film in the Foundation Stage:
www.bfi.org.uk/

This takes you through how to develop simple storyboards for filmmaking:
www.mercedes.wa.edu.au/Media/howto.html

Children's literature and other resources

Jez Alborough's *Where's My Teddy?* (1993), Walker Books.

Emily Bolam's *The House That Jack Built* (1992), Macmillan.

John Burningham's *Come Away From the Water, Shirley* (1983), HarperCollins.

Eileen Browne's *Handa's Surprise* (1994), Walker Books.

Eric Carle's *The Very Hungry Caterpillar* (2000), Hamish Hamilton.

Trish Cooke and Helen Oxenbury's *So Much* (1996), Walker Books.

Julia Donaldson's *The Gruffalo* (1999), Macmillan Children's Books.

Eric Hill's *Where's Spot?* (1980), Heinemann.

Pat Hutchin's *Rosie's Walk* (1968), The Bodley Head.

David McKee's *Not Now Bernard* (1982), Red Fox.

Maurice Sendak's *Where the Wild Things Are* (1967), The Bodley Head.

Martin Waddell's *Owl Babies* (1994), Walker Books.

Bill Martin Jr's *Brown Bear, Brown Bear* (1995), Walker Books.

CHAPTER 2

Teaching fiction creatively at key stage 1

Once upon a time in a land of monstrs there lievd a gyant caterpiller with an enormas mawth and 3 green teeth . . .

(The beginning of Heidi's scary story, aged 6)

Introduction

In this chapter we will consider how to develop children's confidence to create and respond to stories. We will consider the National Curriculum (DfEE 2000) and the *NLS Framework for Teaching* (DFEE 1998) and consider how to ensure that the love of stories so vibrant in the Early Years is continued into Year 1 and Year 2.

Popular culture and home literacy practices

As children enter Year 1, the daily contact between school and family can some-times begin to lessen as children and parents and schools increasingly diverge, with each affecting distinct parts of the child's life: term time/holiday time; school uniform/home clothes; school work/home work. Different ways of talking and playing and different texts help to differentiate and maintain this distinction. All the research evidence continues to show, however, that the closer the links are between home and school literary practices, the more successful the learner will be (see the National Literacy Trust website for a helpful overview of current research in this area). If the school is able to build on and harness the child's enthusiasm and enjoyment of a particular character or story sequence, then their own ability to construct stories and respond to the stories of others will be enhanced as the two unite, and energies and enjoyment can be shared.

Home language and literacy diary

In Chapter 1, we considered the value of asking parents and carers to maintain a diary at home noting down all the activities during the day that relate to language and literacy practices. In KS1 and KS2 it is helpful to begin the school year with a

short activity where the children themselves keep a diary at home for a day, preferably at the weekend or during a holiday. It is important to emphasise that you
are particularly interested in, the full range of language practices the children are
engaged in particularly looking at popular culture such as watching TV and DVDs
and playing computer games, as well as 'extra-curricular' activities such as different language lessons, religious instruction classes, acting lessons and the more
traditional pursuits of sharing books and telling stories. By asking the children
to maintain and share this diary with you, you will be able to broaden your understanding of the interests of the children in your class as well as beginning to close
the gap between the language and literary practices the children 'enjoy' at home
and those they sometimes may 'endure' in school.

Home and school book packs

Most schools have a policy of maintaining dialogue between home and school
with reading bags and sometimes comment books. Try to ensure that these do
not become a one-way, arduous task – one dreaded by parents and children and
teachers alike. Use the bags to send home a range of texts, books and toys.
Encourage texts to come in from home. Plan time in the morning or straight after
school when parents and carers can come in to the classroom to choose books –
this will give you a chance to chat informally with them and for you both to extend
your knowledge of the child as a reader.

Rich and eclectic text provision

To reflect the interests and languages of the children in your class, it is important
to review and extend the provision of fictional texts in your classroom beyond the
usual range of picture books and short novels by well-established writers.

Copies of Disney classic fairy tales on DVD, Beano comics and Harry Potter
computer games will become class favourites, as they are traditionally playtime
favourites. Not only will they encourage reading and writing but will legitimise
the all-important talk about stories among the children themselves and with the
adults in your setting.

Bilingual texts and texts written in other languages should take a prominent
position in the class, highlighting the value you place on speaking and hearing a
range of languages and scripts. This is as important in a class with monolingual
children (to extend their repertoire and experience of language) as it is to reflect
the languages, interests and cultures of children in multilingual classrooms.

Using characters and themes from children's popular culture

In order to build upon children's existing interests, it is important to familiarise
yourself with what is currently popular on children's TV and film. Most popular
children's programmes have great, related websites that are also often useful in
drawing links between home and school story reading and writing practices.

Children's BBC (www.bbc.co.uk/cbbc/), for example, offers a great website with interactive stories, cartoons, games, e-cards and message boards to encourage interaction with popular TV texts. I found a wonderful animated rendering of *A Midsummer Night's Dream* here complete with accompanying text sitting perfectly alongside a 'Fimbles' version of the Three Bears in 'storycircle' – a virtual library of themed stories for the children to watch and listen and play with.

Playing with fictional stories

If we accept the wealth of research in the early years, asserting the value of play as a teaching and learning resource where children can feel confident to rehearse new ideas and innovate upon more familiar ideas (Bruce 2000), then ensuring that opportunities exist for independent imaginative play in KS1 are essential. I find it very worrying when student teachers on our PGCE course go into classrooms in KS1 and are told by class teachers that they used to have wonderful role-play areas but now there's no time, owing to the Literacy Hour or the pressures of the National Curriculum or Ofsted. Time and opportunity to play should not be seen as an added extra for children to partake in at the end of the day if they have finished their work, it needs to form a central and dynamic role in the creative classroom for it is here that creativity is stirred and motivation fed.

And yet as children enter the more structured educational environments in Y1 and Y2, many learn that there is a very clear difference between home and Foundation stage story rituals and games ('play') and school literacy ('work'). As the inspiring American teacher, Vivian Paley states:

> For five years, an intuitive program called play has worked so well that the children learn the language, mannerisms, and meaning of all the people with whom they live. They know what every look means, every tone of voice, who their family is, where they come from, what makes them happy or sad, what place they occupy in the world. Then the children enter school and find, strangely enough, that this natural theater they have been performing, this playfully deep fantasy approach to life is no longer acceptable, is no longer valid. Suddenly they begin to hear, 'Do that playing outside, after your work.' This is a serious problem, for when play is eliminated, the model for story making is eliminated as well.
>
> (Paley 1997)

In order to engage children with reading, writing and telling creative fictional stories, it is important to tap into their instinctive desire to play with stories. When observing children playing during playtimes over 12 years in inner London playgrounds, I would see the most productive play occurring among groups of boys and girls retelling stories from cartoons and films seen at home. The complex narratives concerning huge numbers of characters undertaking quests towards treasure and engaging in overcoming adversities would frequently continue over several weeks' worth of playtimes as the negotiations developed between the children in role. These tales would frequently be so all-consuming that when the bell signalling the end of playtime rang, the children could not bear to halt the narrative and only came back into the classroom under duress. If we could harness this passion for telling stories, this ability to work collaboratively, this ability to lose oneself in the narrative and to create a wonderful world in which to escape to day after day, then our task as teachers would be much easier.

It is helpful to consider a range of play-related activities that could be adapted and developed to encourage this secure environment where risks can be taken and innovative stories developed:

Imaginative role-play areas

Ensuring places for children to develop their socio-dramatic play in a secure environment where you have some input into the scenes involved should be an important element of KS1 provision. In small classrooms, consider adapting a small corner of the room where this vibrant and child-initiated story-making can occur. Plan role-play areas using children's interests as the basis for creative role play. Use the children's current interests to help develop an area where the stories they are keen to tell and develop can be told (see the wonderful work carried out by Jackie Marsh on Batman's central control room, for example – Marsh, Payne and Anderson 1997). Consider other areas of current interest such as:

- A *spaceship* or *time machine* (links with popular films and TV shows such as *Dr Who, Star Trek, Star Wars, ET*, as well as picture-books: *Whatever Next* by Jill Murphy, *Space Dog* by Vivian French, *Quack!: To the Moon and Home Again* by Arthur Yorinks). Reams of silver foil, spray-painted toilet rolls and circular 'windows' with views down towards Earth will enable the children to read and enact their space stories with renewed enthusiasm and imagination.
- *Harry Potter's bedroom* complete with toy owl, Quidditch stick, book of magic spells, posters of wizards past and present – one with moving eyes!
- A *chocolate factory* with sweet-wrapper-covered knobs and levers, taped machine noises and
- *Mona the Vampire's closet* with black capes, fangs and scary stories
- A *wardrobe door* or tunnel which the children must physically pass through before entering a magical world.

It is a good idea to plan the area with the children as they will almost certainly know more about these scenes than you. It will also ensure that the children feel that the area belongs to them. For the wider potential of creative role-play areas in offering opportunities for reading and writing, see also Chapter 6 on 'Teaching non-fiction creatively at key stage 2'.

Computer games

Consider the use of computer games and/or websites related to popular texts. The publicity material on *Harry Potter and the Sorcerer's Stone* Game Boy computer game details some of the interactive activities available. It is interesting to reflect on some of these activities in relation to the NLS text level objectives for Y1 and Y2. Table 2.1 illustrates some of these links.

Although of course you need to be familiar with the material in order to judge its appropriateness for your classroom (sexism and racism are sometimes evident and would therefore not be appropriate for general use unless you want to use them to raise a discussion of the issues), the potential for learning about stories in a dynamic way, affording children the opportunity to become their character of choice can enhance the existing relationship some children have with books.

Table 2.1 *Harry Potter and the Philosopher's Stone* Game Boy and the NLS

Computer game activities	Related NLS Framework Learning Objectives
Play the role of Harry Potter	Y1/T1/T7: to re-enact stories in a variety of ways, e.g. through role-play, using dolls or puppets Y2T2T6: to identify and describe characters, expressing own views and using words and phrases from texts
Sneak, climb, and jump as you explore 3-D environments	Y1/T1/T5: to describe story settings and incidents and relate them to own experience and that of others Y2/T2/T5: to discuss story settings: to compare differences; to locate key words and phrases in text; to consider how different settings influence events and behaviour
Play fast-paced, arcade-style Quidditch	Y1/T1/T5: to describe story settings and incidents and relate them to own experience and that of others
Interact with more than 20 characters	Y1/T2/T9: to become aware of character and dialogue, e.g. by role-playing parts when reading aloud stories or plays with others
Battle evil creatures using all of Harry's abilities	Y2/T1/T6: to discuss familiar story themes and link to own experiences, e.g. illness, getting lost, going away

Interactive whiteboards and story software

Publishers are increasingly recognising the potential of classroom interactive whiteboards to produce talking and moving books where the children can manipulate the characters and scenes by touching the board. This is a wonderful resource for independent work to follow on from whole-class shared reading (see the Billy Goats Gruff interactive CD-ROM from *Come Alive Stories*, for example, which comes complete with wooden character toys, storyline sequencing cards and a sing-along-CD).

Speaking and listening and drama: Creative approaches to telling stories

Opportunities to tell stories to children and for children to tell them to each other continue in KS1 to be a very necessary element of the creative English curriculum. Indeed, as the 'Overview' to fiction states, telling stories is a very necessary element of being a human being. Giving high status to hearing and telling stories must underpin the reading, response to and writing of fictional stories.

Telling stories and the National Curriculum and National Literacy Strategy curriculum frameworks

The *National Curriculum* for English at KS1 emphasises the importance of telling stories to enhance children's speaking and listening skills as well as extending their knowledge about stories. It states that children should experience: 'telling stories, real and imagined' and they should have experience of 'presenting drama and stories to others'. *They should be taught to:*

a   *speak with clear diction and appropriate intonation*

b   *choose words with precision*

c   *organise what they say*

d   *focus on the main point(s)*

e   *include relevant detail*

f   *take into account the needs of their listeners.*

(DfEE 2000)

The NLS Framework has less direct reference to the value of storytelling. For Y1 and Y2 it recommends that children be taught to:

- notice the difference between spoken and written forms through re-telling known stories; compare oral versions with the written text;

- identify and record some key features of story language . . . and using them . . . in oral re-tellings;

- prepare and re-tell stories orally identifying and using some of the more formal features of story language.

(DfEE 1998: 20–31)

Storytelling strategies

The role of the adult in supporting and extending children's ability to tell and respond to stories is vital in terms of both modelling and extending children's experiences. As a part of our PGCE course at London South Bank University, we ask the students to plan a story to tell to a group of children on their teaching practice. In preparation for this, they are asked to practise telling their story to groups of fellow students during a university session. For many this seems initially to be a scary and intimidating directed activity. 'What! We can't *read* the book?' This initial fear of getting it wrong or sounding silly or forgetting the story in front of the class is soon overcome, however, when you see the attention and awe on the children's faces as you begin to take them on a unique journey that could never be reproduced in the same way again. In order to develop your own confidence in telling stories I recommend Elizabeth Grugeon and Paul Gardner's *The Art of Storytelling* (2000) as a very useful starting point. The students on our course identified some useful techniques to support the choosing and telling of stories to a young audience:

- *Choose a story you know very well* so that you don't have to think about the plot or refer to notes that will distract from the flow and break the 'spell'.

- *Choose a story with plenty of repetition* so young children can join in ('I'll huff and I'll puff and . . .'; 'Fe Fi Fo Fum . . .'; 'Can't go under it, can't go over it . . .'). This will ensure the children stay focused and it will help you to structure your story.

- *Practise your story*. It will get better and better each time you tell it.

- *Build up a repertoire* of stories you know very well so that you can tell them at a moment's notice or when the activities you had planned just aren't going to plan.

- *Tell stories regularly* so you encourage an ethos of telling stories in class situations. This will encourage other adults in your setting, parents and children to take risks too.

- *Maintain eye contact* with the children while telling your story. This will ensure the children feel included and will enable them to travel with you on your 'journey'.

- *Enjoy yourself* and thereby encourage the children to enjoy themselves. This is *your* opportunity to be creative!

Children and adults telling stories

Telling stories together can be a wonderful way to create a creative and dynamic classroom environment where each day can afford opportunities to take others or be taken on an adventure. By introducing a range of storytelling activities you will build a repertoire of techniques which can be adapted to support and extend any theme and will encourage confidence in developing and telling stories:

Singing stories   Children can enjoy the rhythms of storytelling and can remember the parts more easily when sung. There are some wonderful recorded examples such as 'There was a princess long ago' and 'The Goldilocks rap'. It is also a good idea to make up your own class story songs. These could be recorded in a book and on story tape during shared writing sessions and could be replayed and reread during independent reading times.

Taking a story on   The adult or confident child can begin a story that should be left at an exciting point to be continued by someone else in the ring. As with all story-telling activities, allow the child the right to 'pass' a turn if they do not have the creative urge. If the story drifts, it may be necessary to take up the story yourself and then pass it on again. The class could use a special object to hold and pass to signify the storyteller (a special shell or stone, for example). This clarifies the role of storyteller and story listener very usefully.

Paired storytelling   Telling stories to a partner can be a useful starter point for less confident children but can prohibit the creative flow of the storyteller and so must be used cautiously. The following ideas can be great fun, however, and can be used as useful 'warm ups' or five-minute 'fillers':

- ABC stories: the children take it in turn to begin the next sentence with the next consecutive letter of the alphabet:

    Child 1:   An enormous bear called Bear went to the zoo one day.

    Child 2:   Bear, Bear, what can you see?

    Child 1:   Colourful birds everywhere

    Child 2:   Do you want to come and play with me?

- Story pairs: alternating only one word each:

    Child 1:   Once . . .

    Child 2:   . . . upon

    Child 1:   . . . a

    Child 2:   . . . time

    Child 1:   . . . a

    Child 2:   . . . scary

    Child 1:   . . . monster . . .

- Story whispers: children sit in pairs close together to take turns in whispering their consecutive part of the story, making it up as they go along. It is useful to allow some thinking time before you begin this one. By whispering the stories you are enabling the children to partake in something exciting, something special and something they may or may not wish to share with others afterwards.

Storytelling bags   This is an opportunity for children to work collaboratively in small groups to plan and perform a story to a wider group or even the rest of the class using the objects in each bag. Stories can be supported in any way (music, drama, puppets, etc.) but must include the given props at some point. Examples of objects might include:

- mobile phone, shoe, and key
- watch, glass, flower
- diary, mirror, feather
- camera, football, shell.

These bags offer wonderful opportunities for children to plan a story together and enable children to support each other's strengths in telling stories. When introducing this technique, it is important to work with each group to help them to take turns, reach conclusions and support their telling.

Retelling stories   In order to illustrate how the oral tradition of telling stories necessitates change and creativity, tell the same story to three children, then asking each one to come back one at a time and retell, but also to improve upon, the story to the rest of the class. What were the similarities and differences?

Children telling stories independently

In order to develop the stories the children tell, they need time and opportunity to practise their stories and work without an audience in the first instance. These stories when refined and rehearsed could then be shared with a larger group or taped and kept in the reading area for children to listen to again. Some activities to return to again and again to support children's independent storytelling confidence:

Story boxes

Helen Bromley has written extensively on her shoe box innovation (Bromley 1999, 2005, 2006) where children are encouraged to enter small worlds represented by scenes created on the inside of shoe boxes. The technique is simple:

1 Find a shoe box.

2 Remove the lid and cut down one or more sides so that the scene can unfold and the story maker can access the inside of the box.

3 Decorate the inside of the box to create the backdrop for the stories (papier maché craters painted with brown paint and sand with plastic astronauts and strange alien life forms for a Mars scene, for example (Figure 2.1); shiny blue fabric loosely stapled around the base, painted sunset on the 'walls' and a small PlayMobil island, tiny fish and a miniature bottle with a message inside for a castaway adventure (Figure 2.2).

4 Fold the sides back up and put the lid back on for the story box to be stored for another day.

5 Decorate the outside of each box to give a hint of the theme inside or, for an element of mystery, wrap the box in unrelated special paper to signify something wonderful inside.

Alternatively, publishers are beginning to produce ready-made story boxes at extortionate prices. Although less time-consuming to develop, they do not necessarily reflect the interests of the children in your class and provide much less fun for the creative practitioner.

The key feature of these story boxes is that the children must initially be left to play uninterrupted, as it is their play in pairs or small groups that will form the basis for their stories. Once stories have been established, discarded, developed and perfected (this will be over several sessions with the box) then the adult may wish to ask the children to share their story – thorough writing, scribing, telling or videoing their story to share with a wider audience. Again, however, it is the process involved in developing narrative structures that is so important here rather than any finite product.

Figure 2.1   Life on Mars?

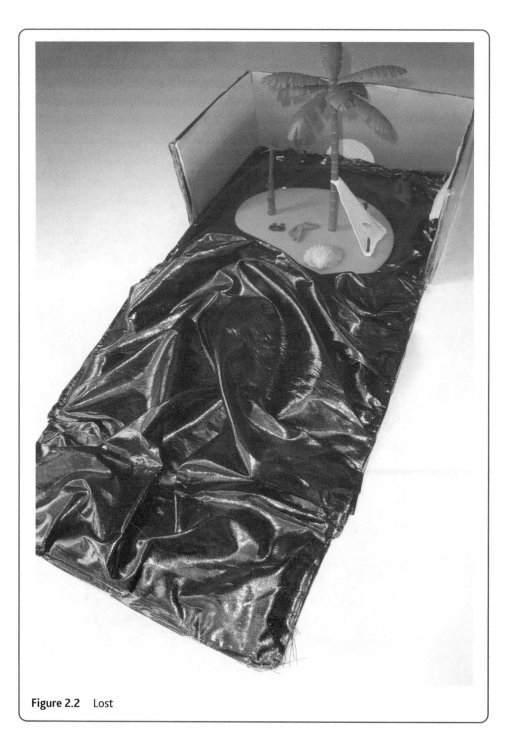

Figure 2.2 Lost

I have found these boxes to be an invaluable resource in the classroom as they can be adapted to fit in with any ongoing theme or can pick up on the children's current interests.

Puppet theatres

Children (and adults!) often feel rather nervous telling rather than reading a story. The security of a puppet or character prop can help to overcome this.

Telling jokes

Giving opportunities for 'joke time' can be a fun way of encouraging children to play with words and meanings. For those of a weak disposition, it may be advisable to check jokes before sharing with the whole class.

Fact to fiction

In order to develop children's understanding of storytelling as entertainment, build up story-telling skills by starting from direct experience and then embellishing and innovating to make the story much more exciting. For example, children tell a partner what they did after school yesterday. They gradually begin to add further details such as a monster with blue hair coming round for tea. Once the story is perfected it could then be retold to a larger group.

Creative approaches to reading and responding to fiction

Reading range

When developing creative practices to support children's reading and responding to fiction, it is important to consider the range of texts available in your classroom. The *NLS Framework* suggests a specific range of genres within fiction:

Y1 T1: *stories with familiar settings; stories with rhymes and predictable and repetitive patterns*

Y1T2: *traditional stories; fairy stories; stories with familiar, predictable and patterned language from a range of cultures; plays*

Y1T3: *stories about fantasy worlds*

Y2T1: *stories with familiar settings*

Y2T2: *Traditional stories; stories from other cultures; stories with predictable and patterned language*

Y2T3: *Extended stories; stories by significant children's authors; different stories by the same author; texts with language play*

(DfEE 1998: 20–31)

The National Curriculum (DfEE 2000) also clarifies the range of fictional texts at KS1:

a   stories and poems with familiar settings and those based on imaginary or fantasy worlds

b   stories, plays and poems by significant children's authors

c   retellings of traditional folk and fairy stories

d   stories and poems from a range of cultures

e   stories, plays and poems with patterned and predictable language

f   stories and poems that are challenging in terms of length or vocabulary

g   texts where the use of language benefits from being read aloud and reread

(DfEE 2000)

If we are to engage children in dynamic interaction with texts that they are interested in we must additionally consider the use of wider reading media:

Books   Selecting good quality texts has never been easier with the wealth of vibrant and multi-layered picture books available. The student teachers I work with are often asking, 'but what makes a good children's book?' The answer, in my view, is often closely aligned to what makes a good adult story book, a good any book: one that captures and then retains the reader's interest, stimulates questions and demands re-reading; one that inspires an emotional response and one that may raise questions or challenge assumptions; one that stays with us after the final page is turned.

Story tapes   Listening to stories recorded by actors, family members or the children themselves is a wonderful way to extend the voices heard in the classroom. If you can place a tape recorder with multiple earphone connections in a corner of the book area it will enable the children to choose and listen to a range of stories independently throughout the day.

CD or DVD interactive stories   The choice of interactive electronic or digital texts is now developing and includes a range of wonderful stories where the children can be involved in the structure and outcome of the stories: see Dorling Kindersley's interactive story CD, *Little Polar Bear*, for example. They are read in a different way from traditional books – nothing to hold or chew, no linear narrative. Here the children are encouraged to actively 'read' the story by exploring the images and text on the screen. The child is often able to extend their knowledge of a familiar text by clicking on the characters and manipulating the actions.

Comics   The range of texts in comic and cartoon format continues in spite of new technologies. Including them in your setting for the children to share and enjoy will help you to bridge the gap between home and school literacies.

Websites related to popular TV programmes   Many TV programmes now have related websites that encourage an interactive and participatory role for the viewer: www.bbc.co.uk/cbbc/index.shtml, for example, offers a wonderful and free resource for use in the classroom. Children can listen to well known stories told by their favourite TV characters. They can sing along with familiar story rhymes and songs and even write their own stories and e-mail them directly to the characters or shows.

Videos/DVDs   Young children are often already very familiar with films of well known stories including Walt Disney fairytale 'classics'. Watching these films in the classroom enables you and the children to beginning to talk about how film texts are constructed. Children are keen to discuss how the story is portrayed differently on film and in the books. For some excellent, inspiring work on using film as text at KS1, see the work carried out by the British Film Institute in their publication *Look Again*. This is a free resource and can be downloaded from their website, or you can order a hard copy direct from them.

Creative reading areas

The storage and display of books can have an enormous effect on inspiring a child to develop their reading practices. Reading areas can be brought to life by engaging a little imagination from the teacher and the children themselves. Consider transforming your reading area to link in with class themes or interests: a Hogwarts library for budding wizards; a space book zone for astronauts; a secret castle turret for fairytale enthusiasts. Adding some special hats or simple costumes, cushions, posters and mobiles can rejuvenate the book corner and make it a place where the children in your class want to go.

Book themes   Books can be effectively stored in plastic boxes with the covers enticingly facing towards the reader. These boxes can be labelled and themed for ease of access and to encourage connections between texts: 'Books we like to read again and again', 'Our top 10 animal stories', 'Stories by John Burningham', 'Pop-up books', 'Stories about being afraid', 'Books to cheer you up', 'Katie's favourite baby books', etc.

Book toys and characters   So many popular children's stories have related toys and puppets for the children to sit with and enjoy telling the stories again and again. As the children become more familiar with the text in their own play, you will soon find them innovating upon the text and developing new and exciting plots and characters.

Book displays   Show off the books you have and borrow from libraries to supplement your stock. If you create a tabletop covered in interesting texts with related toys and equipment – you will ensure that the children's reading interests are challenged and broadened.

CD or tape player with music or stories   Encouraging the children to see reading as something enjoyable and relaxing is a key objective in the creative classroom. Listening to quiet music or spoken stories can enhance the links between enjoyable home-reading practices and help to alleviate the sometimes pressured school-reading practices.

Computer with interactive stories or websites to explore   Including a range of electronic and digital texts into the reading area will extend children's perspective on school reading and can engage those children who feel that reading is not for them.

Reading routines and the literacy hour

The Primary National Literacy Strategy has helped to establish a range of reading routines to ensure children are taught to read through a variety of whole-class and small-group work. These methods are not in themselves creative but they can be employed to develop an interest and enjoyment in stories:

Shared reading   Reading a Big Book together with a group or whole class can help to replicate a warm and unthreatening reading routine where all of the children are focused on one book, reading or humming along with the tunes of the language depending upon their own level of reading experience. Choice of text is here crucial to ensure that the children are challenged and that the book can stand rereading and deconstructing over the week.

Guided reading   Children reading together focusing on the same text with other children at a similar level of reading experience: this is a good time to engage the children in a discussion of the story using genuine open-ended questions to foster a genuine engagement with the themes of the story. It is useful advice in this instance not to ask the children a closed question you know the answer to already (what colour is her hood?), but rather to ask questions you would like to consider or discuss (I wonder what made the woodcutter come into the house at that moment?).

Independent reading   A crucial time in the literacy hour when children should be given the opportunity to reflect, explore and reread stories they have been working on as a whole class and also time to pursue their own reading interests: this is the time for children to:

- browse books in the reading area
- play with stories
- create their own stories in the role-play area.

Reading to children   Reading to children is as vital in KS1 as it is in the Early Years for developing a 'community' of readers as well as enthralling children and demonstrating the joys of reading. As well as reading complete picture-books, it gives you a wonderful opportunity to introduce longer, more challenging books that may take several days to read. Don't forget to use the soap opera techniques of cliffhangers leaving the children wanting more!

Drama activities to develop responses to fiction

Drama is a wonderful way to support and extend children's understanding of, and engagement with, texts. Once the teachers and children understand the techniques, they can be applied to any text. The activities can be developed as part of a traditional literacy hour during whole-class or guided group reading or at separate designated drama times. The following examples are based around one text: *Farmer Duck* by Martin Waddell. It is unlikely all of these ideas would be used on a single text so consider carefully what you want the children to learn from the activity and use accordingly.

Writing on the wall   Before you begin to read the story, draw an outline of the farmer on a (preferably interactive) whiteboard. As you read the story to the children, ask them to tell you how they would describe the farmer. Words to describe how he is feeling about himself will be written inside the outline, words describing how others would describe him will be written outside the outline. These words and phrases will change as the story progresses and the activity enables the children to consider how the character changes as do our feelings towards him (see Case Study pp 72–4).

Mime   Read to page 6. In pairs: ask the children to choose one of the animals on the farm and mime one of the actions to their partner showing the hard work they are involved in. Ask them to consider gesture, facial expressions and body language. Their partner should then try to guess which animal and which job are being represented. This will encourage the children to look closely at the text and to become involved with the action.

Animal talk   Read to page 13. Ask the children to 'talk' to each other in pairs as the hen and the duck using only animal sounds and intonation. Can they understand what the other is saying? How?

Improvisation   Read to page 14. Group the children in 4s or 5s, each child taking one animal character from the story – you could have specially prepared masks or props to help here. In role, the children need to discuss and come up with a cunning plan to help them out of the situation. Initially the children will need some adult support here to help them to work collaboratively.

Freeze frame   Children to choose a key moment in their plan to freeze frame (a still photo of one moment in time). Other children must try to work out their plan from their frozen tableaux.

Thought tracking   During the freeze frame – children to share the thoughts of their character at that particular moment when touched on the shoulder by the teacher.

Hot-seating   The teacher can become the Farmer. The children must plan to interrogate him and find out more about his early life, why he was so lazy and what he is doing now, one year later.

Writing in role

- a postcard from Farmer Duck to the animals
- an advert for a new farmer written by the animals
- a WANTED poster of the Farmer to display on a lamppost outside the farm.

Decision alley   Taking the story on: imagine it is one year later and the farmer, full of remorse wants to return to his birthright! The children must form 2 rows facing one another (the alley). One person must take on the role of the duck. As he walks down the alley the others must whisper out loud why the farmer should or shouldn't be allowed to come back to help the duck make the final decision. At the end of the walk, the duck must consider each thought and be convinced and decide the farmer's fate.

Creative approaches to writing fiction

Writing fiction and the curriculum frameworks

The National Curriculum states that all children must be taught the compositional aspects of the writing process. Pupils should be taught to:

a   *use adventurous and wide-ranging vocabulary*

b   *sequence events and recount them in appropriate detail*

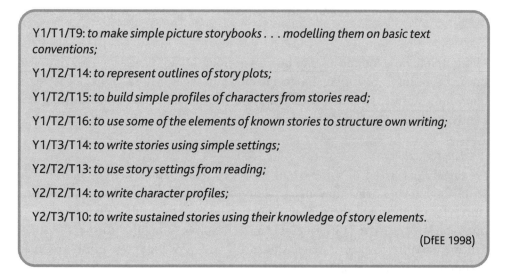

c *put their ideas into sentences*

d *use a clear structure to organise their writing*

e *vary their writing to suit the purpose and reader*

f *use the texts they read as models for their own writing.*

(DfEE 2000)

The *NLS Framework for Teaching* makes explicit reference to aspects of story writing:

Y1/T1/T9: *to make simple picture storybooks . . . modelling them on basic text conventions;*

Y1/T2/T14: *to represent outlines of story plots;*

Y1/T2/T15: *to build simple profiles of characters from stories read;*

Y1/T2/T16: *to use some of the elements of known stories to structure own writing;*

Y1/T3/T14: *to write stories using simple settings;*

Y2/T2/T13: *to use story settings from reading;*

Y2/T2/T14: *to write character profiles;*

Y2/T3/T10: *to write sustained stories using their knowledge of story elements.*

(DfEE 1998)

When developing dynamic and creative storywriting practices, it is important, however, to take a holistic view of composing stories, rather than deconstructing a range of elements into character, setting, structure and then putting them all together at the end of Y2.

Inspirations for creative writing

As discussed in the *Overview* to fiction, children must have a story to tell before they can have a story to write. Be imaginative when considering the wealth of inspirations to support the process of composition:

First-hand experiences

Many well known authors' first novels stem from their own early childhood experiences (Frank McCourt, Anne Fine, Charles Dickens to name but a few).

Young and inexperienced writers need to be encouraged and supported to begin to develop stories from what is familiar to them:

- characters from their family and friends, pets and teachers
- settings based on their home or school, places they have been on holiday or for days out, places where their families live
- take the children on a class visit to broaden their experience of story settings: an old house, a submarine, a wood, a bridge over a busy road or motorway – how does it feel, smell, look? What sounds can you hear? Take photos, recordings; talk to a talk partner. Keep the place somewhere safe in your memory to take out at some later point.
- feelings of being lost and found, being brave or scared, being big or small.

These first-hand experiences can be drawn upon at any time – you do not need Encarta's online encyclopaedia to check your facts. These basic ideas leave the young author free to concentrate on embellishing and transforming the known towards something new.

Reading for writing

As already discussed in some detail earlier in this chapter, before children can write their own stories they need plenty of experience of telling and hearing stories told and read to them. They need to be immersed in the language conventions and structures that differentiate fictional stories from other forms of writing: 'Once upon a time . . .' or 'a magic stalk grew and grew and grew until it reached up into the sky' or 'they all lived happily ever after' contain very different vocabulary and grammar from '1. Chop and peel 3 carrots' or 'On Saturday I went to Sainsbury's and bought some chocolate spread.'

In the earliest stages of writing stories, children will often stay close to the stories they know very well. The innovation and creativity come from building on these familiar stories and beginning to alter, improve and make them their own. Familiar refrains of 'Not now, Bernard' are easily replaced by 'Not now, Ms Ryf' and *Come Away from the Water, Shirley* soon becomes *Come Away from the Fire, Nathan* as they begin to see that characters, settings and plot can be altered and deviation is actually encouraged in the creative classroom.

As discussed in the 'Overview' to fiction, no story is completely new. Indeed, the NLS's flier on *Writing Narrative* calls writers of fiction 'thieves and liars! They plunder their reading and their lives for ideas. They take what they know and then invent some more' (DfES 2001). Inexperienced writers need to be encouraged to:

- retell and rework stories told from home and school
- retell and rework stories read from books, TV, computer games
- retell and rework stories watched on TV, films, DVDs
- retell and rework stories written together as a part of shared writing activities.

Responding to stimulus

Use your own imagination to inspire children to write a story. Consider:

- finding a bottle with a message inside left on your chair before school – how did it get there? Who left it? How could we help?
- hiding an old, torn diary of a mystery girl in a dusty cupboard just before some children are clearing up;
- a class visit to a haunted house or a zoo, which can inspire the story of those who lived there;
- a newspaper report (real or imagined) – the real story of Harry Potter, for example;
- contemporising familiar stories: Little Red Riding Hood walks to granny through the woods – 'Little Pink Hoodie rollerblades to nan across the flats.'

Bookmaking

Making books with children to write their stories in is a highly motivating and stimulating activity giving a genuine purpose for children's story writing. It sends the message loud and clear – your story is valuable. It will be read and reread by others and it will remain important in our classroom or library. It is, therefore, worth spending time and energy on writing, editing and publishing your work.

I have detailed seven really simple books that can be made by the children themselves with some simple instructions displayed in the writing area and some ordinary classroom equipment. A range of paper and thin card can be used – indeed I used to collect paper and card offcuts from when teachers were displaying children's work as any size or colour of paper and card can be used to make a book. Figures 2.3–2.9 illustrate the process of each book.

Folded books

The simplest book to make by the children themselves:

1   Just take a piece of card or paper and fold in half – 4 pages ready to write your story in.

2   To develop this simple book, add different colour pages to distinguish the cover and the inside. Staple vertically along the centre fold with a long-armed stapler to keep the pages together. Alternatively attach by sewing along the spine or by hole-punching the closed book and threading string or ribbon through the holes.

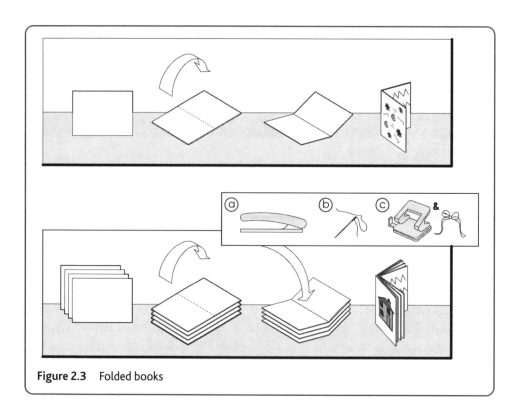

Figure 2.3   Folded books

Folded shaped books

Make as above but shape the paper before you use or staple to tie in with the theme or setting of the story: a haunted house for scary stories, a snowman for Christmas stories, etc. You can use any shape but ensure that you leave sufficient uncut space along the fold to staple so the book stays together.

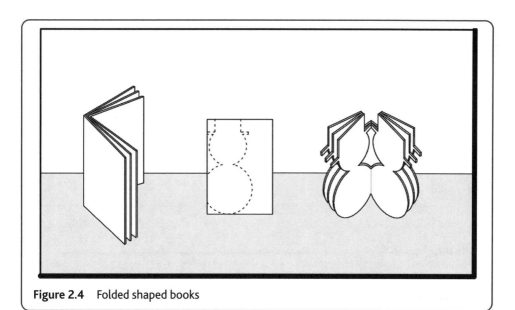

Figure 2.4   Folded shaped books

Zig-zag books

Concertina thick paper or thin card to make a book that stands up. The pages can be used on one or both sides – very useful for displaying books. Stick several pieces together along the fold with tape to elongate the book.

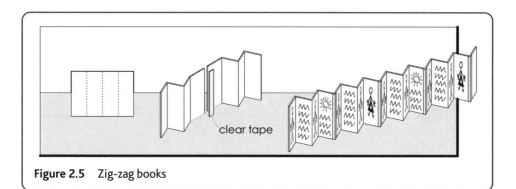

clear tape

Figure 2.5   Zig-zag books

Book in a box

1   Make a cardboard cube from a net and seal all sides except one using tabs or masking tape.
2   Leave one side open so that you can place a simple zig-zag book inside.
3   Glue to the bottom of the box and let it spring out.
4   The outside of the cube can then become the cover with the title, author, blurb, etc. recorded on the different faces.

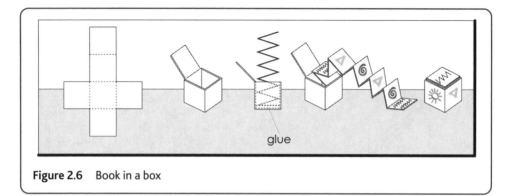

Figure 2.6 Book in a box

Simple pop-up books

You will need thin card for this book.

1 Fold the card in half keeping the fold on your left.

2 Draw a line half-way up and across the book from the open side towards the central fold. Stop 2 or 3 cm from the folded side and then draw half of the shape you want to pop-up.

3 Cut along the line ensuring you leave the fold intact – the book will fall apart if you cut through the centre.

4 Fold the shape down into the book and then back along the crease. Open the page and fold the shape back in on itself. As you open and close the book the shape should now stand up.

5 Write your story on the page below. Further pages can be added with different pop-up shapes on each. Pages can then be stuck back to back to form a longer book.

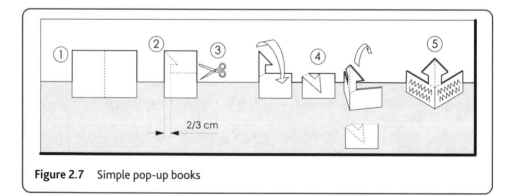

Figure 2.7 Simple pop-up books

The 1 piece of paper book

1 Fold your paper (A4 or larger) in half and then half again and then half again (you should end up with 8 rectangles).

2 Open the paper completely and fold in half along the vertical. Cut horizontally from the fold to the first crease.

3 Stand up paper as demonstrated in the diagram and pinch the pages towards the centre. Fold around the pages to complete the book.

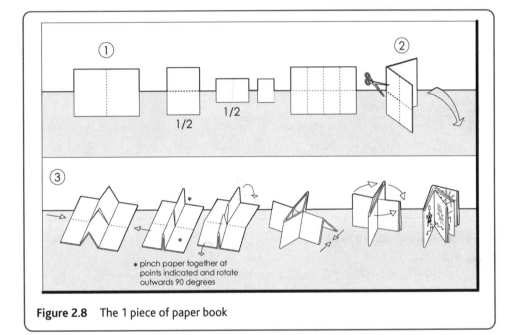

Figure 2.8   The 1 piece of paper book

The unfolding story book

1 Fold a piece of paper (A4 or larger) into 3 lengthways.

2 Fold paper again into 3 width ways and open up.

3 Cut away the corner rectangles.

4 Fold the pages in towards the centre – it doesn't matter in what order as long as you number the pages before you write your story.

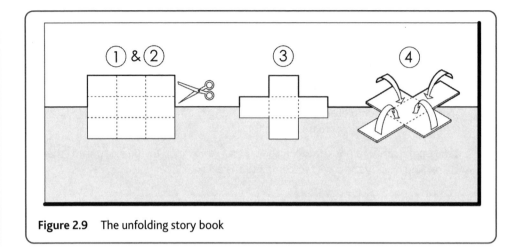

Figure 2.9   The unfolding story book

Using favourite books as models

All of these books can be developed by altering the size, shape and colour of the paper. You could add flaps by folding small pieces of paper and card and attaching with glue (think *Where's Spot?* or *Dear Zoo*). You could add the character to help read the stories by drawing and laminating a picture and then attaching with a hole puncher and a piece of string. You could use hole punchers to make narrative-relevant holes (think *The Very Hungry Caterpillar* or *Peepo!*). You could add envelopes or folded paper to open and reveal further parts to the stories (think *The Jolly Postman* or *Dear Santa*). You can laminate or 'tacky back' to preserve for longer against eager readers. Encourage the children to combine any of these ideas and to explore their own bookmaking techniques – consider the links with DT.

For further wonderful book ideas I recommend Paul Johnson's book *A Book of One's Own*.

Cross-curricular links

A thematic approach to learning can help pupils acquire experience, knowledge and skills in context and can therefore successfully enhance their achievements. It can support a creative approach to teaching by encouraging links between subject areas and by building upon knowledge and experience already gained. It can also allow greater time and flexibility to address several subject areas simultaneously and can promote a more active and participatory view of the school day. 'Making links between curriculum subjects and areas of learning can deepen children's understanding by providing opportunities to reinforce and enhance learning' (DfES 2004b).

Table 2.2 offers examples of activities for a Y2 class related to Inga Moore's *Six Dinner Sid* with the relevant NC links. Many of the activities cross over

Table 2.2 Cross-curricular activities from Inga Moore's *Six Dinner Sid*

National Curriculum subject	Activities	National Curriculum reference
English	Vet the role-play area	EN1 4a; 11a
	Hot-seating Sid	EN1 3c & 3e; 4a & 4b
	Watch and compare book to *Six Dinner Sid* video	EN2 1l; 3a & 3c
	Develop class animation based on story 'The 6 lives of Sid'	EN3 1b & 1f; 2b
	Six dinner children (each child to make their own book based on their own secret lives)	EN3 1a–1f
Maths	The story of 6 – exploring 6 – different ways of making and using 6	Ma2 1a–1f; 2b; 3a
Science	N/A	
Design Technology (DT)	Designing and making cat collars with integral name and address to help keep Sid home	1a–e; 2a–f; 3a & 3b
Information and Communication Technology (ICT)	Digital video animation (see English)	2a; 3a & 3b; 5b
History	Exploring the truth behind Dick Whittington and his cat	1a & 1b; 2a & 2b; 4a & 4b; 6c & 6d
Geography	Map of Aristotle Street leading to a map of locale of school	1b & 1d; 2a–2e; 4a; 6a; 7a
Art and Design	Comparing cat portraits by different artists (Ponkle, Hockney, Warhol)	3a; 4c; 5d
Music	Composing a song for Sid in groups	2a & 2b; 3b; 5b & 5c
Physical Education (PE)	N/A	
Religious Education (RE)	N/A	
PHSE & Citizenship	Exploring the feelings and characters of Sid's 6 owners	1a; 2c; 4a–d

between subjects and certainly these links should be made explicit to ensure holistic learning can take place. It is important to ensure links are genuine, however, and subject areas that do not lend themselves to inclusion should be left out (HMI 2002).

Case study: Reading films in Y1

Liza is an EMAG teacher working in a multicultural primary school in Liverpool. When working with a Y1 class, she was keen to enhance the bilingual pupils' understanding of the whole class text, *Amazing Grace* by Mary Hoffman. Much of the story revolves around Grace's desire to play Peter Pan in the school play, even though she is a girl! In order to support the children's understanding of the text, Liza decided to use Disney's cartoon version of Peter Pan, *Return to Never Land* (2002) to help their understanding of the book's sub-plot. Liza used the British Film Institute's guidance on 'reading films' in their 'free to download' publication *Look Again* (BFI 2003) to support her own subject knowledge with regard to terminology. Liza initially worked on the first five minutes of the film over three 10-minute sessions before showing the whole film to the class at the end of the week.

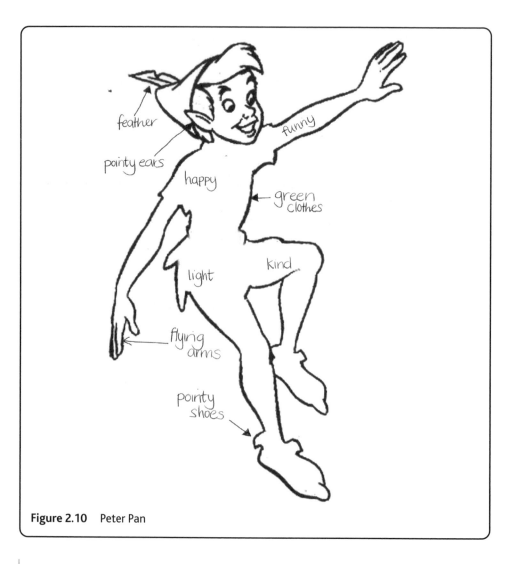

Figure 2.10 Peter Pan

Session 1

Multi-sensory texts

1 She played the children the opening music without any sound. The children then spoke to their talk partners for two minutes to decide what kind of film they thought they were going to watch. They talked about how the music made them feel ('tingly', 'funny', 'happy', 'sad').

2 Liza played the opening sequence again and asked the children to draw on their individual whiteboards what they though they would see as the opening music played (images included a boat, a cat, trees).

3 Finally, Liza played the opening sequence with the sound and pictures. The children then spent two more minutes talking to their talk partners and comparing their ideas before and after the visual clues.

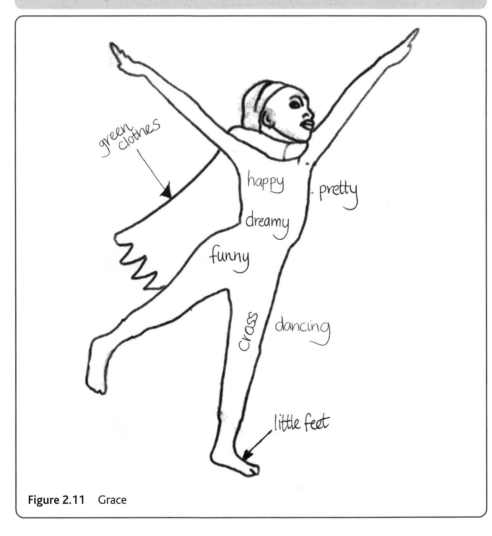

Figure 2.11 Grace

Session 2

Characterisation of Peter Pan

At the end of the opening clip there is a glimpse of Peter Pan at the top of a ship's mast. Liza asked the children to call out any words to describe him which she recorded on a 'writing on the wall' frame (Figure 2.10). Liza prompted the children to consider what he looked like as well as what kind of person they thought he was and why.

Session 3

Comparing Grace with Peter Pan

The children reviewed the group's 'writing on the wall' frame and then Liza reread the class story of Amazing Grace. The children worked in pairs to create their own frame concentrating on Grace's personality. The children compared the two and talked about the similarities and the differences. They displayed the frames in the classroom.

Developing your creative practice

- Design and make a story box to support the independent telling of stories in your classroom.
- Consider a range of storybooks that would complement the box to further inspire the young storytellers.
- Work with groups of children to video a simple story based on their play with the story boxes.
- Consider how to adapt the drama activities detailed in this chapter to a text you are currently using. Incorporate some of these ideas into your literacy lessons to help to bring the text alive.

Creative fiction at key stage 1: A summary

To conclude this chapter, it is helpful to summarise the key areas related to ensuring young children engage creatively with fictional stories.

- Stories can be seen, heard, told and acted as well as read and written.
- Playing with stories can support and extend creative story telling and writing.

- Active participation in drama activities can support a deeper understanding of the text.
- Bookmaking can strengthen the links between reading, telling and writing stories in a purposeful context.

References

Bromley, H. (1999) 'Storytelling', *Primary English Magazine*, 4 (3, 4 and 5).

Bromley, H. (2005) *50 Exciting Ideas for Storyboxes*. Birmingham Lawrence Educational.

Bromley, H. (2006) 'Storyboxes revisited', *Primary English Magazine*, 11 (4 and 5).

Bruce, T. (2000) *Time to Play*. Sevenoaks: Hodder & Stoughton.

DfEE (1998) *National Literacy Strategy Framework for Teaching*. London: DfEE.

DfEE (2000) *National Curriculum*. London: DfEE.

DfES (2001) *National Literacy Strategy Writing Flier 2: Writing Narrative*. London: DfES.

DfES (2004a) *Speaking, Listening and Learning: Working with Children in KS1 and KS2*. London: DfES.

DfES (2004b) *Primary National Strategy: Excellence and Enjoyment: Learning and Teaching in the Primary Years: Designing Opportunities for Learning*. London: DfES.

Grainger, T. and Cremin, M. (2001) *Classroom Drama 5–8*. Loughborough: NATE.

Grugeon, E. and Gardner, P. (2000) *The Art of Storytelling for Teachers and Pupils: Using Stories to Develop Literacy in Primary Classrooms*. London: David Fulton Publishers.

HMI (2002) *The Curriculum in Successful Primary Schools*. Manchester: Ofsted.

Johnson, P. (1990) *A Book of One's Own*. Sevenoaks: Hodder & Stoughton.

Marsh, J. and Millard, E. (2000) *Literacy and Popular Culture*. London: Paul Chapman Publishing.

Marsh, J., Payne, L. and Anderson, S. (1997) 'Batman and Batwoman in the classroom', *Primary English Magazine*, 5 (2), 8–11.

Useful websites

Two American sites offering some great bookmaking ideas:
www.makingbooks.com/projects.html
www.princetonol.com/groups/iad/lessons/middle/paper.htm

The PNS is constantly updating this site, often with some interesting practical ideas. Be careful with some of the related worksheets which can offer rather closed activities:
www.standards.dfes.gov.uk

For useful biographies of popular children's authors see:
www.channel4.com/learning/microsites/B/bookbox/authors

The National Literacy Trust offers some very helpful summaries of current research into parental support:
www.literacytrust.org.uk/

Children's literature and other resources

John Burningham's *Avocado Baby* (1982), Jonathan Cape Children's Books.

Jane Hissey's *Old Bear* (1994), Red Fox.

Mary Hoffman's *Amazing Grace* (1991), Frances Lincoln.

Martin Waddell's *Owl Babies* (1994), Walker Books.

Martin Waddell's *Farmer Duck* (1991), Walker Books.

Eric Hill's *Where's Spot?* (1980), Heinemann.

Rod Campbell's *Dear Zoo* (1985), Puffin Books.

Eric Carle's *The Very Hungry Caterpillar* (2000), Hamish Hamilton.

Janet and Allan Ahlberg's *Peepo!* (1981), Viking/Puffin.

Janet and Allan Ahlberg's *The Jolly Postman* (1986), Viking/Puffin.

Rod Campbell's *Dear Santa* (2005), Campbell Books.

Dorling Kindersley's *Little Polar Bear CD-ROM* based on the story by Hans De Beer.

Come Alive Stories and *Storyboxes* are available to buy from www.yellow-door.net

Disney's Peter Pan, *Return to Never Land* (2002).

CHAPTER 3

Teaching fiction creatively at key stage 2

I like it when we go to nanny's 'cos granddad tells good stories.

(Matt, aged 9)

Introduction

In this chapter we will consider how to interpret and adapt the current frameworks for language and literacy learning to provide an environment where children in KS2 are encouraged to interact with and enjoy a broad range of inspiring fiction texts, oral, written and visual, and to see themselves as creative storytellers, writers and producers, able and willing to experiment with language and form.

Continuing the partnership between home and school at key stage 2

In the previous two chapters we have emphasised the importance of valuing the experiences that children have outside school and incorporating them into a creative approach to learning. There is a considerable body of research into the value of parents' and carers' contributions to children's progress in reading. As a young teacher in Tottenham I was teaching in a school involved in the Haringey Reading Project (1982), which showed that sharing books with children was a significant factor in improving children's reading. Many of the parents did not have English as their first language. They were not teaching decoding skills. It was the interest they showed and the time spent sharing and enjoying books that led to their children's improved performance. We now take for granted the 'book bags' and reading diaries that pass between school and home when children are in the early stages of reading.

More recently Professor Charles Desforges' work (for the Department for Education and Skills, 2003) 'suggests that parental engagement can account for up to 12% of the differences between different pupils' outcomes' (*Excellence and Enjoyment: A Strategy for Primary Schools* (DfES 2003: 47)). It is therefore essential to acknowledge and value the range of different language and literacy experiences children continue to have outside the classroom and to build on and extend the range.

Most schools now recognise the contribution that parents and carers can make and invite them into school to tell stories and sing with the children in nursery and reception classes and to read with the children at KS1. However, as their children gain independence many parents and carers do not have the regular contact that they had when they brought their children into the classroom; many may have returned to work. They may see their contribution as helping with or supervising homework. If we want to ensure children continue to enjoy stories and see reading as an exciting and pleasurable activity that ranks with the many other activities they are involved with outside school, then we need to continue and strengthen the partnership and ensure that we involve parents and the community wherever possible.

A creative approach to maintaining home/school/community links at key stage 2

Language and literacy diary

- Invite children and family members to record their shared and separate language and literacy experiences over a week including watching TV and DVDs, reading newspapers, magazines and comics, sharing stories and anecdotes.

Sharing stories at home

- Ask parents/family members to watch a 'soap' or television programme with their child and discuss their response with each other. For example there may be a moral dilemma facing the characters. Continue the discussion in class.
- Encourage older children to choose a book or tell a story to a younger sibling, friend or relative.
- Ask children to interview a family member so that they can write or record a story for them based on their interests.

Telling stories

- Arrange for a grandparent, parent or member of a local community to come into school to tell a story from their country or region or that has been passed down to them. If the school day is problematic they might provide a tape, video or written version.

Popular culture

- As a teacher, become familiar with the DVDs and computer games that children engage with at home. Plan a unit of work around a popular film or game. Refer to the activities on *Shrek* in this chapter.
- Produce resources for teaching that reflect children's interest in popular culture, for example, a review of a computer game for text analysis or a description of a character or setting from the game as a model for their own writing.

Shared texts

- Encourage children to bring comics, magazines, local and community newspapers into school to include and value the literacy experiences children and their families engage in.

Speaking and listening and drama-creative approaches to telling stories at key stage 2

We all recognise the importance of telling stories to young children but do not always acknowledge the significance of providing older children, especially when they transfer to KS2, with examples of the oral tradition. How many children are told a bedtime story once they are able to read for themselves? How confident are we as student teachers or teachers to tell rather than read a story to our KS2 class, either as a whole class, as a group or an individual? And yet the advantages of telling stories as well as reading to older children are many. Spoken stories have a pattern that enables them to be remembered. They may draw on the rhythm of storybook language ('Long, long ago in the land of . . .') or the dialect and accent of a particular region. Listening to stories enables children to value the spoken word and engage with the teller without the barrier of a written text that has been fixed by an author writing it down.

Teachers telling stories

An important role for us as teachers is to share our own enjoyment of listening to and telling stories with the children in our class, many of whom may come from a culture rich in the oral tradition. One head teacher of a Junior school where I worked would mesmerise children in assembly by sharing with them stories from a range of times and cultures. When asked for the secret of his success, he said that as a boy he had been told stories by his granddad and that when he shared stories with the children it was important that he enjoyed them as much as they did.

Not all of us have had such an experience and we may feel that we lack the skills to captivate older children. The following are suggestions for where we might look to find inspiration and motivation to practise the craft of storytelling.

Video material

In a university session on storytelling at London South Bank University we show PGCE students the video *Story Matters* (Centre for Language and Primary Education 1993). In this video, Bob Barton, an experienced Canadian storyteller, demonstrates the power of storytelling with KS2 children in inner London schools and offers practical advice on how to improve one's own story telling. The techniques that he suggests and demonstrates include familiarity with the material, an awareness of pace, pitch and tone, and sensitivity to the response of the audience. He uses no props, preferring to allow the children to use their imagination, to see the scenes and characters in their mind's eye. This is an important element in developing the creative process. His ability to capture the listener is evident from the rapt look on the children's faces in the video and the disappointment of the students watching the video when it cuts to discussion before the end.

Professional storytellers in school

It is important for students and teachers to have the opportunity to see experienced storytellers working with children as this can help them with their own storytelling. Many schools bring in professional storytellers from different cultural backgrounds who may use music, drama and mime to bring stories to life and both teachers and children can benefit enormously from the experience.

In-service provision

There are also workshops that teachers can attend as part of their continuing professional development to experience and try out storytelling techniques. I remember going to an in-service session for teachers run by Eve Bearne (University of Cambridge Faculty of Education) many years ago where she told a joining-in story called The Button Story. She produced a fabric-covered button from her pocket and proceeded to tell the story of where it came from.

The story was about a rich king and the poor tailor who made the king's clothes. The king wanted the tailor to dress in fine clothes as was befitting his station as servant to a powerful monarch and so he asked the tailor to make himself a beautiful coat, which he did. However, the tailor worked so hard that the garment began to show signs of wear and the tailor had to adapt it over the years: when the cuffs frayed, he shortened the sleeves to provide a jerkin; when the hem was worn he cut it off and turned the jerkin into a waistcoat. By asking the audience to join in and suggest which part of the coat became worn and how to adapt it, Eve was allowing the audience to make the story their own. As the story proceeded, the audience provided the tailor's solution to the problems that arose and the garment eventually dwindled to a fabric-covered button.

This story stayed with me and I have used it in school with a range of year groups in KS2. A structure such as this enables the storyteller to retain as much or as little control as they wish. Each telling involves a creative dialogue between the storyteller and the audience. There is renegotiation from the storyteller and the audience with neither party taking a passive role. Creativity and active participation are embedded in the nature of the activity.

Community links

The less polished storytelling of teachers, parents, carers, grandparents, other adults and children also has significant strengths that we should not overlook. There may be an established bond between the teller and the listener, a shared cultural experience, an understanding of the varied prior experience of the audience that enhances the creative process.

Children telling stories

If children experience significant adults in their lives telling stories as part of an oral tradition, they will begin to recognise its value and learn to develop their own skills as creative storytellers. In the earlier age phases, children are encouraged to retell familiar stories and join in repetitive stories, often as a prelude to writing. From their experience in KS1, children will be familiar with the common features of traditional tales and have a repertoire of familiar stories. At KS2, the teacher who provides a model of different forms of storytelling and shares with the children the devices they use to capture and sustain the audience's interest will enable children to refine their own creative storytelling abilities and begin to transfer these skills to their writing.

Fairy tales, folk tales, ghost stories, myths and legends all originated in the oral tradition. They have been passed down across the years and encompass the supernatural and the extraordinary, elements that will enthral children of this age. They have patterns of language and structures that make them memorable. Children can retell these tales considering how they might sustain the interest of the audience, for example by using pace to create suspense.

The following activities are suggestions to encourage children's storytelling confidence. They can be a precursor to their independent and collaborative writing, but they should equally be valued as part of the oral tradition. Traditional tales can also be used to encourage children to consider the relationship between spoken and written language and to value other dialects and cultures.

Whole class or group story-telling activities

- The children rehearse telling a familiar tale in their own dialect and accent. When they are confident, they might record their story or tell it to a group as a resource for their class or school library.
- Children who are bilingual can tell a story in their own language and record it.

- Children prepare a familiar tale to tell to nursery or reception children putting in sound effects, for example, 'clip clop clip clop over the rickety rackety bridge'.

- Children rehearse and tell an alternative ending to a fairytale to a group or a younger class, for example, 'What happens to Cinderella when the clock strikes 12.'

- In groups children compose a collaborative story using a selection of artefacts (refer to the activity using story bags provided in Chapter 2 on creative fiction at KS1). The artefacts provide a structure and help the children remember the key moments in the story.

- As a class, map out the structure of an oral tale. Children can practise telling the story to a partner from the map. Remind the children that it is not about committing the story to memory. They can improvise and make the story their own. It may vary on subsequent retellings.

We should discuss with children how knowledge of different dialects, accents and languages broadens our language repertoire and helps us to recognise the richness of the language communities around us. Children can research their own language histories and consider how their language varies in different settings.

Just as in KS1, it is important that children at KS2 consider the links between speech and writing and develop an understanding of why stories are often written down. How might children transcribe their oral story? Why might they want to provide a written version? Would they want to illustrate their tape? How? With drawings, cartoons, photographs, puppets, film?

Later in this chapter we consider how we might build on children's spoken language and help broaden their language repertoire by ensuring that we introduce different types of fictional narrative and different ways of presenting them. Familiarity with different fictional genres is essential for children to produce their own creative stories.

Creative approaches to reading and responding to written texts

In this section we explore the concept of 'literacy' and the reading behaviours that we promote and encourage within our classrooms at KS2. It is important that we as teachers acknowledge our own preconceptions about what children should read. Jenny Daniels in *'Girl Talk': The Possibilities of Popular Fiction* (1994) states that 'perhaps the hardest part to accept is that children reading today do not read, and never will read, in quite the same way as we do. This is not a matter of style; rather it is a cultural signifier of a world shaped by us and used by children'.

Children today, a decade after Jenny Daniels' observation, are exposed to not only television and film, but an ever-increasing number of videos, DVDs and interactive computer games and the accompanying 'spin-offs' produced for a lucrative market. It is easy to dismiss this material as poor quality, to devalue much popular culture and seek to redress the balance in school. However, there has always been a gap between what the dominant culture (teachers in this instance) views as 'worthy' and what children often choose. In the past Enid Blyton was banned, comics relegated to playtimes and as a result they became even more popular. Many teachers today believe it is important to embrace the new technologies and work with rather than against children's interest in popular culture and build upon the sophisticated literacy skills that many of them already possess.

Reading fiction and the national frameworks

In the National Curriculum for English (1999), the range of literature that children should read (En2 8) includes:

a   a range of modern fiction by significant children's authors

b   long established children's fiction

c   a range of good quality modern poetry

d   classic poetry

e   texts drawn from a variety of cultures and traditions

f   myths, legends and traditional stories

g   playscripts.

It puts the ICT opportunity in the margin rather than in the main body of the text. It states that 'Pupils *could* use moving image texts (for example, television, film, multimedia) to support their study of literary texts and to study how words, images and sounds are combined to convey meaning and emotion' (my italics). The extensive range of literature under fiction and poetry listed on pages 67 and 68 of the *National Literacy Strategy Framework for Teaching* (DfEE 1998) only includes 'adaptations of classics on film/TV' in Y6 Term 1 and makes no mention of electronic texts.

Excellence and Enjoyment (DfES 2003), on the other hand, recognises as a priority that children should have access to the widest range of high-quality texts but cites four general areas: narrative, poetry, drama and non-fiction, and states that they *should* include multimodal and ICT texts (my italics). It is perhaps a reflection of the dates of the documents that see multimodal and ICT texts being given more status with the move from 'could' to 'should', but it is still the National

Curriculum that is statutory. It is important therefore that as creative teachers we respond to the pace of technological change and ensure that the texts we use are not only of high quality but reflect the increasing range of literacies in the 21st century.

Engaging with whole texts

In order to understand how a genre works, teachers and children need to be immersed in one. At KS2 one of the NC requirements relating to literature is that children respond imaginatively drawing on the whole text (En2 4h). However, under the prescriptive framework of the Literacy Strategy (1998) some teachers considered that there was not enough time to cover whole texts because of the range of material that was prescribed for each term. This resulted in children working on extracts from novels to study 'openings' or 'endings' rather than losing themselves in the 'magic' of a text.

> Children can't *guess* how the magic works. They have to feel it: the gradual opening up of the tension of the story; the arching middle when all the characters and themes have been woven in place; the breathtaking hover before the satisfactory wind-up.
>
> (Anne Fine 2005)

Creative reading areas

However small our classroom, it is important that our class library area is inviting and reflects the range of genres and challenging texts that we want children to read. Children can be encouraged to contribute to the design of the area, in the effective use of space and how the books are arranged and displayed. They can also be involved in the choice of texts.

An important consideration is that children can find and return the books easily and that they are motivated to try new authors as well as find books by an author they have enjoyed. You might include an author focus, where boxes of books are put together that can also be used during lessons. Biographical information about the author, including links to the author's website, might provide an insight into the author's writing. Rearranging the way the books are organised can motivate children to look at books that they have perhaps overlooked. Arranging novels linked by theme or style may help children extend the range of authors or texts they choose. If children are given some responsibility for what is included in the area and how it is organised rather than just tidying it, they will be more likely to use it.

At KS1 children's book areas are often inviting places to curl up with a book. Can we build on the creative practice in EY and KS1 to entice even reluctant readers into the area? Are there story tapes and picture-books for older children, dual-language texts, magazines, animation films on DVDs? Is there a section where children's own writing is published? What use is made of the display boards? Are children's recommendations available? 'If you enjoyed . . . you must read. . . .' Could the book area reflect a setting from a film such as *The Lord of the Rings*, *Tom's Midnight Garden* or *The Borrowers*? Might the fictional setting link with another curricular area, for example, a setting from *Goodnight Mr Tom* could reflect work in history on the wartime evacuation of children?

An inclusive learning environment

As creative teachers we want to promote an inclusive learning environment where a range of learning styles are recognised and children and adults learn with and from each other. It is important that we plan activities that are designed to enable children to respond creatively to narrative, even if their writing skills are still developing or if they are not yet proficient in spoken English. The creative skills and responses that children use in other curriculum areas, such as art, design technology, music, could inform the ways they might access and respond to a work of fiction. These responses complement the more traditional spoken and written responses to texts.

The following suggestions refer to fairytales but can be adapted to whatever genre is being studied:

- **Reading the pictures**. Examples: Anthony Browne *Hansel and Gretel*, Fiona French *Snow White in New York, A Disney Cinderella*. Read the story with the children without the illustrations. Discuss with the children their response to the characters and the setting. Show the pictures. What do they add to our response? Why has the illustrator chosen to work in this way?

- **Illustrating stories**. Ask the children to illustrate a known fairytale reminding them that they may work with the story, add to the tale or choose to work against the tale. The medium they work in may influence how the illustrations are read. There is scope for a sophisticated response that does not depend on advanced transcription skills.

- **Providing a musical score**. Listen to some selections from popular theme music, world music and classical scores with the children. How might children use music to set the scene for their fairytale? They might use musical instruments or use IT to explore and record sounds? What influenced their choices?

- **Set design**. Children select a fairytale and design an alternative setting, similar to *Snow White in New York*. They can develop the ideas of using a story box as described in Chapter 2, 'Fiction at KS1'. Can they design a basic set and add various flats and props to change the scenes? This might link with a theatre visit.

Drama activities to develop understanding of text

As in KS1, drama continues to be an important tool to develop children's understanding of text at KS2. Many of the picture-books produced for older children have sophisticated narratives and drama allows children to explore the deeper meanings beneath the surface features of a whole text and the accompanying illustrations. Drama techniques can also be used to help children to access complex situations in longer novels. If used as part of a literacy hour, the techniques can be modelled in shared reading and developed in guided and independent reading. Alternatively exploration of a fiction text can be the stimulus for work in drama or PSHE.

The following examples are based on the picture-book *Voices in the Park* by Anthony Browne, but the techniques can be adapted to suit any multi-layered text.

Reading the story   The story is divided into four parts and consists of four voices. Read 'First Voice' to the children. It is important as a teacher to model expressive reading to the children even when they are fluent readers. At the end of this section ask the children to discuss with a talk partner what they have learnt about the character. It is important for the children to cite evidence from the text, the pictures, the font. You can move the children on from the known, 'What is the relationship between Charles and his mother?' To the unknown, 'Why might that be?' Read each of the other voices using appropriate accent and dialect and use similar prompts to explore the characters and their relationships. Issues of stereotyping can be explored in relation to class, gender and language. What are the author's intentions?

Describing the characters   Give each table group a character, for example 'Charles' and ask them to make a list of words to describe him. Ask the children to make three lists of words that the other characters would use to describe 'Charles'. How do the characters' feelings change as the story progresses? How do the children's own feelings change? Why might that be?

Improvisation   Ask the children to work in pairs to improvise a scene on a park bench between two of the characters. The children need to consider how they will respond depending on which character they are talking to. This can lead on to discussion about how we act differently with different people. An extension of this is for one pair to meet up with another pair so that all four characters interact.

Hot-seating   In fours one child takes on the role of a character and the others ask questions about their life.

Thought tracking   Children act out a scene in the park taking on the role of one of the characters. At a signal from the teacher, the character says whatever they are thinking at that precise moment.

Interior monologue   As an extension of thought tracking, children become one of the characters and think about their life so far and the future. They can speak their thoughts aloud if they wish when signalled to do so. The teacher might need to model this the first time.

Writing in role

- An invitation to a party from Charles to Smudge or vice versa
- A letter accepting or rejecting the invitation
- A lonely-hearts message from one of the adult characters
- A diary entry from one of the characters of the encounter in the park.

Other strategies for exploring a text

I have used *The Stinky Cheeseman,* a subversive collection of tales by Jon Scieszka and illustrated by Lane Smith, to provide examples of strategies to extend children's understanding not only of a particular text but of the conventions of a genre, in this instance traditional tales. *The Stinky Cheeseman* is a collection of alternative tales in which both author and illustrator subvert not only the tales themselves but the conventional layout of a book. For example, the contents page does not come at the beginning, the narrator who is the little red hen pops up throughout the text, on the cover and in other characters' stories and mocks the bibliographic details on the book jacket, 'Who is this ISBN guy?' The subversive humour appeals to both adults and children and encourages creative interaction with the text, the genre and publishing conventions. In order to appreciate how an author overturns the reader's expectations, familiarity with the original form is essential.

The suggested activities listed below may be carried out with the whole class or with a group and the strategies may be used with most genres. Again it is not intended that you use all the strategies with one text but that you choose those that are appropriate to the text that you are using. The strategies that I describe are: prediction, analysing the text, changing the text, questioning, sequencing, deletion or cloze procedure and visual representation of the text.

Playing with the form   Explore *The Stinky Cheeseman* through whole-class introduction to the text. How many stories are there? How does the author break the rules? Why?

Who is the narrator? What is the narrator's role? This can lead on to an interesting and sophisticated discussion on authorial voice and who the author empathises with.

Prediction   When we encourage children to predict what is going to happen next, we are asking them to be active rather than passive listeners. They already engage in this activity when they discuss with their friends what is going to happen in the next instalment of their favourite 'soap'.

Read the first page of *The Ugly Duckling* with the class. Discuss the genre. What type of narrative is suggested by the opening? How do you know? Encourage the children to refer to the text. How does the traditional version end? Remind the children that this author is subverting the text. Think how the author might end the story. Ask children in pairs to consider both content and style and to write their own subversive ending.

Analysing the text   Text marking is an important strategy to encourage close reading of a text. The following activity helps children to practise their higher-order reading skills with the support of a partner. The ensuing discussions bring out the social aspect of reading.

Hand out photocopy of *The Princess and the Bowling Ball* and a version of the traditional story of *The Princess and the Pea*. Ask the children in pairs to mark the text highlighting with different colour pens the similarities and differences in order to draw out common features. Alternatively the texts can be put on to a split screen on the computer or interactive whiteboard and children can use the highlighter tool.

Changing the text   With the children make a list of other traditional tales that they know.

What experience do the children have of other different versions of a story? Consider film versions, alternative versions.

Ask children in pairs to rewrite a traditional tale in a similar 'post-modern' style to that used by Jon Scieszka (NLSY6 T1 TL6) to manipulate narrative perspective by: writing in the voice and style of a text; producing a modern retelling; writing a story with two different narrators). Who is the audience for the tale?

The use of a parallel writing frame where children can cross-check the events and storyline may be used to scaffold some pairs' work. As a teacher you may wish to support a group version of a tale, using the interactive whiteboard or a computer.

Collect, illustrate and publish the tales using one of the bookmaking ideas from Paul Johnson described in the previous chapter on 'Fiction at KS1'. This can be kept in the reading area or the school library.

Mix-and-match stories   Read *Cinderumpelstiltskin*.

Children to work in groups of four to develop a 'text message' or phone conversation between two characters from different fairy tales. Each pair takes a character and explores the background of the character and considers why they acted in a particular way.

Questioning   The little red hen appears throughout the text, popping up in the most unlikely places. How does the little red hen feel?

It is important to encourage children to ask their own questions of the texts they read. As teachers we need to model open-ended questions and responses as children often find this difficult. Aidan Chambers' *Tell Me* questions (1993) are a useful starting point. While some of the answers may be evident in the text, others may be hidden and more difficult to discover.

Reading between the lines is important if children are to fully understand the complex, challenging texts they encounter. The answers to some questions may not reside in the text and may be answered differently by different readers. Other questions may await answers from the characters themselves. Children can be encouraged to empathise with the characters' hidden motives through the use of drama, for example through hot-seating and thought tracking as discussed in the suggested activities in this chapter for *Voices in the Park*.

Sequencing   Children in the Foundation Stage and KS1 are encouraged to sequence stories orally, through pictures and in writing to demonstrate their understanding of the stories they hear or read. At KS2, the narrative structure of texts may be complex and children need to see how an author uses different devices such as time or stories within stories.

Using the interactive whiteboard, if available, or a computer, work with the class to map the structure of the whole book, *The Stinky Cheeseman*, noting how it differs from their expectations.

Ask children in groups to map one of the stories contained within the book, noting examples of references to other texts.

Ask children in pairs to fill in a simple six-frame storyboard depicting selected images from the tale. Which images do they select and how do they sequence them? What influences their decision?

Cloze procedure   Cloze procedure, where selected words are omitted from the text, is a useful strategy to encourage children to read for meaning, using semantic and syntactic cues. It can provide teachers with an insight into children's knowledge about language and literature. Texts and deletions should be differentiated according to learning objectives and the ability level of the group.

Children should read through the whole text before selecting words to insert. Missing words should not be supplied, as there is not necessarily a 'right' answer. As well as encouraging children to respond to the whole text in their quest for meaning, cloze procedure can be used to encourage a creative response to text within the confines of a text type.

Hand out *The Other Frog Prince* as a cloze passage. Ask the children to work in pairs to provide a creative interpretation of the text. The following example illustrates one child's imaginative response:

Once upon a _____ there was a frog.

One day when he was _____ on his lily pad, he saw a beautiful princess _____ by the pond. He hopped in the water, swam over to her, and poked his head out of the _____.

Once upon a *lily pad* there was a frog.

One day when he was *sun bathing* on his lily pad, he saw a beautiful princess *break dancing* by the pond. He hopped in the water, swam over to her, and poked his head out of the *junk food litter*.

Visual representation   As teachers we can explore children's understanding of a text by asking them to present it in another form, rather than asking them questions that they can answer by spotting the pattern of words within the text. Teachers often employ this strategy when using non-fiction texts with children. Further information on the value of presenting information in different formats is included in Chapter 6. However, this device can also be used to help children see the bigger picture with fiction texts, whether it is the mood and essence of the story or the setting or the interrelationship between characters.

Ask children to design a book jacket, including cover pictures and blurb for *The Stinky Cheeseman.*

Encourage drawing or painting a picture to explore settings or a character's dilemma or relationships between the characters in one of the tales.

Children can adapt these activities to clarify meaning when composing their own stories for an audience.

Reading and responding to film

As well as encouraging children to respond creatively to written texts, it is important that we provide opportunities for children to respond to film (NC En2 8).

Shrek DVD/video

Working with popular culture, I have taken the film *Shrek* as an example of how you might use popular culture and film to extend children's higher-order reading skills and promote a creative response to narrative. At the time of writing, *Shrek 2* had just come out in the cinema and many of the children had the video or DVD of the original. The ideas presented are intended to encourage you to work creatively with films/DVDs that the children are interested in, so it is important to keep up to date with current feature films.

Shrek is full of allusions to a range of fiction and non-fiction genres. Through song, language and image it draws on other texts and genres both implicitly and explicitly. Popular conventions and established narrative structures are interwoven throughout without any particular discourse being privileged. It can be appreciated on a range of levels and thus appeals to children and adults of all ages.

The following activities are examples I have used to develop children's under-standing, enjoyment and appreciation of a film text. It also provided a stimulus for children's own creative writing of fiction and non-fiction genres.

Introducing the text

- Play the opening scene of *Shrek*

  Working with the class, ask the children what they think of the opening where the pages of an old-fashioned book are turned over on screen. Probe on the font, the language etc. Bring out the blurring of film and book conventions.

- Play the first ten minutes. How many characters do the children recognise from other stories? Collect their responses on a flip-chart.

Getting to know the characters

- Role on the wall: provide outlines of the Shrek and the donkey. Children to write words to describe external and internal characteristics, e.g. green, sensitive.

- How are the characters developed? Look for evidence. List under Speech and Actions.

  What do the children notice about the way the characters speak, for example, accent, register, code switching, dialect? They might also wish to consider gestures, facial expression and body language.

  What advantages and disadvantages does animation provide?

- Donkey describes Shrek as a 'fool' and 'a lean green fighting machine'. Children to provide phrases to describe characters, perhaps to accompany paintings or still images. They could be in speech bubbles (link to punctuation).

- Paired improvisation.

- Donkey and Shrek meet to discuss what they should do about the quest. How would they speak, act, react?

Intertextuality

- Children list examples of references to fairytales, for example, 'He huffed and he puffed and he served an eviction notice.'

- Children write an eviction notice or letter – for example, the council evicting a family because of a new motorway. What features of language would a council representative use?

- Watch sequence 'Do you know the muffin man?'

  In pairs children take a nursery rhyme, for example 'Sing a song of sixpence' and turn it into dialogue as shown in the film. They can act it out for another pair or some pairs can show their version to the class in a plenary.

  Example:

  Sing a song of sixpence

  A pocket full of rye.

  Four and twenty blackbirds baked in a pie?

  When the pie was open the birds began to sing.

  Wasn't that a dainty dish to put before the king!

An extension to this activity would be to ask children to provide two different versions. This an opportunity to show how we convey meaning in spoken language and how punctuation is used to convey meaning in written texts.

Links with television and computer games

- Show sequence of Bachelorettes

  Children provide some more examples of bachelorettes or bachelors from fairy tales. Children to act out a *Blind Date*-type programme in studio with audience and cue cards – for example, *Applause*.

- View WWF scene and Fighting Princess scene

  Children look at reviews or the synopsis of a video/DVD or Play Station Game.

  What makes you watch a film, video? Subject matter, form, actors?

  What makes you choose a computer game? Graphics, level of skill, subject matter?

  How are the reviews similar or distinct from book reviews? What makes you choose a book? Author, subject matter, etc.?

  In pairs children write their own review of a film or game. If using the computer they might wish to consider the font and size of type.

Language study

- Show sequence 'Why is Shrek like an onion?'

  Children compose riddles on fairytale characters to compile a riddle book.

- Collect examples of metaphors, e.g. 'Wear your heart on your sleeve.'

  Children to illustrate metaphors.

Confronting /challenging stereotypes

- In *Shrek* the ogre is gentle, the dragon is female, the princess is ugly after sunset, a fighting princess.

  Children can compare this with Disney versions of fairytales – language and illustrations.

  Children to write/draw a comic strip in Disney style and an alternative version.

Further ideas

- Donkey says 'Celebrity Marriages Never Last'.

  Write a tabloid account of one part of the story, using a desk-top publishing package if available.

- Agony Aunt letters.

- Look at the structure and style of the story. It switches between the old-fashioned and the popular. Compare it with 'soap operas'.

  Write an episode of the story in the style of *EastEnders*. Shrek says 'Can't we sort this out over a pint?' Continue.

  Provide photos of examples of film posters. Children could use still-image or clip art to produce a poster.

There are many ideas that we as teachers can adapt from commercially produced material. On the Shrek website and DVD, for example, there are interviews with characters, an Image Gallery, Movie Trailers and Games.

These ideas can be used to extend children's response to what they have seen and often complement ideas and activities that we may already be using. For example, interviews are similar to hot-seating and might develop into another drama technique such as conscience alley, where the character has to weigh up the consequences of an intended action and make a decision. Still images lend themselves to freeze frames or composing a film poster. Children could use significant stills to make a poster or a film trailer, using a digital camera.

Using film to introduce classic texts

As well as working from children's interest in popular culture, animation and film can lead children to explore challenging texts within the dominant literature. One way of promoting this understanding is to look at film versions of 'classic' texts. Working with film can help children to understand how texts work. One of the NLS objectives for Y6 is to explore the differences between stories told on screen and in print (Y6 T2 TL1). Many children's 'classics' have been produced as videos/DVDs or made into television series. Rather than seeing children's love of video as negative, we can harness their interest in film to introduce them to challenging texts that they may feel have little relevance to their lives and experience. Many adults first encounter 19th-century novels through TV or film adaptations.

Many years ago when I was teaching in Haringey, my Y6 class all read and enjoyed Mary Norton's *The Borrowers* and John Masefield's *The Box of Delights* because they were on television and video. More recently *The Lion, the Witch and the Wardrobe* has come out in the cinema and children in the Y6 class I was visiting were all queueing up to read the three copies that were available. Children are often inspired to read a text that they might be resistant to or have thought too difficult by encountering it through film or DVD. Comparing the way different media convey a story enables children to reconsider the choices that authors and film directors make and the creativity that is involved.

Writing fiction: A creative approach

In order to be creative writers of fiction, children need not only to have their own culture valued, but also to have experience of a wide range of texts. Immersion in oral stories and exploration of the characteristics of different written genres and film through a range of creative activities as exemplified in this chapter must provide the basis for developing children's writing at KS2.

Equally important is an awareness of purpose and audience. When children write non-fiction they are often engaging in functional writing and the audience and purpose is often very explicit, for example a thank-you letter to a relative. However they may be less aware of the purpose and audience for their creative story writing. In order for children to see themselves as authors who have a story to share, it is important that they know how authors work. Many children's authors have websites containing on-line interviews where they share their ways of working, including where they get their ideas from. As a result of a visit to school from one local author, the children in my class always carried a notebook where they jotted down ideas that might be useful for a future story. They were encouraged to be observant and look at their surroundings and characters they knew or encountered as possible material.

The National Literacy Strategy training materials advocate the importance of familiarising children with story structure and the authorial techniques for narrative writing. However, children are often encouraged to write in a formulaic way, focusing on scene-setting, characterisation, problem-setting and resolution from Y3 through to Y6. Although these components provide a base from which to model narrative writing, as their writing develops children need the opportunity to experiment with creative interpretations of the story components and experiment with the sequence of these components. As we have demonstrated, challenging texts often play around with structural elements and interweave different elements in unconventional ways. They make demands on both the reader and the writer. Just as young children need to know that what they write will have an audience, older children should learn to recognise the needs of more diverse audiences. They need opportunities to engage in extended writing, to plan, draft, edit and publish work that they are pleased with.

One of the most positive strategies that the NLS training materials advocated was the importance of teachers, through shared or guided writing, modelling the thought processes that accompanied the compositional aspects of writing a story. In the past much of the emphasis on redrafting was on the transcriptional aspects of writing with children expecting their initial ideas to remain unchanged. By focusing on the process of writing rather than the finished product, children are enabled to take risks and experiment as authors. The use of the interactive whiteboard and word-processing has made the drafting process easier. The 'Track changes' facility allows the writer to revert to earlier ideas if they choose.

If we are to develop creative practice we must demonstrate how the various elements of a text intermingle both by pointing out how established authors work in shared reading and by modelling the process in shared writing:

> I feel 'very shy' does not quite convey what I want to say about this character. If I change it to 'painfully shy', the reader might understand how miserable she feels going into her new class.

If children become used to drafting their stories in the compositional stage, they will know that ideas are often rejected, edited out or changed. The process of reviewing, editing and changing the sequence of events should be seen as a response to the needs of the audience.

The use of response partners where children respond and comment on a partner's work is a useful device for helping children to be aware of the needs of the audience. Again, as a teacher it is important to model the process:

I understood how angry M felt because you described the way 'she clenched her fists.' I saw you doing that when you tried to get inside the character through role play.

Teaching story components creatively

Although it is important that children have the opportunity to produce whole texts for an identified audience, there are strategies that we can provide to enable children to improve elements of their writing without resorting to a formulaic approach. For example, children may have thought of a problem they are going to include in their story without having considered the setting. The process of writing a story is not necessarily linear.

The examples below are intended to encourage students and teachers to use a creative approach to teaching and learning that builds upon children's interests in order to develop and extend their language and literacy skills. These components of narrative should not be seen as necessarily sequential.

Scene setting

There are many ways to encourage children to set the scene in their stories and to choose vocabulary and syntax to convey mood and atmosphere for the audience. As teachers we might provide music, visual images, taste or smell to suggest words or phrases to convey an atmosphere.

One student teacher I was supervising used a school trip to a stately home to inspire and support children's creative writing. As they soaked up the atmosphere in the chill of the stair well and considered the secret lives of the ancestors' portraits that hung on the walls, they were collecting the material that would inform their stories when they returned to school. They were authors researching their material.

Characterisation

It is by exploring in detail the range of techniques that an author uses that children learn to use methods other than just direct description of physical or personal characteristics. This is most easily achieved by asking questions of a text that rely on inferential knowledge. This might be carried out as a prelude to shared writing. Children can highlight all the information they have about a character using the interactive whiteboard or a photocopy of a text. They might consider dialogue, other perspectives, adverbs, actions, expressions, and interaction between characters before seeing the teacher demonstrate taking the story on using the author's chosen techniques. By seeing the teacher model the thought processes of the author, the children learn how and why a character is presented in a particular way and why the reader empathises or dislikes a character at a given point in the story. They are learning about the process of writing and can try out some of the ideas for themselves.

Problem setting and problem solving

Children are familiar with the dilemmas facing characters in the stories and films they see and the computer games that they play. Improvisation in drama sessions can encourage children to think creatively about the types of problems that may be encountered in a particular genre and different possible solutions. As a teacher you might set a problem for the children to resolve in groups. Children may act out or freeze-frame a problem. What actions are required? What contribution do the protagonists make to resolve the problem? Groups can set problems or provide solutions for other groups. The stylistic choices that need to be made to convey the seriousness or urgency of a situation might then be explored through shared and guided writing.

Extended writing

It is crucial that children have the opportunity to combine the components of narrative that they have been learning about in formal and informal ways to produce their own stories for an audience. This cannot be achieved in a single lesson but will need a longer period of time, if the end result is to be a story that they are proud of.

Case Study: Personalised story books

One successful example of practice with a Y5/6 class was a project that involved them writing for children in a Y2 class. As a follow-on to the successful paired reading that was already established in the school, where older children listened to a younger child read and enjoyed stories with them, they engaged in a writing project.

In a short interview the Y5 children asked their young partners what types of story they liked to read, listen to or watch on TV, as they were going to write a story just for them. The Y2 children showed them their favourite books. They talked about their favourite cartoons and videos. The children made notes on what their partners told them to help them plan the story. They had to interpret the answers on what their partner would like, including

'the goodies win', 'a princess', 'a scary monster', 'cartoon characters', 'me in it', 'a magic forest', 'happy ever after', 'fighting', 'a castle', 'a flying horse', 'I like comics'.

The information helped them to decide on genre, structure, characters and setting.

The children researched the genre of the story that they were writing. This entailed reading favourite books, immersing themselves in a particular genre, looking at the language, layout, illustrations. They had to plan, draft and review their stories. Over a period of six weeks' intensive activity, they produced personalised stories for their partners.

All children were able to take part: some produced lavishly illustrated stories with little written text, others produced short-chapter books, some dual-language texts, some reworked familiar tales. No child was excluded. Where necessary they were supported with the compositional aspects of their story when they got stuck or suffered from 'writer's block', as we called it. They used each other as 'response partners'. Some children needed help with the secretarial aspects of their work. Some books had a separate illustrator, as the children learnt to recognise and value each other's skills.

The children wrote their own biographical details inside the cover. They included a dedication 'This book is for . . .'.

In the final week they worked in pairs to review each other's books and with the help of their partner wrote a brief blurb: 'Will Mark overcome the dragon? Read on to find out.'

Many of the children in the class had not been encouraged to see themselves as authors and were unenthusiastic and uninspired when writing stories. Over this six-week period, they learnt to be inventive and creative and for the first time saw themselves as authors writing for a specific, known audience. Drafting, reviewing and editing were an essential part of the process that led to their 'book launch', where they signed their 'first edition'. The subsequent sharing of a book that both the younger and older child 'owned' was beneficial to both children's self-esteem.

A project such as I have described can be incorporated into a unit of work whether or not there is a formal structure such as the literacy hour. It provides children with the opportunity and incentive to work on an extended piece of writing. The children can make the books in Design and Technology and illustrate them in Art if the practice in the school restricts the content of the literacy hour. If the school is promoting a more cross-curricular approach such as advocated in the Primary National Strategy, the process may be more fluid.

Writing in the style of an author

It is important to provide opportunities for children to have experience of longer novels and consider stylistic features. At KS2 it is important to explore with children how an author makes their stylistic choice (Y5 Term 3 Text level 9). This can only be accomplished by close reading of a text and exploring how the scene is set, how the characters think, behave and speak and why. If as a teacher we model aloud the thinking process that we engage in, if we try to continue an author's story using similar stylistic devices, we are introducing children to a writer's craft and their creative thought processes. In turn children can take the story on and explain how they made their choices.

Co-authoring

One teacher working with Y6 children in a South London school chose Lemony Snicket as an author focus. The teacher conveyed his enthusiasm for the books and the children were passionate about them. While reading *Book The Eighth* in *A Series of Unfortunate Events* as a class novel, the teacher introduced the idea of co-authoring. On the back cover the author had stated his intention 'to write it down as best I can'. The children were to write another chapter or scene for the book that they imagined the author might have edited out. Perhaps it was too terrible to recall even for Lemony Snicket!

At strategic points during the novel, the teacher discussed with the class what might happen next, why a character behaved in the way that they did, possible alternatives to events. The children were so involved with the Baudelaire children and with their enemy, Count Olaf, that they had lots of suggestions and would carry on their discussions beyond the classroom. The children worked in mixed ability groups to write other scenes that might have been included if they were co-authoring.

Some children who had difficulties with transcription had brilliant ideas. The group scribes used large sheets of paper to jot down suggestions. Once they had their skeleton plan the children were supported in the writing process through opportunities for improvised role-play, hot-seating, thought tracking, decision alley and group discussion. Many chose to write in role about the same events as seen from another character's viewpoint, thus providing another perspective. One group introduced a flashback to explain why a character was behaving in a particular way. Another included Sunny's baby language that adults could not understand.

After some redrafting, one member of each group typed up the additional scene. Some groups included illustrations in the style of Brett Helquist. All groups included a proviso, similar to the author's, for the reader on the lines of 'Clearly you do not want to read about such things.' The teacher read out the 'missing' scenes as they were finished, reminding the class where they would have come in the story. The scenes were kept in a file in the book corner and enjoyed almost as much as the novel itself.

Throughout this extended project the children were reflecting upon the text and gaining an understanding of book structure, stylistic features and authorial choice. They were given some autonomy and enabled to be creative within the confines of a style of writing. They were practising writing in a style that had captured their imagination, as a prelude, it is hoped, to finding their own voice.

Making films – another form of narrative

By using children's visual literacy we can develop children's understanding of the conventions of both books and films and enable them to experiment with different ways of producing narratives.

As a class you might look at the opening film scenes of a book that they have read, such as a Harry Potter novel, and ask the children to find details from the book that have informed the selection of material.

- Why did the film maker make his or her choices?

- Would the children have chosen to focus on the same incidents?

- List the way the author of the book has evoked atmosphere. For example, words, phrases, sentences.

- How was the atmosphere conveyed on film? Music, still image, fading out?

- What techniques were used in the film? For example, close-up, angle, lighting.

Children can experiment with hand-held video cameras or digital camera, to try out different opening shots for one of their own stories. Using a 'voice over' provides the opportunity to consider the authorial voice in both film and novel.

Many DVDs have out-takes and interviews with the characters and many children will be familiar with these. This is a useful way to show children how much editing takes place by accomplished film makers. As with writing, the process of reviewing, editing and changing the sequence of events in response to the needs of the audience will be an important part of the process of making a short film or photo story. The children will be constantly switching from producer to audience. By using and extending children's visual literacy we can develop children's understanding of the conventions of both books and films and enable them to experiment with different ways of producing narratives.

An inspiring resource to encourage and give you practical advice on how to use film with your class is *Look Again! A Teaching Guide to Using Film and Television with Three- to Eleven-Year-Olds* (BFI Education 2003).

Developing your creative practice

- Consider how you might use an artefact to devise a joining-in story for children at KS2.

- Design a reading area for a KS2 classroom that reflects a creative approach to the organisation of resources, taking into account children's interest in popular culture and multimodal texts.

- How might you use one of the creative arts to deepen children's understanding of a text?

- Select a written fiction text or film that you wish to use with a class and devise activities to encourage children to engage in a creative response to the text.

Teaching fiction creatively at key stage 2: A summary

To conclude this chapter, we have summarised the key factors in ensuring that children enjoy reading fiction and become creative storytellers and writers:

- The oral tradition is an important part of our heritage and should be included in the curriculum we provide.
- It is important to build on children's interest in popular culture and technology and value the literacy skills that they already possess.
- Children should engage with whole texts that challenge their thinking and extend their imagination.
- Children should be encouraged to take risks and move beyond formulaic writing.
- Providing audiences for children's storytelling and writing increases motivation and encourages them to see themselves as authors.

References

BFI Education (2003) *Look Again!: A Teaching Guide to Using Film and Television with Three- to Eleven-Year-Olds.* London: BFI Education.

Chambers, A. (1993) *Tell Me: Children, Reading and Talk.* London: Thimble Press.

Daniels, J. (1994) ' "Girl talk": the possibilities of popular fiction' in Styles, M., Byrne, E. and Watson, V. (eds) *The Prose and the Passion: Children and their Reading.* London: Cassell.

DfEE (1998) *The National Literacy Strategy Framework for Teaching.* London: HMSO.

DfEE (2000) *English in the National Curriculum.* London: HMSO.

(DfES (2003) *Excellence and Enjoyment: A Strategy for Primary Schools.* London: HMSO.

Fine, A. (2005) 'Read, read more, read everything' in *Waiting for a Jamie Oliver: Beyond Bog-standard Literacy.* Reading: National Centre for Language and Literacy (NCLL).

Gamble, N. and Yates, S. (2002) *Exploring Children's Literature.* London: Paul Chapman. (Chapter 7 'Genres and traditional stories' provides a useful overview and background information.)

Tizzard, J., Schofield, W. and Hewison, J. (1982) 'Collaboration between teachers and parents in assisting children's reading', *British Journal of Educational Psychology*, 52, 1–15.

Wilson, A. (2004) *Language Knowledge for Primary Teachers.* London: David Fulton Publishers.

Useful websites

http:www.standards.dfes.gov.uk/
is invaluable for keeping up-to-date with reports on current research on all aspects of language and literacy teaching, the latest government initiatives and developments within the Primary Strategy. There is also useful information on latest publications and teaching resources.

http:www.bfi.org.uk/education/resources
currently provides excellent on-line materials for teaching folk tales creatively at KS2 and the opportunity to purchase the accompanying DVD. There are practical supportive suggestions on how to use the material in the classroom and suggested activities for children. There are also suggestions as to how the material might be used as informal educational activities for families, an area that we have emphasised throughout this book.

Children's literature and other resources

Jon Scieszka's *The Stinky Cheeseman* (2002), London: Viking Press.

Anthony Browne's *Voices in the Park* (1999), London: Picture Corgi.

Lemony Snicket's *A Series of Unfortunate Events: Book the Eighth: The Hostile Hospital* (2003). London: Egmont.

PART 2

Creativity and non-fiction: An overview

It's hard to believe that there was ever a time when I had not seen such an illustration before, but evidently I had not for I clearly remember being transfixed.

(Bill Bryson remembering first seeing a diagram of the earth's interior, 2003)

The role of non-fiction in our daily lives cannot be overestimated. First, review your day so far. Now rerun the day concentrating on your engagement with non-fictional texts to help you through your day. It may include some of the following:

- checking the weather on *Teletext* before choosing what to wear
- reading subtitles on News 24
- writing a text message to a friend
- checking the gas bill and hoping for possible errors
- reading an advert for a new film on the tube
- choosing a cereal packet from a wide selection in your cupboard
- leaving a note for the milkman to cancel the milk
- downloading a song on your MP3 player
- following a recipe for a birthday cake
- reading the newspaper over somebody's shoulder on the bus
- checking your route on the A–Z
- scanning your e-mails for one you want to read
- skimming down the bewildering list of coffees to find a hot one with milk.

And all of these before you even get to work! Indeed our daily lives revolve around our interaction with a plethora of non-fictional texts. They enable us to: recall and recount; persuade and instruct; inform and explain; discuss and analyse the world around us.

What is non-fiction?

Non-fictional texts are enormously diverse in form and function as illustrated on p 103. They can help us to record our memories (diary) and find our way around (map). They can help us to convince others of our beliefs (political pamphlets) and dictate how we spend our money (adverts). They can tell us about things we want to know (websites) and show us how to do something we don't understand (flat-pack bed instructions).

The *National Literacy Strategy Framework*'s glossary of terms (DfEE 1998) does not give a single definition for non-fiction. Indeed the Primary Strategy's approach to the teaching of non-fiction is perhaps the most prescriptive of all their teaching advice. They present non-fiction as composed of 6 discrete text types:

1 Recount

2 Instructions

3 Non-chronological report

4 Explanation

5 Persuasion

6 Discussion.

Each of these is described and explored in a series of glossy pamphlets produced by the DfEE. The 'fliers' describe the main features of each text type and explore the fairly simplistic approach of immersion (plenty of reading of said text type), analysis (drawing out and considering any common key features) and writing (through shared and guided and independent writing activities). This process is explored more fully in *NLS Grammar for Writing* (DfEE 2000a). Although this is an appealing model of encouraging children to gain access to a range of different non-fiction genres, it does not account for the complex nature of many real non-fictional texts (as opposed to the perverse publisher-manufactured texts designed, written and produced to fit the text type descriptions).

Consider, for example, a recipe by Madhur Jaffrey:

In their own mountainous homeland, Kashmiris eat *haak* all through the year. In the summer and early autumn, they pluck the leaves right off the stalk and cook them very simply in mustard oil with a touch of asafetida. The asafetida has traditionally come from their neighbour, Afghanistan. As the chill winter sets in with a staying determination, *haak* is dried in plaited wreaths to preserve it for the snowy winter months.

(Jaffrey 1983)

Her vivid descriptive account is very much an integral part of the instructions to help us cook. Which boxes does it tick? The creative teacher will utilise these pre-scriptive materials to support a discussion of texts but will ensure that the texts read and written are not stifled by an impoverished text in order to demonstrate a point.

Fact or fiction?

It is important to consider the differences between fiction and non-fiction. Fictional narratives tell us a story – they may contain elements of fact and be presented in such a way as to convince the reader or watcher of the events unfolding, but they are not literally true.

Non-fiction is, by its nature, biased. It is constructed by one person to give us their perspective and can therefore be used to one's advantage or disadvantage. A holiday brochure sells one hotel above another, a recipe favours one type of red chilli over another, a diary entry will only record what the author really wants to be read, an e-mail will tell your side of the story first, a TV review will be peppered with the critic's own prejudices, the European atlas will distort distant, less powerful continents to enhance its own geography. Understanding the power of non-fictional texts through a range of questioning and active activities will support children's ability to be creative users and creators of factual texts.

Non-fiction offers a text that is factual and *presented* as truth. It can be presented and read as impartial and serious and authoritative. The creative teacher will recognise the opportunity here to build on the experience children already have in interacting with non-fiction texts and the importance of encouraging a questioning and challenging stance towards them. As our lives become increasingly dominated by powerful and sophisticated images and texts, it has never been more important to develop critical and analytical reading strategies.

In the earliest stages of textual analysis, children in the Foundation Stage may begin to look at some of the surface differences between factual and fictional texts. They could sort books into piles with help from adults determining any distinguishing features to help them classify ('stories usually have pictures; non-fiction books usually have photos'). They might begin to consider TV adverts for toys: 'How can we tell they want a boy to buy this?' As children move into KS1 and KS2, this analysis can be developed by looking at more detailed differences in texts (use of language and grammatical structures) as well as exploring how we are made to feel about certain texts (sweet packaging or shopping bags, for example – what do they tell us about the sweet, the shop, us?).

Teaching non-fiction creatively

The key to creative teaching of reading, response and composition of non-fiction texts is, therefore, an understanding that factual texts are as creative as fictional ones. Authorial decisions with regard to contents (inclusions and, critically, omissions), point of view, text type, organisation, tone, etc. are all crucial aspects in creating and responding to texts.

In the following chapters we consider a range of ways to ensure that non-fiction is not left on the shelf. In Chapter 4, we discuss the importance of role-play and drama to explore real-life scenarios and to build upon young children's first-hand experiences of the 'real' world. In Chapter 5 we focus on drama as a tool to draw on fiction in order to explore non-fiction. We consider how to engage children in writing in role in order to explore a number of text types in a meaningful and active way. In Chapter 6 we focus on the importance of reading and writing across the curriculum with explicit links made to other National Curriculum subject areas.

Speaking and listening

As with the telling of fictional stories, so the telling of factual stories and events, the giving and receiving of instructions, the recounting and reflecting on events past and present are all crucial in defining who we are. As the greater part of information is passed to us verbally (TV and radio news, word of mouth, educational and promotional DVDs, telephone, etc.), much of the creative work in the classroom will also be oral. The following chapters explore a range of activities designed to engage the children with non-fiction through some of the following activities:

- drama and role play
- interviews and presentations
- film and video
- adverts and jingles
- podcasts and radio reports
- commentaries and interviews.

As children are actively engaged in making, and responding to, non-fiction, so their understanding of issues and events deepens.

Reading and responding to non-fiction

Ways of reading

Consider for a moment snuggling down on the sofa with your novel, opening the crisp cover and beginning at Chapter 1. You expect to be introduced slowly to the settings, themes and characters as the narrative weaves a spell and you become immersed as the story unfolds. Wanting to know what happens, caring for the characters and (with a book you enjoy, anyhow) following the story onwards until the climax and then the resolution are all part of the pleasure of the read. Early Years and primary school teachers are historically very good at supporting children on this narrative journey, modelling the process through shared and guided reading and through reading stories regularly to the children.

And yet the scenario is rather different when reading an information text. Now consider how you read your newspaper, the bus timetable, an 'E-bay' search for new shoes, your MP3 instruction booklet, a diagram of the heart in your medical encyclopaedia. Each demands of the reader slightly different skills in order to draw out the information we want to know. These skills include:

- using contents pages, alphabetic indexes, glossaries, dictionaries
- reading the blurb on the back of the text
- reading diagrams and maps
- skimming and scanning
- scrolling and searching.

These skills are sometimes referred to as 'higher order reading skills', implying a hierarchy of skills that is rather unhelpful when teaching emergent readers. These are vital and necessary skills across the age phases that can be learnt alongside narrative reading strategies. It is important to recognise that most five- and six-year-olds are quite familiar with accessing information across a range of media (few children will fail to find the favourite TV listing out of a complete TV guide, for example).

The creative teacher will avoid at all costs those purposeless exercises where the children have to use a dictionary to order a list of unrelated words or copy down a number of explanations taken from a glossary. These do little to inspire a deep understanding of the reading skills as they have no real context and no percepti-ble purpose beyond 'what the teacher wants me to do'. Reading for information is essentially driven by the need to know something and this must be the key objective when supporting children's access to non-fiction texts.

The EXIT model

David Wray and Maureen Lewis have written extensively on supporting children's reading and response to non-fiction (Wray and Lewis 1997). The culmination of their research resulted in the publication of the EXIT model of teaching non-fiction to pupils (EXtending Interactions with Texts). Much of this research formed the basis of the NLS module on teaching non-fiction, as it was recognised that children needed guidance in accessing non-fiction texts as well as support in writing non-fiction. Because the EXIT model is process-driven and is not intended as a linear approach, there is scope for teachers and children to be creative in their adaptation of the model to take account of both the text and the reader's needs. The process stages of the EXIT model are:

- activating prior knowledge
- establishing purposes
- locating information
- adopting an appropriate strategy
- interacting with the text
- monitoring understanding
- making a record
- evaluating information
- assisting memory
- communicating the information.

This model recognised the limitations of dry comprehension questions where children could supply the right form of words regardless of whether they understood or cared about the content of the passage. For example:

The female fox is called a vixen.

What is the female fox called?

The female fox is called a vixen.

In contrast, in the EXIT model children are encouraged to ask the questions that they are interested in, the intention being that they are therefore motivated to find out the answers. This model offers a useful starting point for the creative practitioner to use across the Primary age phases and it can be applied to the reading that children engage with in all areas of the curriculum. Each of the following chapters adapts aspects of this model with explicit examples of age-related practice.

Constructing non-fiction

By building on the experiences of speaking and listening and reading, children will need to become experts and constructors of their own non-fictional texts. This understanding that you have something valuable to tell people is a powerful motivator. The following chapters look at making non-fiction in a variety of complementary media including writing, film and video making and drawing. These

include children in a nursery class developing an information booklet on the Teletubbies to help their teachers know about their favourite TV characters, writing
texts to accompany audio guides for an art gallery in KS1 and the development of
a living history museum in KS2.

The creative classroom environment

The selection and inclusion of a range of non-fiction texts in the Nursery through
to Y6 is critical in ensuring that non-fiction is developed effectively. Classroom
resources should include:

- a range of picture books and technical guides
- multimodal texts
- up-to-date information texts offering a range of global perspectives
- electronic texts and restricted internet access.

It is important to look at texts critically to ensure that they are relevant and inclusive and current. For example, books on Africa should reflect the contemporary
society in the cities as well as looking at rural mud huts; atlases need to be updated
regularly to reflect the changing names and boundaries of countries and states for
very significant political and cultural reasons; books on the jobs people do should
reflect the social, gendered and ethnic make-up of 21st-century Britain. Some texts
that do perpetuate stereotypical views and beliefs should be kept separately by the
teacher to help inform discussions on bias and stereotyping.

Inclusive practices

Learning styles and special educational needs

As creative teachers we want to promote an inclusive learning environment where
a range of learning styles are recognised and children and adults learn with and
from each other. Each chapter looks at a range of teaching and learning methods
to support children's access to non-fictional texts including:

- open-ended questions where children can contribute their ideas and be
  valued for their thoughts at their own level
- a secure classroom environment where risk-taking is celebrated and
  innovation admired
- development of a range of ways of recording and constructing non-fiction
  texts, not just by writing

- explicit modelling and teaching of a range of reading strategies to access non-fictional texts
- interactive whole-class or group work including shared and guided reading
- paired work with children working with similar and mixed-ability partners to encourage discussion and pooling of ideas
- individual independent work where children can practise their telling, reading and writing of non-fictional texts
- thinking time where the children are given the opportunity to reflect and consider, enabling all children to respond
- the use of a range of information and communication technologies to broaden the range of non-fiction including interactive multimodal texts
- visual aids such as big books or interactive whiteboards
- physical props such as models and maps to support children's access to information
- drama techniques and extensive use of role-play across the age phases to actively explore the meaning of texts.

These activities will support a range of learning styles including kinaesthetic, visual, physical as well as literary. Through the use of these teaching methods, children with different levels of experience and confidence, including those with special education needs, can access the curriculum.

Gender

Non-fiction is traditionally seen as the domain of the boys (Barrs and Pidgeon 1993) and yet it is vital to ensure girls and boys enjoy access to texts that address their interests and activities that enable children to use their knowledge and experiences.

The interests of boys and girls are established as soon as the child is born and he is placed in his blue baby-gro' with astronauts all over or as she opens her eyes to admire her musical mobile with soft bunnies dancing between pink flowers. These icons of 'girlness' and 'boyness' are systematically reinforced and further defined from birth through overpowering advertisements of clothes, toys, TV programmes, comics as well as the parents' and friends' own gendered interests.

The creative teacher needs to understand how these gender-specific interests have often been developed in order to develop strategies to broaden the interests of the children in the class. In the past teachers have been encouraged to select boy-friendly non-fictional texts to engage the boys in reading (Ofsted 2003; DfES 2003) without considering what happens to the girls. The important factor here is to ensure that texts and activities relate to the children's own experiences and interests.

The PNS states the following strategies will make a difference to boys' success in writing:

- provide real purposes and audiences for boys for writing;
- ensure a wide range of texts linking with boys' interests including visual literacies;
- ensure boys are given opportunities for oral rehearsal before writing;
- provide effective feedback to boys orally before writing.

(DfES 2005)

The creative teacher will recognise the benefit these actions will give to the whole class. A successful creative classroom will ensure that girls' and boys' interests and contributions are valued. So, in addition to the above recommendations, we would add, in relation to teaching non-fiction:

- ensure activities are open-ended and can be moulded and adapted by the children to include reference to their popular cultural interests;
- opportunities to share texts collaboratively as well as independently;
- opportunities to share reading interests and expertise from home.

Bilingual pupils

The activities discussed above will additionally support bilingual pupils. In particular the use of visual aids and role-play will enable children to participate in their response to the texts. Many books, software and internet sites are also available in a wide range of languages and as dual texts.

References

Barrs, M. and Pidgeon, S. (1993) *Boys and Reading*. London: CLPE.

DfES (2001) *Writing Fliers 1–6*.

DfES (2003) *Using the National Healthy School Standard to Raise Boys' Achievement*.

DfES (2005) *Raising Standards in Writing*.

Jaffrey, M. (1983) *Eastern Vegetarian Cooking*. London: Jonathan Cape.

Lewis, M. and Wray, D. (1998) *Writing Across the Curriculum: Frames to Support Learning*. University of Reading.

Ofsted (2003) *Yes He Can: Schools Where Boys Write Well*. London: HMI 505.

PNS (2005) *Raising Standards in Reading – Achieving Children's Targets*. London: DfES.

Wray, D. and Lewis, M. (1997) *Extending Literacy: Children Reading and Writing Non-fiction.* London: Routledge.

Useful websites

The Primary National Strategy hosts a range of useful and less useful resources including all of the curriculum documents and supporting literacy materials in downloadable form: www.standards.dfes.gov.uk

They also have an interesting area to discuss some of the latest research on gender and achievement with an emphasis on how to support boys' writing: www.standards.dfes.gov.uk/genderandachievement/

David Wray's website offers some helpful material and articles related to his EXIT model including texts to use with children to support their understanding of bias: www.warwick.ac.uk/staff/D.J.Wray/exel/exit.html

The Wordpool offers a range of helpful information on children's books: www.wordpool.co.uk/wfc/art/nonfictlh.htm

CHAPTER 4

Teaching non-fiction creatively in the Early Years

Put the Cheerios in a bowl.
Put the milk in the bowl.
Put the sugar in the bowl.
Eat it all up. Yummy!

(Flo giving instructions, aged 3)

Introduction

In this chapter we will consider what non-fiction means in an Early Years educational context and we will consider how to build upon children's positive home experiences of making sense of the world by engaging creatively with non-fictional texts. We will look at how to use the existing frameworks for language and literacy teaching as outlined in the *Curriculum Guidance for the Foundation Stage* (DfEE 2000) and the *National Literacy Strategy Framework* guidance for YR (DfEE 1998) in a creative and innovative manner in order to maintain and extend young children's response to, and development of, non-fictional texts.

Non-fiction in the Early Years

The principal aim of creative teaching of non-fiction in the Early Years is to generate an understanding of the importance of information-led texts and experiences in order to help the children to start to make sense of the world around them. It is about beginning to consider *how* these texts can be explored to help us find out about things we want to know and it is about beginning to explore how these texts can be constructed to help us share information in the way we want to.

Cereal packet contents, birthday cards, shopping lists, burger restaurant logos, toy catalogues, TV titles – just a few of the non-fiction texts very young children encounter and discriminate between every day. Reading, writing, watching and encoding these texts form the core of functional language use. Life can be very hard for people who are not familiar with these communication systems. In addition to these crucial day-to-day texts, non-fiction covers a huge range of different types of texts including instructional texts (fairy cake recipes), persuasive texts (advert for delicious, delectable dainty cakes), explanatory texts (the history of cake making), recounts (my first birthday cake . . .).

The role of the Early Years educator in a creative classroom is to support this interaction with non-fictional texts by:

- encouraging the child's natural inquisitiveness
- enabling the child to frame questions
- supporting the child in searching for possible answers
- allowing the time and opportunity to explore and question the information
- sharing any findings
- celebrating the process of enquiry.

This cycle (importantly, beginning in no particular order) builds on the crucial work developed by Lewis and Wray (1998) refined in their EXIT model and disseminated by the National Literacy Strategy. This chapter looks at practical ways to engage children creatively with a range of non-fictional texts in order to deepen their understanding and enjoyment of discovery.

Building on home literacy

The very first texts that a baby will encounter will very often be those everyday vital forms of communication. The young child will begin to recognise the packet of their favourite cereal, they will recognise the logo on a piece of clothing, they will dance to the theme music and point to the titles of a familiar TV programme, they will pick up a mobile phone and 'talk' in a range of voices and registers. They are in fact demonstrating a competence and confidence in accessing non-fictional texts and thereby making sense of the world around them. Young children born in the 21st century are frequently sophisticated users of technology-based information and multimodal texts, in particular – sometimes more confident than the adults working in their setting. Children of two and three years old using DVD players to watch their favourite programmes or reading and writing e-mails or mobile phone text messages are not unusual occurrences. The children are used to using a rapidly expanding cache of communication tools in order to access and pass on information.

And yet, as children enter our nurseries and reception classes, the overwhelming emphasis is upon telling, reading and writing fictional stories. The majority of picture-books tell a story; the end of each session is usually incomplete without the adult reading a story; the book corner is vividly promoting stories and fictional accounts through posters, pictures, toys and, of course, the bright and engaging colours and images on the covers of the books themselves.

In order to extend and complement the young child's interaction with non-fictional texts, it is vital to consider ways of bridging the home and school experiences by developing our understanding of the children's interests and competencies outside the classroom. Consider the following activities as a way of ensuring and developing a meaningful dialogue between home and school:

Home 'literacy' diary

If we go back to this idea discussed in the Early Years fiction chapter – we can see the enormous range of non-fictional language and literacy activities Zac, aged 3, is engaging with, even before 9 o'clock in the morning:

- selecting his cereal from the cupboard
- checking e-mails with mum
- practising writing his name on the computer
- looking at the CBeebies website
- searching for the letters in his name on car number plates
- reading shop signs.

Asking parents and carers to note down a 'literacy' diary for just one day can be enormously enlightening for staff in the Early Years setting and can give some good ideas for tapping into children's own interests and aptitudes as well as illuminating the breadth of the literacy curriculum at home as well as in school.

My favourite things

Ask children with the help of parents and carers to keep a scrapbook or sketchbook of their favourite things – pictures of special toys taken from catalogues, photos of pets and family members, wrappers from sweets or delicious foods, birthday cards, postcards, tickets from outings and journeys and so on. Children can add to these books at home and school and should become unique to each child. These books often become a child's most prized possession as they share it with family at home and friends at school and can provide an excellent record of a child's interests and enthusiasms as well as a powerful early reading book.

Travelling Teddy

Many Early Years classrooms have a treasured teddy, doll, benign monster or other beloved stuffed animal. This classroom friend must be treated as a most special and much desired addition to the class by adults and children alike in order to generate the enthusiasm and interest necessary to keep this activity going so that all the children who want to can participate in turn. Each week the teddy must pack its tiny bag or suitcase with help from the children (complete with a range of communication tools including items such as a diary, camera, blank stamped postcard, scrapbook and passport) and then travel home with one of the children (it must be a volunteer) for the week. The class should agree on the expectation of this visit: a video diary perhaps or a postcard sent from the child's home telling the class about their week (with help from the child's family, of course) or a few snapshots to go in Teddy's scrapbook or even a daily e-mail. Each week the class could welcome Teddy back and the host child could be encouraged to share their adventures. It can be a great opportunity to encourage the children to introduce words and phrases from other languages into the diary or scrapbook and to celebrate the diversity of events in the children's lives. The important element here is to ensure effective communication between the home and the setting and to allow the child an opportunity to share home activities in school. It is also an excellent routine to support and extend children's ability to recount to an audience.

Non-fiction and the Early Years curriculum frameworks

The DfEE's *Curriculum Guidance for the Foundation Stage* stresses the value of 'planning an environment that reflects the importance of language through signs, notices and books' (DfES 2000: 44) and encourages and values the use of environmental print: 'Children's surroundings offer natural opportunities to look at and learn about printed language, such as on food packets, road signs and labels' (DfEE 2000: 45).

Children are expected to 'use language to imagine and recreate roles and experiences' (DfEE 2000: 58) and to 'show . . . how information can be found in non-fiction texts to answer questions about where, who, why and how' (DfEE 2000: 62) and to 'attempt writing for different purposes, using features of different forms such as lists . . . and instructions' and 'write their own names and other things such as labels and captions' (DfEE 2000: 64).

The *National Literacy Strategy Framework for Teaching* (DfEE 1998) outlines the explicit content of work to be undertaken during the reception year. Under *range*, it refers very broadly to 'simple non-fiction texts, including recounts'. Under reading, it states that pupils should be taught to 're-read frequently a variety of familiar texts, e.g. . . . information books . . . captions, own and other children's writing' (*YR T6*).

Through shared writing, 'pupils should be taught to understand that writing can be used for a range of purposes, e.g. to send messages, record, inform' and, through guided and independent writing, children should be taught to:

- 'experiment with writing in a variety of play, exploratory and role play situations
- write their own name
- write labels or captions for pictures and drawings.' (*YR T11*)

And, importantly, 'to use writing to communicate in a variety of ways, incorporating it into play and everyday classroom life, e.g. recounting their own experiences, lists, signs, directions, menus, labels, greeting cards, letters' (*YR T15*).

Overall the Early Years curricula recognise the value of non-fiction to enhance 'functional literacy' but there is very little emphasis on critical literacy and the need to question information presented as factual. This would seem to be an oversight in the light of several major initiatives in this area (see work being developed by UKRA and the BFI, for example).

Playing with facts: Exploring non-fiction through speaking, listening and drama

As discussed in the chapters on fiction and poetry, the importance of planning opportunities to talk about ideas and play with non-fictional themes cannot be underestimated. It is through carefully planned oral work that children and adults will be able to rehearse and extend their thinking together by building on each other's ideas without being restricted by the permanence or technicalities of written texts: 'Here the talk is fluid and open-ended. Participants may change their views or change direction many times; they can revisit ideas and the talk may be interspersed with asides, comments and anecdotes' (DfEE 2003). Being given the opportunity to explore factual texts and ideas verbally allows the children time to rehearse their thoughts on a subject and encourages a dialogue about information. It is an essential precursor to critical analysis of texts and the beginnings of the right to question.

Framing questions

Searching for information needs to begin with a question that demands answers. How did you do that? Where does granny live? Why is the sky blue? These are all genuine questions asked by four- and five-year-olds with some regularity. The young infant will have been asking questions of their parents and carers for as long as they could be understood. The parents' patience and commitment will often tirelessly support the child in finding the answers and will often lead the child towards the means to find the answers ('Watch me'; 'Let's look at a map'; 'We could Google it'). The Early Years educator similarly needs to build upon this infectious curiosity in order to support the children's quest for information. A key factor in this process is to support the framing of questions. In the first instance these questions will be very simple and will take plenty of practice. As the children become more familiar with the routines, they will enjoy taking the role of teller or questioner.

The role of the adult in the following examples, and in the general discourse throughout the school day, is to model the use of effective questioning and response to questions. It is important to demonstrate the use of a range of open and closed questions. Closed questions demand a single right answer (How many cats do you have? What time do you go to bed? Who is taking you home tonight?). Open questions invite a range of possible answers (What do you think might happen next? How could we carry these sweets home safely?). Both types of questioning are valuable but, if we are to encourage creativity in thinking and response, we need to encourage children to answer with real thought rather than parroting the answers they think we want to hear.

Talking Chair

A particularly useful classroom routine is the 'Talking Chair'. Children are brought together at regular weekly intervals to listen to one child's news from home. The children know when they are to have their turn and so can prepare what they want to share with the other children. They sit on the special chair (indicated by a particular cushion or cloth, perhaps) and the adult then invites the child to tell their news. The other children are encouraged to listen and then invited to ask the teller questions to find out more about their recount. The children asking the questions would need some visual prompts to support them initially (a display or poster of question words – Where? When? Why? Who? How? – could be shared at the beginning of each session, for example) but gradually the session becomes a more meaningful exchange generating a genuine interest in each other.

Circle time

The children sit in a ring with clearly defined and agreed 'rights' (the right to pass, the right to be heard when holding the shell, the right to be safe, for example) and pass a special object around. Only the holder of the object may speak and the others must be the listeners. The purpose of the sessions is to develop thinking and questioning times on a particular subject – 'I feel happy when . . .'; 'I feel angry if . . .'; 'If I could change one thing in this school I would . . .'. The work undertaken by Jenny Mosley in this area is excellent (Mosley and Sonnet 2001).

Costumes and hats

A small box of dressing-up clothes or hats can be a very helpful impetus to encourage young children to ask questions and consider the diversity in people's jobs, cultural, historical and religious observances and heritage, as well as creating an opportunity to challenge children's stereotypical views. Consider taking out a fire-fighter's helmet, for example, or a Muslim boy's Tigiyha: 'Who might it belong to?'; 'Where might you wear it?'; 'Can you describe it?'; 'Why do you think people wear it?'. It is important that the adult leading the discussions is well informed on any religious or technical information connected with the clothes and hats in order to sensitively support the children's investigations. Access to a relevant website or information book is also very helpful here.

Hot-seating

This can work well in conjunction with the ideas discussed above in 'Costumes and hats' as initially the teacher takes on the role of a character in order to be questioned by the children. In a unit of work on pets, for example, the teacher could become a vet. The children need time and support to plan and ask relevant and revealing questions that they really want to know the answers to. After much practice, some children may wish to research the role and take the 'hot-seat' to be questioned by other children.

Using drama

Role-play areas

Creative role-play areas offer the potential for children to explore activities and scenarios from 'real life'. They can mimic and rehearse 'grown up' experiences through narratives developed in play situations. If the children are to become absorbed in meaningful play in these areas it is essential that the areas are familiar to the children in their everyday lives at this stage in their development. Preparatory visits to real-life venues will enable the children to help plan and resource the area as well as supplying a wealth of memories from which to plunder during their future independent play.

Planning opportunities to speak in role and to experience roles outside of their lives is an essential part of Early Years education. Watch the children in your setting as they pick up the telephone and talk to the 'doctor' in a rather formal, ever-so-polite voice and then turn to the 'crying baby' with soothing cooing and baby talk. This ability to interchange between levels of formality in speech demonstrates an already sophisticated linguistic ability to alter the way we talk to different audiences for maximum effect.

Reading and writing in role will give real and often urgent reasons to write (entering an appointment in the diary; writing a prescription for a sick cat; taking the class register) and to read for a genuine purpose (who is next in the line to see the doctor; what do I want to eat?). The functional aspects of literacy that they are so familiar with outside school and often observed from the adults around them, can thus become a reality within the confines of the classroom itself.

Table 4.1 shows some examples of reading, writing and speaking and listening opportunities in a range of role-play areas. It is important to consider that different

Table 4.1 Non-fiction through creative role-play areas

	Reading	Writing	Speaking and Listening
Baby clinic	Help leaflets (e.g. bathing your baby)	Help leaflets (e.g. bathing your baby)	Mums and dads and babies chatting in waiting room
	Appointments book	Appointments book	
	Baby health books	Recording info and weights in baby health books	Health visitors, midwives, nurses and doctors giving advice
	Picture books to share with babies		
	Magazines	Picture books to share with babies	
	Information posters and notices on notice board	Information posters and notices for notice board	Babies talking to each other
	Labels on medicines and injection vials	Prescriptions	
	Baby health websites		
	Phone messages and memos		
	A range of information books and software about babies		
Flower shop	Shop signage	Shop signage	Telephone orders
	Flower and plant labels	Flower and plant labels and plant care advice	Florists
	Plant care posters and leaflets		Customers for Valentine's Day, weddings, funerals, Mothers' Day, etc.
	Price lists	Price lists	
	Flower display brochures	Cards to attach to 'Interflora' flowers for every occasion	
	Invoice book		
	Telephone book		
	Maps for deliveries		
	Florist websites		
	Name badges		
	A range of reference books and software on plants and flowers		
Fire Station	Fire safety posters and booklets	Fire safety posters and booklets	Emergency telephone receptionist
	Fire instructions	Fire instructions	

H & S information	H & S information	Fire fighters
Incident log book	Incident log book	Members of the public needing help
Rota lists	Rota lists	
Timetables	Timetables	
Maps	Fire engine manual	
Stay Wise website	Labels for uniforms	
Fire engine manual	Name/rank badges	
Labels for uniforms	Thank-you letters and cards	
Name/rank badges		
Job application forms		
Thank-you letters and cards		
Phone messages		
A range of information books on firefighting and emergency services		

role-play areas offer different curricular emphases and should be planned accordingly. These arenas present ample opportunities to extend interactions with a range of fictional and non-fictional text types.

These examples are offered as a starting point to help you consider the enormous potential for language-based activities within these role-play areas. For a detailed case study of the creation and energetic development of a mechanic's garage in a YR class, see the wonderful work undertaken by Nigel Hall (Hall 1999).

Small world play   Engaging young children with figures and scenes from realistic and familiar forms (zoo animals, hospital, park, burger bar) in miniature form can support them to explore and manipulate imitation real-life situations. Children will rehearse the language used by the adults they have seen in these situations and will begin to explore cause and effect when they take decisions on behalf of their characters.

Teacher-in-role

The role of the adult in these role-play areas is frequently debated among Early Years educators. Unsolicited interventions can inhibit the children's play and can pressurise children into performing for you rather than independently exploring these imaginary real-life worlds for themselves. It is important therefore to approach any intervention in role and to seek an invitation, wherever possible, before entering the children's highly self-regulated arena.

The drama technique of 'teacher-in-role' enables the adult to inhabit a character from the unfolding play in order to affect the drama as well as to reinforce the value of the children's endeavours and to support them to extend and resolve dilemmas without interrupting the flow. The teacher could, for example, enter the post office to buy her car tax in Urdu. She would be encouraging the children to consider the most effective way of communicating with her as well as raising the status of the play.

Mime Engaging children in a play without words is an excellent way to extend their use of non-verbal gestures and clarity of physical movements. It enables the children with the chance to consider how to represent people or creatures by reflecting on their key attributes – the movement of a caterpillar, the actions of cooking, etc.

Creative approaches to reading and responding to non-fiction in the Early Years

Text provision

The classroom setting itself can be a wonderful resource to demonstrate the importance of information texts and to see 'environmental' print in action. It is vital to share with the children in the setting the power of reading for information through a range of invaluable classroom routines in a range of community languages wherever possible – just as the children expect to see outside school. Examples could include:

- welcome notices
- labelling of children's pegs, trays, message boxes, etc.
- fire drill and emergency procedures
- instructions for cooking or IT equipment
- class agreements or expectations of, and between, children, staff and parents
- class/group/key worker lists
- registers and rotas
- directions and maps
- wall diaries and calendars
- display captions and questions for consideration on interactive displays
- signs and symbols (no-smoking/smiley face, etc.).

This list is just a snapshot of the many and varied opportunities for texts to be displayed and shared in the classroom. Using and displaying photos, diagrams, arrows and real objects to support the reading process for monolingual and bilingual adults and children can exemplify many written texts. Texts should be written and read by both the adults and the children in the setting.

Selecting information texts

It is essential to ensure that book areas represent the children's interests in non-fictional texts as well as storybooks. It can be helpful to ask the children in your setting about the kind of information books and electronic texts they would like to see (budget permitting, of course). Firm favourites with young children usually include reference to animals, the human body, food and babies. Other essentials could include atlases, children's encyclopaedias, dictionaries and word books in a range of community languages, simple texts on single issues (weather, trees, planets, dinosaurs).

Helen Arnold gives some clear advice on selecting effective information books for children in the Early Years:

- They should not be packed with facts
- The illustrations should relate clearly to the text
- There should not be extraneous fantasy or story elements
- Language should be simple but not patronising
- Close observation should be encouraged
- The purpose of the book should be clear
- Texts which ask rhetorical questions or give instructions which cannot practicably be carried out should be avoided. (Arnold 2001: 181)

I would also add:

- The content of the texts should be examined for stereotypical portrayals
- Texts should build on the current interests of the children in the class.

Range of texts

In addition to information books designed for young children, the creative practitioner needs to see the opportunities for expanding the traditional stock of classroom reading matter by building on the children's experience of, and interest in, texts from the immediate environment and including a wide range of non-fictional texts in the book area. Texts might include:

- environmental print, including collections of shopping bags, sweet wrappers, food names, local shop and street names

- websites (available for almost any subject – collect useful sites in 'favourites' and limit access to these so that you can thoroughly check suitability and safety)

- wall friezes and posters

- information leaflets (available from everywhere you go – from zoos to the post office – many specifically developed for children)

- CD-ROMs and DVDs (software such as Dorling Kindersley's *Amazing Animals*).

Reading areas

We discussed the importance of developing a stimulating and relaxing reading area or book corner in the chapter on Early Years Fiction. In addition to those ideas discussed, it is vital to include displays and labels supporting children's access to information texts. You could consider:

- **themed book boxes** such as 'Books about minibeasts', 'Information about dinosaurs', 'Stories about real people'. These boxes could include a range of media including information leaflets, software or DVD boxes (keep the software safe and clean near the computer);

- **interactive signs and displays** written by children as well as adults – 'Our top 5 favourite information books are . . .', 'Can you find out where Jamaica is in the atlas?', 'Search our new computer program and find out where polar bears come from';

- **'Non-fiction book of the week'** celebrated with a display including cut-out speech bubbles with children's comments about the book, related props and books on a similar theme. Consider the Haynes car manual on the Mini Cooper with a child's tool box, toy car and recorded comments from the children: 'The cars are grrrrrrrrreat!'

- **uniting fiction and non-fiction texts** – for example, in connection with an interest in space, you might highlight Roaring Rockets (part of the wonderful Amazing Machines Series) by Tony Mitton and Ant Parker, and display with Nick Butterworth's Q Pootle 5 and Arthur and Adrienne Yorinks's Quack!: To the Moon and Home Again;

- **games** related to texts (e.g. animal lotto; alphabet race game; bilingual toy snap – see more detailed examples below in the section on 'Response to texts').

Reading for a purpose

Searching and reading for information needs to be driven by the need to know of the reader in order to maintain interest and energy for the quest. The creative practitioner will manipulate real events to occur (sometimes through luck but more often through imagination, drama and make-believe). The creative practitioner will therefore understand the importance of:

Answering genuine questions 'Today we are going to look at this book and find out about frogspawn' is very different from: 'When I looked in the nursery pond this morning, I found this strange jelly stuff and I'm not sure what it is. Can you help me to find out what we should do with it?' Through careful questioning and a little drama, the children can be taken on a wonderful investigative journey where their input is valuable and there is a reason to pick up the book or search a website.

Following instructional texts As instructional texts are written to help us to make or do something we want to do, it is vital to ensure that children are encouraged to, and enabled to, follow them practically, i.e. make sandwiches, books, puppets, sandcastles or whatever in order to fully understand the purpose and requirements of such texts. This will in turn support the children's own construction and writing of similar texts.

Engaging in a stimulating correspondence Children often respond enthusiastically when engaged in a genuine or convincing but imaginary correspondence. In Nigel Hall's edited book, *Writing with Reason* (1989), Jeanne Price describes a lovely interchange between the class ladybird in the centre of a display in a nursery class and the children. The exchange begins when the children enter the nursery one day and one child spots a large envelope addressed to the class sticking out from the display board. As the teacher opens the envelope and reads the note from the ladybird asking the children to guess her name, the children are immediately drawn in to a lengthy, meaningful and prosperous make-believe relationship. The children are eager to read the notes from the ladybird as well as engage in prolific writing in response. The creative practitioner uses the children's inspired imagination to drive the correspondence and to introduce a range of text types (including speech bubbles, lists, notes, etc.).

Other starting points for this type of correspondence might be:

- a message in a bottle from a lost whale needing instructions
- an e-mail from a child in another country (there are several genuine sources for this kind of international correspondence: see the MirandaNet website for example)
- a postcard photo of a favourite classroom toy superimposed on a familiar landmark background (the London Eye, the Eiffel Tower, the Statue of Liberty).

Reading routines

Reading non-fiction to children

It is often harder to read non-fiction texts out loud to groups of children than fictional stories while maintaining your fluency and their interest. There are several important reasons for this: first, the very nature of the text can make it personal to the needs and interests of the individual reader – I might want to know the alligator's swimming abilities but you might want to know what it eats. Second, the text itself is often not written or designed to be read aloud – diagrams, photographs, tables and grids hold much of the information and are designed to be pored over by the individual reader. Third, many information texts are often not designed to be linear or sequential. Indeed the purpose of the index and contents pages is to help you navigate the text in a way that can inhibit fluid and sustained reading. Finally, many instructional texts require you to follow the instructions as you are reading – recipes, car manuals, book-making instructions, knitting patterns, etc. Their interest is predominantly in the doing, not in the reading alone.

Nonetheless, it is still important to share a range of information texts with the children in your setting in order to expand their experience of texts and to engage those children who prefer factual texts. There are several text types more suitable to reading with a wider audience such as letters and e-mails, diaries and recounts – narratives of real-life people. The creative teacher needs to reflect critically on the suitability and 'readability' of the text before sharing it with a wider group.

Shared reading

Reading together with a group of children with a shared text is a very useful technique to model for the children how to look for information. A typical shared reading session might include the following exchanges: 'Aisha has asked me where the rain comes from. I'm not sure if I can answer that without some help. Can anybody help us find out? Where could we look? What could help us?' Encourage the children to help you source the information. Possible places might include:

- books from class, school or local library
- information booklets
- websites
- other children or adults
- TV, DVD or CD-ROMs.

Each of these sources has its own reading strategies – often quite distinct from reading fiction or poetry. Skills include using a contents page or index or glossary; reading diagrams or tables; using a search engine and scrolling through information; framing meaningful questions; searching frames sequences. Many of these techniques will be familiar to some of the children in your setting but many will not. Explicit 'talk alouds' with the practitioner talking to the children as she or he demonstrates the process of accessing information will begin in the early years. This will be developed in KS1 and into KS2 and beyond with an emphasis on the 'higher order reading skills' including skimming and scanning and summarising.

In the Early Years, much of the reading itself will be undertaken by the assisting adult but should always be led by the child and the child's interests. What is important here is the opportunity to begin to locate the information needed and to experience the different ways of reading.

Response to texts

Once the children have rehearsed and reflected on what they want to find out and have been supported to find the information, it is important to plan activities that will engage the children in an exploration of the text and allow them to make sense of their findings. Questions and answers are frequently used to assess the children's understandings but it is really only when the child is given the opportunity to use the information that they can clarify their understanding and demonstrate their knowledge. Activities could include:

Games   These can be simply developed by the children and/or the adults to complement the themes and interests of the children in your setting.

- *Lotto* games (can be designed for any theme) where each child has a card with several pictures and needs to collect the matching or connecting cards.
- *Alphabet name game* where you pick a theme (animals, toys, food, sweets, TV programmes) and then spin a wheel or throw alphabet dice to determine a letter. The child must try to think of a word to match.
- *Bilingual snap* – this could include pictures and words in English and other community languages in your setting (ask parents, carers and older siblings for help here).
- *Memory pairs game* where the children need to make connections between pairs (e.g. animals and their babies, people and their hats, etc.).
- *Sequencing cards* where the children have to sort and organise information (e.g. the life cycle of a butterfly, getting dressed, etc.).

Bookmaking   As discussed in some length in the KS1 Fiction chapter, making and writing simple books enables the children to reword and transform their investigations for others to read. Consider very simple, repetitive texts where the children record one fact on each page (*The Farm* by Princess: The cow eats grass. The horse eats hay. The chicken eats grain. The pig eats everything!).

Cooking   Cooking from stories is a good way of developing links between fiction and non-fiction. (See some great ideas such as fruit kebabs from *Handa's Surprise* in Sally Featherstone's *The Little Book of Cooking from Stories*, 2002.)

Non-fiction story boxes   As discussed in the Fiction chapters, story boxes (inspired by the work of Helen Bromley, 1999) are a wonderful way to engage children in a small world and through their play explore and use their knowledge and experiences to help tell stories. Possible ideas for non-fiction boxes might include:

- a minibeast garden
- a farm
- a dinosaur landscape
- the moon.

Creative approaches to writing non-fiction in the Early Years

Reasons to write

The majority of non-fiction text work undertaken in the Early Years classroom will be oral and through shared reading and play. In order to support children's emergent writing of non-fiction texts, there needs to be a powerful reason to write The creative practitioner will not, however, always wait for a real situation to arise. He or she will need to inspire their children to write through real or convincingly imaginative reasons:

- a letter that needs sending to invite someone to your party
- a card for somebody's birthday
- instructions on how to feed the fish
- a recipe for your favourite pizza topping
- a map to help find the treasure you have hidden.

Adults writing

Non-fictional writing is predominantly about passing on information. As adults we are constantly using writing to communicate to others around us:

- scribbled notes to the teacher next door asking who's on playground duty
- completing the codes in the attendance register in black and red pen
- writing in a child's home school PACT book
- texting a friend at coffee break
- writing a list of children who have visited the role-play area
- writing names in the 'golden book' for assembly.

Examples of writing undertaken by the adults in the setting should not be hidden but should instead be recognised as effective models demonstrating the importance of writing: 'children will learn about the different purposes of writing by seeing practitioners write for real purposes such as making lists, greeting cards, books to recall a visit or event, and labels for displays and models' (DfEE 2000: 46).

Writing areas

Developing an area in your classroom where children can access a range of writing implements and materials in order to write for a self-chosen purpose is an essential component of the creative Early Years classroom – indeed, I would maintain, any creative classroom. In a large room, a corner with several tables is ideal, preferably with plug points for a computer and wall space for a notice-board or message boxes (see below). The area should be made as attractive as possible by including a range of enticing writing accoutrements such as:

- writing mats on the tables (laminated alphabet wrapping paper works well)
- a range of alphabets and dictionaries in community languages wherever possible
- examples of scripts in a range of community languages
- an alluring selection of pens, pencils, chalks and gels organised in attractive pots or boxes
- a wide selection of paper including coloured paper and card, squared and lined paper, plain and patterned cut into different sizes and shapes (off-cuts from classroom displays are good for this)
- a collection of old birthday/Christmas/Eid/Diwali cards with the message covered up
- blank postcards (you can often collect free advertising postcards from cinema, bar or restaurant foyers)
- envelopes
- simple bookmaking materials such as a child-friendly hand stapler, standard and shaped scissors, hole punch, tags, ribbon, etc.
- a computer (a laptop is ideal here) with word-processing software, e-mail facilities and, importantly, a working printer
- a Dictaphone.

Message boards   It is important to have a place in your classroom where the children and adults can independently post notes and messages to each other. It offers an ideal way to offer children a genuine purpose for their writing as well as being a practical way of sharing information within the setting.

Message boxes   These individually named boxes mounted on the wall with each child and adult's photograph mounted alongside to support access – preferably transparent so the children can see if they have a message – are inspired by the wonderful work developed in the Early Years centres in Emilia Reggio, Italy. Here the children are encouraged initially to exchange tokens and objects. These are gradually supplemented with written notes and cards and letters through their own individual box. The importance of these communications is acknowledged:

> In this way, communication skills find the 'right' opportunities for developing, passing from the object to the message to standard writing, in a reciprocal interplay that eludes any sort of formal structure. This is a very different kind of communicative situation from the usual ones that are confined by external rules and curriculum plans . . . So, perhaps paradoxically, the most fascinating aspect of this type of communication is the world of interconnections that the children construct around objects, graphics, and words, in an 'open' communicative space that offers freedom and room for experimentation.
>
> Bonilauri, S. and Filippini, T. (Reggio Children 1996 : 173)

The children and adults can access their box freely throughout the day and are enthusiastically used to sending and receiving messages. One example of an exchange shows the depth and meaning of these communications – love letters in the spring between Agnese (5.6 years) and Luca (5.5 years) who can only write his name so asks Carla (5.8 years) to scribe for him:

> Dear Agnese, I'm very very in love with you, but sometimes you make me mad because you play with the other kids, and I don't like that, because who can I play with then? I can never break away from you, tomorrow I'm going to marry you, and I'll scare you too and chase you with the black cape on. Lots of kisses from Luca Tondelli.
>
> (Dictated by Luca, written by Carla)

And the delicious reply:

> *Dear Luca, I can't marry you that day that you said because I'm too little! And also I'm never going to get married because I don't want to. I'll play with you if you don't bother me with all your little kisses – they're too many and I'd rather have a lot less. One day I'll invite you to my house. Send me another message and I'll answer you again. Bye from Agnese.*

Bookmaking   Developing information books ensures that your ideas and thoughts are important and accessible and permanent. In the Early Years, these books will often follow a simple repetitive structure on each page. For example:

A *recount* might look like:	I went to the farm and I saw a pink pig
	a brown cow
	a yellow duck
	a brown horse.
Instructions might look like:	Put on some butter.
	Put on some cheese.
	Put on some tomato.
	Put on some onion.
	Eat it.

A *persuasive* text might look like: I like Smarties best because they are sweet and chocolatey and nice colours and yummy.

Written texts can be supported by photos, drawings or even sound effects if using a multi-media authoring software program (e.g. Textease).

Opportunities for extending children's experience of non-fiction in outdoor provision

External visits and external visitors Most community-based services and businesses will have funding and a commitment to be active and responsive to their local school's requests for an opportunity to visit your class or indeed for your class to visit them. I took my class to visit a local pizza restaurant and they were shown how to make the pizzas and indeed allowed to eat them; a veterinary nurse visited my reception class to help us prepare our veterinary surgery. She came with bags full of leaflets on caring for your pets as well as some old x-rays of a dog's broken paw.

Environmental text trails Give the children magnifying glasses and take them on a top-secret investigation of the outside area and locality searching for environmental print – it is everywhere from fire hydrants to road signs to graffiti to local lost-cat leaflets on trees. Take photographic records to help make a dossier book or display of the findings.

Treasure hunts With adult help, the children have to plan, write and read each other's simple clues (laminate so they can stay outside for several weeks) to navigate a path around the outside area. 'Find me under a tree with big branches' or 'Look for the blue tractor with the wobbly wheel.' It is a great way of extending children's experience of writing instructional texts as well as working co-operatively to resolve a problem.

Signage Encourage the children to participate in the development of signs in the outside area (consider directions/instructions/adverts/announcements in words, symbols and images) as well as contributing to the parents' *information board.*

Case Study: A YR information booklet on the Teletubbies

James teaches in an inner city primary school with a culturally mixed intake of children with over 70 per cent of children on free school dinners and 31 per cent on the SEN register. He is the class teacher of a Reception class during their final term in the Foundation stage. He was keen to encourage the children to see themselves as experts as well as wanting them to unite images and text in a WP document. James wanted the children to work together over two weeks to develop a guide for the teachers in the school. The guide was to be developed to help familiarise teachers with the children's passion of the moment: the Teletubbies.

To begin the project, James brought in some Teletubby toys to share with the children. As he placed them on the carpet with all of the children sitting around, he deliberately named them incorrectly much to the indignation of the children, who soon squealed the correct names and James proceeded to get all of the information about the toys wrong until in true pantomime fashion, he got quite upset and asked the children what they could do to help him. The children said they could tell him all about each character but James said he might keep forgetting and someone suggested that they write it all down. James said this would help him and perhaps the information could be shared with the other teachers in the school. So the seed was sown and the project was introduced to great excitement.

James brought in some simple instructional leaflets on a range of subjects from looking after your guinea pig to a range of ice creams on offer from a large manufacturer. The children worked in small groups with James to decide three simple headings to help them structure their leaflet:

Name of Teletubby:

Description:

Other information:

The children were immersed in all things Teletubby for the fortnight including: watching videos; small world play with a Teletubby island; Teletubby music CD; Teletubby display where the children brought in any related objects to share and the official Teletubby website was in constant use.

James developed a basic information leaflet pro-forma on his computer using a desk-top publishing package entitled *All About . . .* (Figure 4.1). He shared this with the children and helped them to scribe their information on each character. The

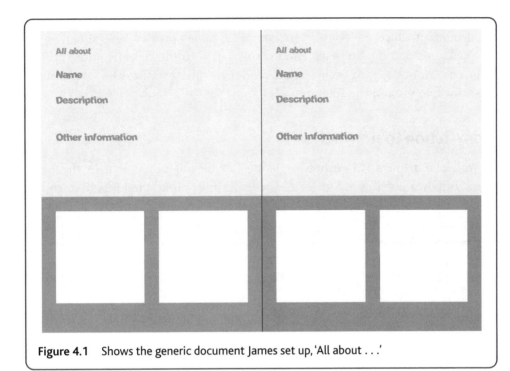

All about

Name

Description

Other information

All about

Name

Description

Other information

Figure 4.1   Shows the generic document James set up, 'All about . . .'

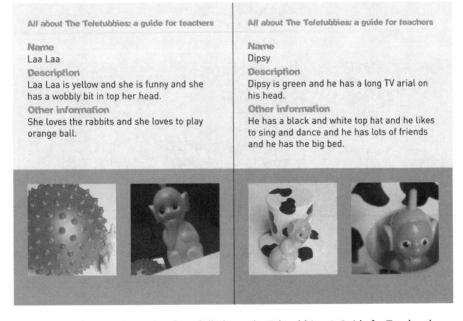

All about The Teletubbies: a guide for teachers

Name
Laa Laa

Description
Laa Laa is yellow and she is funny and she has a wobbly bit in top her head.

Other information
She loves the rabbits and she loves to play orange ball.

All about The Teletubbies: a guide for teachers

Name
Dipsy

Description
Dipsy is green and he has a long TV arial on his head.

Other information
He has a black and white top hat and he likes to sing and dance and he has lots of friends and he has the big bed.

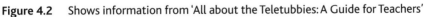

Figure 4.2   Shows information from 'All about the Teletubbies: A Guide for Teachers'

children took photographs of their Teletubbies and imported their photos into the document. Once the pages were complete, James printed several copies for the book area and one for each adult connected with the class (Figure 4.2). The children continue to quiz their teachers and the support staff to check how much they now know about the Teletubbies.

From fiction to non-fiction

It would be artificial to entirely separate fiction and non-fiction in the Early Years (is it ever possible?). Stories are a wonderfully stimulating way of introducing and developing factual and cross-curricular activities in a creative and imaginative manner. The following ideas in Table 4.2 suggest a starting point to help you consider the range of non-fiction work leading from some popular pictures books.

Table 4.2 Fiction to non-fiction

Fictional text	Examples of related non-fiction activities
Rod Campbell's *Dear Zoo*	Letter writing Zoo brochure Animal care booklets Zoo websites Visit to zoo or city farm City farm role-play area Recipes for animal-shaped biscuits
Nick Butterworth and Mick Inkpen's *Jasper's Beanstalk*	Bean diary Growing instructions for seed packet Short video for BBC's *Gardener's World* on growing beans Flower index Tool catalogue Robin internet investigation Visit to garden centre or arable farm Garden centre role-play area Garden storybox with minibeast characters
Janet and Allan Ahlberg's *Peepo!*	Instructions for baby bedtime routines Interviewing and recording older visitors talking about their childhoods Old and new toy catalogues Video diaries of children's bedtime routines (recreated through drama) Visit to baby clinic or maternity ward Baby clinic role-play area Pin-hole camera

Developing your creative practice

In order to extend your creativity in the teaching of non-fiction in the Early Years, reflect on your current practice and have a go at the following activities:

- Review the provision of non-fictional texts in your settings – do they offer something for a range of interests for both boys and girls?
- Select a favourite fictional picture-book and consider the range of opportunities to lead into non-fiction study.
- Plan a local visit for a group of children. How could you develop a role-play area to help extend children's understanding and experience of the visit?
- Plan an event to begin an imaginative correspondence in your setting. Consider how you could capture the children's imagination in order to engage the children in writing and reading letters, e-mails, cards, etc. Consider how you might extend the scenario to engage the children in a non-fictional investigation.

Creative approaches to teaching non-fiction in the Early Years: A summary

To conclude this chapter, it is helpful to summarise the key areas related to ensuring young children engage creatively with non-fiction:

- Non-fictional texts are all around us and are often the first and most powerful texts encountered by young children.
- Play is the essential medium to explore and extend young children's interests in, and interactions with, non-fiction.
- Shared reading and writing are useful tools to model searching for and disseminating information.
- Reading and writing non-fictional texts should be driven by the need to know and the desire to inform.

References

Arnold, H. (2002) 'Penguins never meet polar bears' in Whitebread, D. (ed.) *Teaching and Learning in the Early Years*, 2nd edn. London: RoutledgeFalmer.

British Film Institute Primary Education Working Group (2003) *Look Again! A Teaching Guide to Using Film and Television with Three to Eleven Year Olds*. London: DfES & BFI Publication. (Download a free copy from: www.bfi.org.uk/education/teaching/lookagain/)

Bromley, H. (1999) 'Storytelling', *Primary English Magazine*, 4 (3, 4 and 5).

DfEE (1998) *The National Literacy Strategy Framework*. London: DfEE.

DfEE (2000) *Curriculum Guidance for the Foundation Stage*. London: DfEE/QCA.

DfES (2003) *Speaking, Listening and Learning: Working with Children in KS1 and 2*. London: DfES.

Featherstone, S. (2002) *The Little Book of Cooking from Stories*. Lutterworth: Featherstone Education Ltd.

Goodwin, P. (1999) *The Literate Classroom*. London: David Fulton Publishers.

Hall, N. (ed.) (1989) *Writing with Reason: The Emergence of Authorship in Young Children*. London: Heinemann Educational Secondary Division.

Hall, N. (1999) 'Young children, play and literacy: engagement in realistic uses of literacy' in Marsh, J. and Hallet, E. (eds) *Desirable Literacies*. London: Paul Chapman Publishing.

Lewis M. and Wray, D. (1998) *Writing across the Curriculum: Frames to Support Learning*. Reading: University of Reading.

Mosley, J. and Sonnet, H. (2001) *Here We Go Round: Quality Circle Time for 3–5 Year Olds*. Trowbridge: Positive Press Limited.

Reggio Children (1996) *The Hundred Languages of Children* (exhibition catalogue). Municipality of Reggio Emilia.

Useful websites

The British Film Institute website is a great resource with some free downloadable materials and images for educational purposes:
www.bfi.org.uk/

A useful online encyclopaedia from the USA, which would need adult support to access.
http:encarta.msn.com/

The author of *The Gruffalo* gives plenty of information about herself here. Unfortunately there is no link to e-mail her directly:
www.juliadonaldson.co.uk/

This is a useful website on children's health designed for children to access:
www.childrenshealth.org.uk/

The Fire Brigade offers some helpful advice for children on fire safety:
www.staywise.co.uk/

Interflora offers some great visuals to enhance your role-play florist:
www.flowersdirect.co.uk/

This gives some useful information on Islam for children:
http:atschool.eduweb.co.uk/carolrb/islam/islamintro.html

The website for the UK Reading Association is particularly helpful on current research on critical literacies in the primary schools:
www.dfes.gov.uk/readwriteplus/teachingandlearning

This site contains some free downloadable resources to support circle time in the classroom:
www.circle-time.co.uk/site/home/

The MirandaNet website promotes international e-communication and offers a range of stimulating ideas for teachers:
www.worldecitizens.net/wecitizens/index.htm

This is a quirky site with very clear information on how to make and use a pinhole camera:
www.pinholephotography.org/

The official Teletubbies website:
www.bbc.co.uk/cbeebies/teletubbies/

Children's literature and other resources

Janet and Allan Ahlberg's *Peepo!* (1981) Viking.

Pamela Allen's *Mr Archimedes' Bath* (1980) Bodley Head Children's Books.

Nick Butterworth and Mick Inkpen's *Jasper's Beanstalk* (1992) Hodder Children's Books.

Nick Butterworth's *Q Pootle 5* (2000) HarperCollins.

Rod Campbell's *Dear Zoo* (1985) Puffin Books.

Eric Carle's *The Very Hungry Caterpillar* (1994) Hamish Hamilton.

Kathryn Cave (@ Oxfam) *One Child One Seed* (2003) Frances Lincoln Publishers.

Beatrice Hollyer's *Let's Eat! Children and their Food Around the World* (2003) Oxfam.

Tony Mitton and Ant Parker's *Roaring Rockets 5* (1997) Kingfisher.

Martin Waddell's *Owl Babies* (1994) Walker Books.

Oxfam's Discovery Flaps Series *Come and Play with Us!*

Arthur and Adrienne Yorinks's *Quack!: To the Moon and Home Again* (2003) Harry N. Abrams, Inc.

Dorling Kindersley's *Amazing Animals* DVD.

CHAPTER 5

Teaching non-fiction creatively at key stage 1

Triceratops is a herbivore (that means he doesn't eat animals) and he has three huge spikes on the top here and his skull is more than six feet long and he likes to eat trees and he is more than 65 million years old!

(Told very excitedly by Paul, aged 7)

Introduction

In this chapter we will look at how to develop the vital elements of functional non-fictional literacy from the Early Years, in order to support young children's ability to discriminate, locate and record information effectively. We will look at how to continue to build on the vital non-fictional literary experiences and interests that the children are developing out of school in order to motivate and stimulate their enthusiasm and engagement in school. We will look at how to use the existing frameworks for English teaching as outlined in the *National Curriculum* (DfEE 2000) and the *National Literacy Strategy Framework* guidance for Y1 and Y2 (DfEE 1998) in a creative and innovative manner in order to maintain and extend the children's construction of, and interaction with, a range of non-fictional texts.

Popular culture and out-of-school non-fiction

If you talk with six- or seven-year-old children outside of school, you will soon be amazed by their enormous knowledge of factual information on subjects that particularly interest them: dinosaurs, DVD players, sea creatures (sharks and whales, in particular), celebrities, rabbits, cars, mobile phones, space, ponies, tap dancing, and so on. This wealth of knowledge is often untapped within the classroom as the mismatch between the QCA schemes of work and the children's current interests seem to rarely meet. I remember teaching a Y2 class a unit based on the QCA scheme of work about electricity when the children in my class were otherwise enthralled by the World Cup and its associated frenzy.

The creative teacher sometimes needs the confidence to respond to the children's interests and abandon the most detailed plans in favour of the motivating force of the children's powerful interest in their popular culture. In this case, the World Cup offered endless fascination and engagement with maps and locales, languages, national anthems, kit designs, flags, as well as the game itself. The vital elements of the National Curriculum can be met in more than one way and it is vital to ensure that the creative practitioner respond to the needs and dreams of your children if you want to retain their interest and support their learning.

Current and popular non-fictional interests of the children in your class will often be triggered outside of school through a range of highly charged and powerfully financed media such as:

- films (e.g. dinosaurs after *King Kong* or *Jurassic Park*, for example)
- cartoons (e.g. bats and nocturnal creatures after *Mona the Vampire*)
- music (e.g. Indian dance after Bhangra)
- toys (e.g. baby care after *Baby Born*)
- adverts (e.g. cars)
- sport (e.g. Football World Cup)
- computer games (e.g. caring for dogs after Sony's *Dog's Life*)
- TV-related websites (e.g. sport section on CBBC website)
- news (e.g. 2004 tsunami in the Indian Ocean).

The creative teacher will be able to consider the opportunities these media sources have to offer, while also importantly recognising their limitations (stereotypical racist and sexist portrayals, unrealistic violence, western-world-centric information). The creative teacher will plan opportunities to utilise children's interests and to plan activities to challenge the often-stereotypical imagery.

Table 5.1 considers the range of texts suggested by the Literacy Framework for Y2 and some corresponding popular texts examples.

Non-fiction and the National Curriculum and National Literacy Strategy frameworks

The National Curriculum at KS1 makes explicit reference to non-fiction, particularly with regard to reading:

Table 5.1 Non-fiction and popular culture at KS1

NLS reference	NLS suggested non-fiction range	Examples of texts drawn from popular culture
Y2 T1	Instructions	Gameboy manual Construction toy/board games instructions
Y2 T2	Dictionaries	Web-based Encarta/spell checks Dinosaur/pet/sport dictionaries
	Glossaries	Football/ballet/minibeast terms
	Indexes	Toy catalogues
	Other alphabetically ordered texts	Telephone directories Video and CD collections and lists Popular culture alphabet frieze: Adidas, Barbie, Coca-Cola (*Marsh and Millard*, 2000)
	Explanations	Reviews of TV programmes/sporting events
Y2 T3	Information books including non-chronological reports	Pop/gossip magazines TV programme-related websites Car websites/adverts Collectable cards (Pokemon/football world cup, etc.)

Reading for information

Pupils should be taught to:

a   use the organisational features of non-fiction texts, including captions, illustrations, contents, index and chapters, to find information

b   understand that texts about the same topic may contain different information or present similar information in different ways

c   use reference materials for different purposes.

Non-fiction and non-literary texts

The range should include:

a   print and ICT-based information texts, including those with continuous text and relevant illustrations

b   dictionaries, encyclopedias and other reference materials.

There is less explicit reference to writing non-fiction, with purposes for writing detailed as:

> **a** to communicate to others
>
> **c** to explore experience
>
> **d** to organise and explain information.

And the range of forms is to include: 'notes, lists, captions, records, messages, instructions'.

The NLS Framework (DfEE 1998) promotes the teaching of non-fiction with explicit and prescriptive reference to reading and writing at text level for each term in KS1. The emphasis is on functional literacy for written communication from labels and captions to the specific strategies needed to read information texts (indexes, diagrams, glossaries, etc.).

Playing with non-fiction

As discussed in KS1 Fiction, playing at KS1 needs to remain a central provision for supporting and extending the curriculum in a creative classroom. Using play to explore non-fiction as an independent activity in the literacy hour is an invaluable teaching and learning routine to ensure children develop their thinking and experience in an enjoyable and motivating manner. Play, as discussed in previous chapters, does need extensive planning, however, and should not always be left to the children to self-initiate. The teacher's role is crucial in extending scenarios, supporting interactions between the children and scaffolding children's language development.

It is important to play with non-fictional texts as well as fictional stories for several reasons:

- Play can allow children to demonstrate what they already know about the subject.
- Play enables active exploration of the meaning of the text when the children inhabit the 'real' worlds.
- Play allows the children the opportunity to question the information presented.
- Play can exemplify how texts are constructed.
- Play can highlight the integrated nature of non-fiction across curriculum boundaries.

Imaginative role-play areas

Role-play is crucial in supporting and extending children's understanding of non-fictional texts. Creative role-play areas can be based on any theme or interest developed in the classroom and should, importantly, be developed with the children from the outset. Table 5.2 shows how you might develop an imaginative area such as a garden centre to inspire a range of English-related activities following a class visit to a local centre. This example shows the breadth of incidental literary activities employed by the children as part of their play and how they begin to address the corresponding National Curriculum English content (DfEE 2000).

In order to extend the children's involvement in a range of non-fictional text types it is important to add challenges to their play. This can be done in a number of ways:

Adult-in-role   For example, the teacher could come into the garden centre quite distraught with a dying pot plant. The children must placate you and give you explicit instructions on what you need to do to bring your plant back to life.

Complication   For example, as the children begin their group play a letter could be delivered by the head teacher voicing concerns about the mess caused by the garden centre and calling for the closure of the centre. The children could thus be inspired to write letters, e-mails or begin a petition or campaign to 'save our garden centre'.

Whole-class/group work   For example, the children could write a job description for a new sales assistant as part of a whole-class shared writing session using generic job descriptions as a model.

Non-fiction story boxes   See the guidance in KS1 Fiction to make these wonderful small worlds out of an empty shoe box (Bromley 1999). In addition to supporting children's construction of fictional narratives, story boxes can engage children with a range of information texts across curriculum areas. They allow the children time to work with a partner or small group to enter into a small world and explore environments and actions through play.

The boxes work most effectively when designed and made by the children and work particularly well when supported as a joint project with older KS2 children. Initially, as with the fictional story boxes, children should be allowed time to play and explore the worlds independently with a gradual intervention of specific learning outcomes:

So, for example, a pair of children could explore initially the Seaside box playing out stories of crabs playing in the sand. The task could then include reference to a text on seashore creatures as the children are asked to explore where certain creatures live at the seaside (snails, jellyfish, crabs, molluscs, etc.) and to place the creatures in their rightful habitat. The activity would give the children a reason to

Table 5.2 The garden centre

NC English strands	Language and literacy opportunities	NC links at KS1
En 1 Speaking and listening	Phone calls with suppliers Discussions with, and advice to, customers Tea-time chats with colleagues	**Drama** 4) To participate in a range of drama activities, pupils should be taught to: a. use language and actions to explore and convey situations, characters and emotions b. create and sustain roles individually and when working with others. **Language variation** 6) Pupils should be taught about how speech varies: a. in different circumstances (for example, to reflect on how their speech changes in more formal situations) b. to take account of different listeners (for example, adapting what they say when speaking to people they do not know).
En 2 Reading	Memos Phone messages Diary Planting instructions Plant names Plant reference books Gardening glossary Garden centre websites Signage	**Reading strategies** 1) To read with fluency, accuracy, understanding and enjoyment, pupils should be taught to use a range of strategies to make sense of what they read. They should be taught to: l. focus on meaning derived from the text as a whole m. use their knowledge of book conventions, structure, sequence and presentational devices n. draw on their background knowledge and understanding of the content. **Reading for information** 2) Pupils should be taught to: a. use the organisational features of non-fiction texts, including captions, illustrations, contents, index and chapters, to find information b. understand that texts about the same topic may contain different information or present similar information in different ways c. use reference materials for different purposes. **Reading** f. respond imaginatively in different ways to what they read.

(*continued*)

Table 5.2 The garden centre *(cont'd)*

NC English strands	Language and literacy opportunities	NC links at KS1
En 3 Writing	Memos Phone messages Diary Planting instructions Receipts Caring for your plants – instruction cards Signage	**Composition** 1) Pupils should be taught to: a. use adventurous and wide-ranging vocabulary e. vary their writing to suit the purpose and reader f. use the texts they read as models for their own writing. **Presentation** g. the importance of clear and neat presentation in order to communicate their meaning effectively. **Language structure** 7) In composing their own texts, pupils should be taught to consider: a. how word choice and order are crucial to meaning. **Breadth of study** 10) Pupils should be taught the value of writing for remembering and developing ideas. 12) The range of forms of writing should include narratives, poems, notes, lists, captions, records, messages, instructions.

search for information with the motivational and presentational aspects offered by the use of the story box.

The cross-curricular emphasis on the teaching content of non-fictional texts cannot be understated and it is helpful, therefore, to consider how story boxes can enable an exploration across subject areas. Table 5.3 shows some ideas for story boxes across a range of National Curriculum subjects. The children's exploration could be extended with the use of corresponding information texts to support and extend their play.

Games

Interactive websites and games   Many websites offer free-to-download games and activities related to a range of non-fictional texts. See the interactive quiz on the seashore at ... for example, or the games related to sharks on the Discovery Channel website at http:dsc.discovery.com/games/

Table 5.3   Story boxes across the curriculum

NC subject area	Related themes for story boxes
Maths Exploring money and weighing Exploring shapes	A sweet-shop Shape city
Science Exploring animal habitats	Under the sea; In the garden (a minibeast world)
Geography Exploring environments	A rainforest; the seaside; a volcano; the Moon's surface
History Exploring past times first hand	Dinosaur world; the Victorians; when Mum and Dad were young
Art and Design Exploring the work and lives of artists	An artist's room decorated in the style of the artist's paintings (e.g. Van Gogh's bedroom; Niki de Saint Phalle's bathroom)
RE Exploring and comparing places of worship	A mosque or church or synagogue with corresponding miniature artefacts
PE Exploring the rules and strategies of a game	A sports pitch or ground or court with mini-players and equipment (e.g. a mini version of table football/Subbuteo or an ice hockey rink

Board games   These can be commercially produced on a theme or developed bespoke by you or the children on a specific theme related to work being undertaken in class. You may, for example, develop a simple board game based on Monopoly exploring your local environment to support and extend research into the locale.

Language play   I-spy; Animal, vegetable or mineral; who am I? Twenty questions (Yes or no), Quizzes. Consider adapting the range of car games to support and extend children's reasons to look for information.

Playtimes

It is important to recognise that play during the children's regular 'free' times during the school day are vital for them to explore and make sense of real and make-believe worlds with minimal adult intervention. Ensuring time for this totally unstructured play is an essential part of creative development.

Speaking and listening and drama

Clarifying knowledge; framing questions; exploring findings; presenting to others: these are all key areas for children to undertake when researching an area of interest. They are also all areas that demand a great deal of talking and listening in order to bring the enquiry to life.

Use of talking partners

This is a crucial teaching strategy useful for all areas of learning in the creative interactive classroom. It enables the children time to talk to a partner to help them explore their ideas and allow time to articulate a thoughtful response. Talking partners are an especially useful tool to break up whole class shared reading and writing sessions by allowing the children time to talk about their ideas one to one without the need to talk in front of a large group, which can be quite threatening to many children. For children at KS1, it is helpful to use talk partners regularly but for short periods of time (two or three minutes is usually sufficient during whole-class sessions – longer if used as part of group work).

Drama techniques from fiction to non-fiction

Using drama to develop children's understanding of information texts is as critical as using it to develop perspectives on fictional narratives. The following examples are based upon one wonderful fictional text, *The Snail and the Whale* by Julia Donaldson. The activities draw the reader away from fantasy through the use of complementary information texts and are intended to demonstrate how drama techniques can be used to deepen children's understanding of the pertinent issues raised:

Role-play areas   Links with an aquarium, an oceanographer's or marine biologist's sea station, a pet shop, a zoo, a vet.

Dynamic duos   The snail and the whale – children work in twos to explore the differences between the two animals. Each child must work together to find out five important facts about each other using websites, books, DVDs.

Animal language   Children listen to whale sounds on CD and discuss what they think the whales could be saying to each other. Children to work in pairs to 'talk' in whale, relying on intonation and gestures to help understand each other.

Writing in role   This can enable the children to use a range of different text types:

- a thank-you letter to the snail from the whale
- an e-mail to the whale in response
- a message in a bottle asking for help
- a diary of events from either character
- a newspaper report of the events
- a poster demanding an end to speedboats in the bay.

Guided action Talking the children through a re-enactment of certain key parts of the text can enable them to explore certain issues in more depth. Consider how the children could work in small groups to develop a plan to save the beached whale, for example.

Radio/Pod casts Children could work in groups to plan and rehearse a 1-minute broadcast on the beached whale. Look at a clip from the BBC news website (http:news.bbc.co.uk) of the whale in the Thames with the children first to discuss how other broadcasters have done this before working in small groups to consider the key events, develop a convincing newsreader 'voice' and present within the time. This project could take several sessions to complete.

Video diaries The class could keep a 'diary room' after the currently popular Big Brother TV series. The children can access the diary room at a certain time each day but must be in role as the whale describing her/his thoughts as the drama unfolds.

Dance drama Transforming information to dance can be a rewarding experience. As the children develop their understanding of whales and snails, so their confidence in reflecting on the movements and responding to the music will increase.

Video Filming re-enactments or small-world play can enable the children the opportunity to review their own work and performance. It is important that any showing of the children's drama be agreed by them in advance and that the audience be shown how to respond positively to others' work.

Hot-seating Once children have been immersed in their investigations on a particular theme and consider themselves to be experts, it can be very rewarding for them to use drama to transform their knowledge and inform others. The children could prepare to be 'hot-seated' as a marine biologist, for example, after spending time researching information about the snail and the whale.

Creative approaches to reading and responding to non-fiction at key stage 1

Text provision

This should include a range of multimodal reference material where children can be enticed to browse and discover, as well as where specific information can be located. The information should reflect the interest of the children and should provide up-to-date information wherever possible (unless for use as a historical text, of course). The range should include a selection from:

- information picture books (big books and individual copies are important to support shared, guided group and independent reading)
- library books (to supplement your classroom stock related to a particular theme or subject area)
- internet access (with identified and vetted websites)
- encyclopaedias (book and CD or internet-based)
- dictionaries, thesauruses and topic-related dictionaries (e.g medical with plenty of vivid diagrams and photos)
- gossipy and hobby magazines
- maps (a selection from the local area, London Underground maps, bus maps, cycle routes, etc.)
- diagrams and timetables
- recipe books
- manuals (Haynes car maintenance are particularly popular)
- advertisements (from posters and TV)
- TV listings (free magazines in most weekend newspapers or web-based)
- children's film and book reviews (web- or paper-based)
- children's newspapers or news websites (e.g. BBC's Newsround)
- sports magazines and programmes
- films
- cartoons.

Ways of reading non-fiction

As discussed in the introduction to non-fiction (page 107), the EXIT model developed by David Wray and Maureen Lewis (1997) offers a useful model of the range of experiences needed to search for, read, understand and impart information from non-fictional texts. They should not be read as stages to pass through to enlightenment, instead they are intended to support the reader to access and use information texts most effectively. The following examples look at each stage with reference to activities at KS1 with the emphasis on the active learner.

1. Activating prior knowledge

- Talking partners: 'Tell the person next to you three things you already know about electricity.'

- Drawing or making models of what you already know about dinosaurs

- Group 'mind maps' or 'thought showers' with the teacher asking the children to call out any related ideas connected with rain and scribing their ideas. Links between the random ideas can then be made.

- Role-play (see above)

- KWL grids could be developed as part of share writing where the teacher can prompt and scribe a record of what the class already *knows* about healthy eating, what they *want* to find out and, later, what they have *learnt* from their enquiry.

2. Establishing purposes

- Using a question tree to generate explicit questions the children want answering. Children consider each question word to help prompt a range of questions: *Where* do caterpillars sleep? *Why* do they make a cocoon? *When* do they lay their eggs? *What* colour are their eggs? *How* long do they live? Attempt to answer the questions posted on the tree by the end of the project.

- Role play – the creative teacher will enjoy establishing a make-believe situation demanding help from the children in solving a problem ('When I came into class this morning I found an animal's egg under my chair. I need you to help me to find out what creature left it there and what we need to do to help it to go back home').

- Preparing questions (and answers) for a Mastermind quiz about the Moon.

- Preparing questions for hot-seating or interviewing an expert visitor (Al's great-granny, for example, who remembers coming to the school when she was a little girl in 1945).

- Preparing a presentation or talk or show to an audience (younger or parallel class, parents and friends, invited guests) on world religions.

- Inspiring the need to know more through:
  - watching a film or video
  - reading a story (e.g. *Katie and the Sunflowers* would support an initial enquiry into the work of the post-impressionist painters, for example)
  - going on a class visit (the rights and wrongs of zoos, for instance)
  - looking at a real object or artefact or creature (e.g. a wooden washing board) and tracking down what it is.

3. Locating information

- Understanding the range of places to search for information needs to be made explicit to the class.
- The resources need to be well organised and diverse in order to attract enquiry and appeal to the range of learning styles favoured by the children.
- Familiarity with searching tools – library indexes, search engines, contents pages, interview techniques, etc.

4. Adopting an appropriate strategy

- Shared and guided group reading can offer a very supportive model to share explicitly the strategies used to read different kinds of texts. 'Think alouds' where the teacher literally talks through the process: 'Now I want to find out what snails eat so I'm going to start looking for it in this book with a snail on the front. It would take me a long time to read the whole book so I need to find a way of looking for this information. Let's take a look at the contents page. Let's read it together to see if this helps us . . .'
- Adult support to read the content of the texts to the child when it is beyond their independent decoding ability.

5. Interacting with the text and 6. Monitoring understanding

- Restructuring texts will enable the reader to clarify the key points and will encourage dialogue particularly when activities are carried out with a partner or in small groups:
  - diagram to prose
  - recipe to a map
  - diary to a cartoon
  - instructions to a photo story.
- Transform fact to fiction and fiction to fact (*Owl Babies, Mr Archimedes' Bath, The Very Hungry Caterpillar*).

- Develop a cloze procedure on a text where children are encouraged to discuss and substitute omissions. It is important not to give possible answers as this will inhibit broad and creative thinking.

- Introduce text marking. Rather than taking lengthy notes, children should be encouraged to photocopy texts or download from the website and literally mark the text with highlighter pens or by circling information. 'Highlight everything you can find about the cat's favourite foods in blue.'

- Drama activities (see activities on pp 146–7).

7. Making a record

- Adding key findings to a class list as part of shared writing.

- Using a Dictaphone to record information and keep for later on.

- Share and exchange findings with a partner.

8. Evaluating information   Ensuring children begin to question the texts that are presented as factual by adult writers needs plenty of adult support and adult-led activities. See the activities suggested under Critical literacy on pp 155–6.

9. Assisting memory   In order to ensure that children retain some of the information they have found out, it is essential to make the process meaningful and purposeful by ensuring a real reason to search for information (1) and an audience to pass on the information to (10).

10. Communicating the information   Ensuring that the purpose identified at the beginning of the process is celebrated and disseminated at the end of the investigation makes it all worthwhile and ensures clarity of thinking as well as maintaining a focused search for information. This is discussed in more detail in the section below on writing and constructing non-fictional texts. The range of ways to communicate the information could include:

- bookmaking, brochures, pamphlets, newspaper
- oral presentation
- drama
- video
- tape or podcast.

Creative approaches to writing and constructing non-fiction texts at key stage 1

Children are engaged in writing non-fiction regularly outside of the school environment: text messaging to friends, e-mailing family abroad, e-cards to favourite, TV celebrities, cards, notes, shopping lists, letters are all fundamental forms of communication for the very young 'inexperienced' writer.

Writing non-fiction in school can be perceived quite differently, however: closed comprehension questions in practice KS1 SATs booklets on spiders or the countryside; copying huge chunks of 'facts' from 'seen better days' books with dense and impenetrable texts in order to demonstrate all you know about the Romans; writing about what you did at the weekend – every Monday – even when nothing much happened or you don't want to share what happened with your teacher and the whole class anyway. The creative practitioner needs to recognise the difference beween these experiences and build on the instinctive need of all of us to communicate and tell people what we know.

Models for writing

In order to foster a creative classroom environment where children are confident to explore the range of non-fiction writing opportunities, it is important to extend clear and comprehensive models for children's writing.

Books

Starting from an effective non-fiction text can support young and inexperienced writers by giving them a voice and a framework from which to begin. The range of non-fiction books is huge as is the style, form and layout. Consider these examples as useful starting points for children's own writing:

> *Window* by Jennie Baker: a text with no words but with a powerful meaning. A mother with her baby looks out of a window. As the years go by we see out of the same window with the baby boy as he grows to fatherhood. The environment is altered dramatically over the time, leaving questions in the mind of the reader. This is a useful text to demonstrate the power of images to construct information.
>
> Janet and Allan Ahlberg's *The Jolly Postman* offers a range of text types within the fictional arena of a postman delivering communications to and from various fairy tale characters. The range of texts presented includes simplified versions of familiar real-life texts: a party invitation, a postcard, a letter of apology, a catalogue.
>
> *A B Sea* by Bobby Kalman, and *A is for Artist* by Ella Doran and Silence, offer great models. The alphabet offers a tight and familiar structure to explore any theme.

Our Gran by Kathy Swift offers a personal history complete with photos, drawings and memories comparing her gran as a child with now. It offers a useful model of writing from the personal and the value of uniting written texts with images and objects.

Writing frames

Lewis and Wray have written extensively about the value of using writing frames to support the less experienced writer in writing to a 'text type' format (1997, 1999; Wray and Lewis 1997). They argue that by giving children a clear structure within which to write on a particular genre, children will be relieved from the terror of the blank page and, with explicit prompts, able to write their ideas independently. They include examples such as:

Recount genre

Before I read about this topic I thought that . . .

But when I read about it I learnt that . . .

I also learnt that . . .

Furthermore I learnt that . . .

The final think I learnt was that . . .

Explanation genre

I want to explain why . . .

There are many reasons for this. The chief reason is . . .

Another reason is . . .

A further reason is . . .

So now you can see why . . .

(Lewis and Wray 1999: 95)

Although the authors clarify that these frames must be used with a clear purpose and at points of difficulty or when beginning to write in an unfamiliar genre, the creative practitioner needs to consider whether writing frames liberate or inhibit creative writing. Although we believe there is a place for explicit support of children's writing, it is important not to put unfamiliar and decontextualised words in the children's mouths.

Shared writing

The NLS's *Developing Early Writing* (DfES 2001) stresses the value of using shared writing as a vehicle for supporting and extending children's writing. It is a particularly useful teaching technique if used with a range of participatory activities including talk partners, thinking time and drama bursts. There are three broad types of shared writing:

- *Teacher demonstration* – this is where the teacher makes the writing process explicit using 'think alouds' articulating her or his thought process as she or he writes
- *Teacher scribing* – inviting contributions from the class through carefully framed questions and responses and thereby encouraging and developing individual responses
- *Supported composition* – encourages the children to explore a sentence type or phrase on individual or paired whiteboards that can be rehearsed and fed back to support the whole-class composition.

Reasons to write

Standards of writing have improved as a result of guidance from the national strategies. However, although pupils' understanding of the features of different text types has improved, some teachers give too little thought to ensuring that pupils fully consider the audience, purpose and content for their writing.

(Ofsted 2005: 6)

The creative practitioner will revel in developing real and imaginary real purposes for children's factual writing. 'We are all going to write down what we know about caterpillars now. Open your English books . . .' is very different from: 'Some children have been squashing the caterpillars in the school garden for fun. Urrrrrgh! What can we do to save our caterpillars? Make a poster to display in the school garden? What a great idea!'

- Leaflets on caring for pets for distribution at the local vets (facts carefully checked, of course!)
- Alphabet books for children in the Nursery
- Up-to-date books and maps on the local environment for the library
- Animated texts reporting on outings published on the school's website for parents to view
- Letters to the headteacher pleading for new PE equipment
- Private diaries to be written and read in private (no marking or peeping)
- Shopping lists for the Christmas party
- Writing-in-role (see examples of writing-in-role on pp 146–7).

These are a few offerings to encourage children to realise that writing non-fiction is important and has an impact and can be more effective than other forms of communication.

Constructing non-written texts

It is important to consider the many and varied texts that are not written down. These include:

- TV interviews
- radio documentaries
- audio guides (see the Case Study in Y2 below)
- news podcasts
- audio descriptions for partially sighted people (www.bbc.co.uk/ouch/closeup/audiodescription_guideto.shtml#whatisad offers some useful advice on developing verbal descriptions of film and TV).

Constructing these texts demands many of the same researching and planning methods as writing and enables children to develop additional co-operative and creative skills.

Critical literacy

Monitoring and questioning what we read or 'critical literacy' is a challenging but vital part of reading and writing information texts. As children are increasingly targeted as consumers and with the explosion and circulation of unsolicited information, understanding how and why texts are made is an essential part of learning how to read and write (Marsh and Millard 2000). Critical literacy is essentially about comparing texts with our reality. This 'reality' will of course be different from reader to reader but of fundamental importance is the understanding that texts can tell us what the writer wants us to know. This can be very different from what we know to be so.

Non-fiction texts tend to have an authority quite different from fictional stories. They look serious and important and adults wrote them so they must be true. Challenging this accepted truth is an exciting and vital part of the creative classroom environment.

Jennifer O'Brien and Barbara Comber offer a useful framework of questions for 'reflection about texts' that could be altered slightly to enage with any written or visual text:

What kind of a text is this?

How can we describe it?

Where else have you seen texts like this?

What do these kinds of texts usually do?

Who would produce (write/draw) a text like this?

Who do they produce (write/draw) for it?

For what kind of readers (viewers/listeners) is this text intended?

(Barratt-Pugh and Rohl 2000: 156)

Further activities to encourage questioning critical readers and knowing writers could include:

Reading and writing catalogues   Collect images from catalogues and explore the differences between boys' and girls' toys – why do girls' toys always have to be pink? Who says so? Developing research into real favourite toys and activities in the class. Any surprises? The children could develop class posters of Toys for All or Toys for Girls – the Truth!

Reading and developing greeting cards   Collect and collate images and words on greetings cards designated for particular people. Explore images of dads or grandparents, for example – my granny doesn't like roses and kittens, she likes motorbikes! Write alternative greetings and celebratory cards for use in the writing area.

Reading and filming TV adverts   How does the music make me feel? What is the filmmaker trying to sell me? How do I know? What do I need to tell the audience if I want to sell my bike?

Reading and making sweet wrappers   Look at a range of popular sweet wrappings and any related advertising. What do the pictures/words/fonts/colours tell me? Design and make and market a new sweet using the information gathered.

Case study: Y2 audio tour for school art gallery

Stella is an experienced class teacher of a Y2 class in Wales. She is also the school's art co-ordinator and is keen to heighten the school's art profile. After a class trip to the Tate Modern gallery in London, she was inspired to transform a bare and rather dingy school-corridor into a public gallery where children's artwork could be displayed by each class on a rota system. As part of the preparation for the half-termly 'private view', she discussed with the children the value of the audio guides they had seen at the Tate gallery.

Stella borrowed an example from the gallery and shared a brief excerpt with the children describing a picture they had spent some time looking at in the gallery. The language was quite difficult for the class but she selected her excerpt carefully.

The children were then asked to select one piece of their favourite art work each from their portfolios. They worked in pairs over a two-week period mainly in the Literacy Hour to develop their own audio guide for visitors to the school and children from other classes.

The children were initially encouraged to talk about their artwork to a partner without showing them the image itself. They were given three open discussion points to help guide their descriptions. Stella modelled the descriptions with a picture of her own first:

> > Tell me the story behind your picture
>
> > Tell me how you made the picture
>
> > Tell me how your picture makes you feel

The children then shared their pictures and talked again with their partners. The partners were encouraged to ask any questions they wanted to know about the picture and how it was made.

This oral rehearsal with 'talk partners' enabled the children to practise and refine what they wanted to say before recording their thoughts using standard classroom tape recorders. The children could re-record as often as they needed until they felt happy with their efforts and until they had managed to keep their description to under one minute each (egg timer used).

The tape was copied and two pairs of headphones and two redundant Walkman personal stereos (kindly donated by teachers pleased to update to MP3 players) were used for visitors to listen to the audio tour.

Figure 5.1 shows Karma listening to Frank's picture: 'Think of *Men in Black*. Do you remember the bit on the roof with the helicopter? The light from the top shined really bright and the night lit up like a bonfire night. That's what I was thinking about when I started this drawing. I did it four times before I was happy with the helicopter. It was hard to draw the wings to make it look like it was flying. This picture makes me feel happy and scared and exciting. It is one of my best drawings because I didn't have to draw people.'

Figure 5.1   Karma listening to Frank's picture

Developing your creative practice

In order to extend your creativity in the teaching of non-fiction at KS1, reflect on your current practice and explore the following activities:

- Search the WWW for suitable websites you could use with the children to help them access information relevant to the themes and interests of your class.

- 'Read' a short film or advert or picture with your class.
- Develop an alphabet frieze with your class drawing on images and icons from the children's popular culture.
- Plan an event to inspire your class to write passionate letters of complaint.

Creative approaches to teaching non-fiction at key stage 1: A summary

To conclude this chapter, it is helpful to summarise the key areas related to ensuring children engage creatively with non-fiction:

- Children at KS1 already know a huge amount about reading and constructing non-fiction texts as part of their everyday lives.
- Children need clear and motivating reasons to write purposeful and effective texts.
- Non-fictional texts are as creative as fictional ones.
- Critical literacy is a vital component of reading and writing non-fiction in the 21st century.

References

Barratt-Pugh, C. and Rohl, M. (2000) *Literacy Learning in the Early Years*. Buckingham: Open University Press.

Bromley, H. (1999) 'Storytelling', *Primary English Magazine*, 4 (3, 4 and 5).

DfEE (1998) *National Literacy Strategy Framework for Teaching*. London: DfES.

DfEE (2000) *National Curriculum*. London: DfES.

DfEE, (2001) *Developing Early Writing*. London DfES.

Lewis, M. and Wray, D. (1997) *Writing Frames*. Reading and Language Information Centre, University of Reading.

Lewis, M. and Wray, D. (1999) 'The problems and possibilities of non-fiction writing' in Goodwin, P. (ed.) *The Literate Classroom*. London: David Fulton Publishers.

Marsh J. and Millard, E. (2000) *Literacy and Popular Culture*. London: Paul Chapman Publishing.

Ofsted (2005) *English 2000–2005: A Review of Inspection Evidence*. London: HMSO.

Wray, D. and Lewis, M. (1997) *Extending Literacy: Children Reading and Writing Non-Fiction*. London: Routledge.

Useful websites

Dorling Kindersley's website offers a useful range of popular non-fiction titles tapping into children's interests. This section is particularly designed for 5–7 year olds:

www.dorlingkindersley-uk.co.uk/static/cs/uk/11/childrens/intro57.html

To explore the wonderful work of the artist Niki de Saint Phalle:
www.niki-museum.jp/english/index.htm

A useful resource for researching table football as well as for ordering mini-footballers: www.subbuteoworld.co.uk/

A simple seashore quiz suitable for Y2 developed by the British Marine Life Study Society:
www.glaucus.org.uk/splash1.htm

Children's literature and other resources
Janet and Allan Ahlberg's *The Jolly Postman* (1986) Viking/Puffin.

Pamela Allen's *Mr Archimedes' Bath* (1980) Bodley Head Children's Books.

Jennie Baker's *Window* (2002) Walker Books.

Eric Carle's *The Very Hungry Caterpillar* (1970) Hamish Hamilton.

Julia Donaldson's *The Snail and the Whale* (2003) Macmillan Children's Books.

Ella Doran and Silence's *A is for Artist: An Alphabet* (2004) Tate.

Simon James' *Dear Mr Blueberry* (1996) Aladdin Paperbacks.

Bobby Kalman's *A B Sea* (1995) Crabtree Publishing Company.

James Mayhew's *Katie and the Sunflowers* (2000) Orchard.

Kathy Swift's *Our Gran* (1991) Longman Group.

Martin Waddell's *Owl Babies* (1994) Walker Books.

Seashore: 3D Window into the Fascinating World of Nature, Virgin Sound and Vision CD-ROM.

CHAPTER 6

Teaching non-fiction creatively at key stage 2

I need to be able to argue in case I get a parking ticket like my mum did

(Katy, aged 10)

Introduction

In this chapter we will consider how to build on the opportunities for engaging with non-fiction that children have experienced in Early Years settings and at KS1, as well as the knowledge and skills that they bring with them from their daily lives. At key stage 2 we need to extend children's functional literacy to enable them to sort through and interpret the vast range of information that they encounter and to use spoken and written language as a tool that will empower them. Our aim should be to provide children with the skills that they need to become reflective and critical readers and creative writers.

Non-fiction at KS2

Children of this age will increasingly gain their information and knowledge about the local, national and global society in which they live from a range of media sources, such as newspapers, radio, TV, advertising and the worldwide web, as well as more traditional information texts. A lot of the information may be contradictory, having been produced to persuade, put across a political viewpoint or to sell a product or lifestyle. Opinion may be presented as fact. Many of the texts that they encounter will not fit neatly into a text type. They may contain features from several genres (a persuasive text such as an advertisement may pose as a scientific report).

As KS2 teachers our role is to help children select the most appropriate resources and navigate through the material to help them understand the world and pursue their interests. Children need to understand how non-fiction texts are constructed and how the author's purpose influences what is produced. One way to develop this understanding is to provide opportunities for children to use research to construct their own information texts for an identified audience.

Children at KS2 need access to a wide range of texts and media forms and reasons to engage critically with them. The creative teacher will build on and extend children's interests and provide real-life situations for children to respond to (for example, stating the case for an after school club) and encourage them to consider the various forms such a response might take (letter, e-mail, banner, petition, website), taking into account the intended audience.

To review how the National Curriculum (1999) and the *National Literacy Strategy Framework* (DfEE 1998) and the guidance in *Excellence and Enjoyment: A Strategy for Primary Schools* (DfES 2003a) address teaching non-fiction, I have set out what I consider to be some of the salient points.

The National Curriculum for English at key stage 2

The statement on page 50 of the document addresses in general terms what children need to learn to be effective speakers, critical readers and writers:

> In English, during KS2 pupils learn to change the way they speak and write to suit different situations, purposes and audiences. They read a range of texts and respond to different layers of meaning in them. They explore the use of language in literary and non-literary texts and learn how language works.

En1 Speaking and listening

The details in the Programmes of Study set out under the separate headings of Speaking, Listening, Group Discussion and Interaction and Breadth of Study almost all relate to using language for functional purposes rather than literary ones. They mostly inform the non-fiction writing conventions that children of this age are expected to understand and use.

En2 Reading

Under En2 Reading there is a sub-section specifically on Reading for Information, which includes reading information on screen.

Reading for information

3. Pupils should be taught to:
a   scan texts for information
b   skim for gist and overall impression
c   obtain specific information through detailed reading

d draw on different features of texts, including print, sound and image to obtain meaning

e use organisational features and systems to find texts and information

f distinguish between fact and opinion (for example, by looking at the purpose of the text, the reliability of the information)

g consider an argument critically.

There are also detailed requirements for developing pupils' understanding and appreciation of non-fiction and non-literary texts, which include 'engaging with challenging and demanding subject matter' (5g).

9. The range should include:

a diaries, autobiographies, biographies, letters

b print and ICT-based reference and information materials

c newspapers, magazines, articles, leaflets, brochures, advertisements.

En 3 Writing

There is repeated reference to purposes for writing, the needs of the reader and different forms of writing, which include reports, explanations, opinions, instructions, reviews, commentaries.

We believe that The National Curriculum provides a sound framework for teaching about non-fiction at KS2. It recognises the importance of being able to use organisational systems to gain access to information and the teaching of higher-order reading skills such as skimming and scanning to facilitate this. It highlights the importance of using challenging texts and the broad range of material suggested includes both linear and non-linear texts and ICT-based reference materials. However, the significant and substantial developments in technology in recent years are not reflected and the creative teacher should also build on children's home literacy and their exposure to computer games, videos and DVDs, mobile phones and text messaging. It is important to work with multimodal texts as well as more traditional texts to prepare children for the 21st century, in which they are citizens.

Perhaps most importantly the National Curriculum also states what children should be able to do once they have accessed information, which is to be critical of the material and consider its reliability. As teachers we must recognise how important this is, but should not underestimate how difficult it can be, even as adults, to recognise when and how we are being manipulated. Throughout this chapter, I will suggest activities that help children to develop critical reading skills.

The National Literacy Strategy

As with Fiction and Poetry, it is the National Literacy Strategy *Framework for Teaching* (DfEE 1998) that provides the details of when and what should be taught. Text-level work includes a section on 'Non-Fiction' with subsections on reading comprehension and writing composition and there are clear links between reading and writing through the range of forms that are suggested. Children's understanding of how texts work will develop as they experiment with producing their own texts to communicate for a range of purposes and with a growing awareness of the needs of the audience.

However, because of the range of forms and the amount of material that was to be covered each term in structured daily literacy hours, the complexity of many texts was ignored and only those texts that fitted the organisational features of the genre that was to be taught were presented. The NLS training materials (*Reading and Writing for Information*, DfEE 1998) provided teachers with a table of the structures and features of a range of non-fiction genres. The particular text types they referred to were recount, report, explanation, instructions, persuasion and discussion.

Although there is a disclaimer that the material is not 'a rigid set of rules', inevitably many children's books were published to exemplify these text types and many teachers presented the features as if they were rules. Yet in the real world genres are often blurred and do not follow a strict formula. Wray and Lewis (1997), who have written extensively about teaching non-fiction, acknowledge that, 'There are of course many other kinds of non-fiction genres and many examples of mixed genre texts' (1997: 118) but still seem to suggest that children should understand the main characteristics of the identified genres to help them with their writing. Once those features have been identified, children's writing can be scaffolded through the use of writing frames and this has led in some instances to a formulaic rather than a creative approach to composition, as I discuss later in this chapter.

I tend to agree with the sentiments of Angela Wilson (1999) who in a brief overview of genre theory in her discussion of the non-fiction genres specified in the National Literacy Strategy concludes that though writers are operating within a social context and are aware of social pressures and expectations, the human mind is inventive and very few text types will stay fixed for long (1999: 35).

Excellence and Enjoyment: A Strategy for Primary Schools

There is far more scope and encouragement to teach non-fiction creatively under the existing and planned freedoms set out in *Excellence and Enjoyment: A Strategy for Primary Schools* (DfES 2003). Schools can decide how to arrange learning in the school day. 'There is no requirement for subjects to be taught discretely – they can be grouped, or taught through projects – if strong enough links are created between subjects, pupils' knowledge and skills can be used across the whole curriculum' (p.17). The principles of learning and teaching in this document reiterate a cross-curricular approach and emphasise promoting creativity as 'a powerful way of engaging pupils with their learning' (p. 31).

This is important as much of the work on non-fiction at KS2 will either be through cross-curricular themes or undertaken in other curriculum areas, for example report writing in science. What is vital is that children are interested in the topic if they are to have the motivation to research and present materials whether as individual, group or class projects.

Reading and responding to non-fiction

In the introduction to this section we explored in some detail the differences and similarities between fiction and non-fiction texts and the notion of facts as opposed to fiction. If our aim is to empower children, it is important that the texts that we use with children at KS2 reflect the variety of texts that they will encounter in their lives as children and as adults. For example, non-fiction that is written as a narrative (diary, letter, biography) may have elements of subjectivity and a persuasive non-fiction text (advertisement) might not be based on facts. The significant difference between responding to fiction and non-fiction that children at KS2 should be aware of is that with texts that are presented as fiction *there is no need for the reader to question the validity of the text*, whereas with non-fiction *the reader needs to check the accuracy of the text*, whatever format it is presented in.

Activities to develop children's understanding of genre

Consider the following activities as a way of developing children's understanding of genre.

Classifying texts by features
Explain to the children that they are 'feature' detectives. The world is becoming too chaotic and some order needs to be restored. Their job is to ensure that writers obey the rules. Provide each group with a list of features for a different text type. Ask the children to sort a range of texts and select the ones that fit their given category: recount, report, instruction, persuasion, explanation and discussion. They can highlight examples of the features that they find. As a class consider whether some texts fit into more than one category? Are there any texts that do not fit at all? Why? How effective are such texts?

Exploring different forms of writing
Collect a selection of recipes. The children can help with this. Ask the children to examine the recipes to identify the features of instructional texts from their list.

What other features from different text types can they identify? For example, a recipe might include a description of the locality from where it originated. Why has the writer chosen to include the information? A recipe might be written or embedded in another form, as a recount for example: 'As a child I loved to make "upside down" pudding. We used to get up early to . . .'

The most important question we should encourage children to explore is the purpose of the writing or the writer's intentions and how successful they have been in communicating that purpose to the intended audience. Children may have their own reading preferences and how they assimilate information might reflect these. When they come to present their own texts they can consider different ways of presenting information clearly, reflecting on themselves as readers and what they know of the intended audience.

The EXIT model of teaching non-fiction

As discussed in the introduction to this section, the EXIT model of teaching non-fiction to pupils (Wray and Lewis 1997) formed the basis of the NLS module on teaching non-fiction at KS1 and KS2.

Although children may engage with different stages of the process at any time depending on their reading skills, the type of text and the task that they are engaged in, there are four areas in particular that might be developed at KS2. These are:

- locating information
- interacting with the text to assist understanding
- considering issues of validity and bias
- presenting information to different audiences.

In the following section I suggest how we might teach the skills that children need for these stages in a creative way.

Locating information

It is important to remember that the term 'text' as used throughout this chapter, indeed throughout this book, refers to 'language organised to communicate (which) includes written, spoken and electronic forms' (NLS Glossary) but also to still and moving image. Our understanding of the 'text' will depend on the knowledge that we bring to it. This may be culturally specific. As teachers we must be aware of the skills and experiences that children bring to school and build upon them.

While recognising the importance of teaching where and how to get information, we need to consider the way children today receive information. As we have already mentioned, there is a vast range of information available through paper-based texts, the media and ICT. With such information overload, teachers have an important role in helping children to decide where they might find the information the need. Children will have some understanding of contents, index and glossary from their work in KS1. They may have used simple search engines. At KS2 children need to develop their understanding of such tools and evaluate how effective they are.

Currently there is a preoccupation with pupils' ability to decode texts and 'synthetic phonics' is to become a statutory teaching strategy in our schools in the light of the Rose Report www.standards.dfes.gov.uk/rosereview/finalreport/. While not denying the importance of decoding skills, although how these should be taught is contentious, the higher order skills of skimming and scanning, inference, personal response and critical reflection need to be taught concomitantly. Children at KS2 who have difficulty with print texts or children in the early stages of learning English may employ higher order reading skills with still or moving image. The creative teacher will develop these skills and help children to transfer their knowledge to print texts too.

Skimming and scanning

Many children today have videos and DVDs in their bedrooms. They are accomplished at finding their way round films to select their favourite scenes to revisit or to share with friends. They rewind, fast forward, pause, freeze scenes. These skills are very similar to the skills that children need to find information from print, whether it is hard copy or on a screen, and we can build on them. I tell children that skim reading is like fast-forwarding their video. They are familiar with the material and stop when they notice a familiar image. They then play the scene slowly to gain more detailed information. This is what is meant by scanning. It is important that children are encouraged to create and develop their own strategies and share them with their peers. One child in my class compared scanning to a person on a till scanning the barcode on an item to get the details from it.

Accessing electronic texts

The growth of the internet and ICT texts has had a considerable impact on the way we access information. Children today have access to electronic non-fiction texts when they are using the Web to research material or CD-ROM information texts. Many children at KS2 will already have some strategies for negotiating web pages and interactive books but they may need guidance in negotiating the material effectively, as well as critically reflecting on it. To encourage children to use ICT as a research tool we must teach them how to access the information.

The Teaching Ideas website www.teachingideas.co.uk/welcome provides information on the use of the internet with children. Children can use this site to practise using the tools that they need to navigate the material. The instructions are clear and they have to click on hyperlinks to negotiate the pages. Children can transfer the skills that they have learnt to other websites. Once they have the basic tools to access a site, they can evaluate the accessibility of web pages and the information they provide. This will involve higher-order thinking skills as well as reading skills as they compare and contrast, decide on what is relevant and what should be discarded, judge, rate and justify. As with paper texts essential information may be hidden among less relevant material. It may be conveyed in different ways: through diagrams, graphs, photographs.

Evaluating materials

The following activities are designed to help children select appropriate resources and locate information using higher-order reading skills. To provide an additional purpose for the activities they are linked to writing for a 'real' audience.

Tell children that they are to review some non-fiction books for a publishing company. Provide a selection of information texts on a topic that the children are interested in. Ask them to write the titles at the top of their page. Once children have formulated some questions they want answered, they work with a partner to locate the information. As well as noting where they found the answers, children can record their answers to the following questions:

- How helpful were the books in signposting the information?
- How long did it take to find the information?
- How often did they use the contents, the index?
- What did they use if these features were not present? For example, chapter headings, table of illustrations.

Use this information to compile a class letter to the publisher or editor suggesting any improvements that would make the material more accessible.

A similar activity to the one outlined above can be carried out with websites or digitexts. Children can record and evaluate ease of access, navigation and success in locating relevant information. A further question to explore is:

- What are the advantages and disadvantages of interactive, electronic texts?

Use the information collected on a specific resource to write a review for the publisher or for another class who might be using the resources.

Interacting with the text to assist understanding

Although there has already been a lot written about the need for children to engage with texts in an interactive way, in this section we revisit some of the key skills that we consider important at KS2, focusing on both traditional paper-based texts and electronic texts. The creative teacher will provide opportunities for children to practise these skills using material that they are interested in.

Text marking

An activity such as text marking, where children highlight or underline information that addresses and possibly answers the questions that they are asking, is a skill that we continue to need as adults. Children can practise these skills using newspapers, magazines, photocopied pages or the highlighting tool on the computer. Different colours can be used to note different types of information. They might be finding out information about their favourite pop group, football team, hobby. The extensive media coverage of the World Cup is an excellent source of material. Children should be reminded that essential information may be hidden among less relevant material. Also it may be conveyed in different ways: through charts, tables, diagrams, graphs, photographs. Children are more likely to engage with this type of activity if they work with a partner and share their findings with another pair, with a group or with the class.

Note-taking

Note-taking is another skill that children need to practise. At secondary school they will be required to make notes on the spoken and written information presented in the various subject areas. Role-play situations can provide interesting opportunities for KS2 children to practise taking notes. Children can act as reporters, police officers, court officials to record key information. How might they transcribe the words? Are 'text messaging' conventions helpful? Replaying a television programme or a video on a topic that the children are studying and allocating sections of programme for different groups to make notes on for the rest of the class makes the task of collecting information more manageable.

Reading for the main idea

Wray (2004) suggests asking children to highlight the main idea in a paragraph and to share and justify their choice. Such an activity is a useful way of helping children to understand paragraphing. The cut and paste facility on the computer enables children to experiment with moving the main idea around and considering how effective the different positions are. Rather than accepting how information is presented children are asking 'What would happen if . . .?' and discovering and challenging how choices are made.

Restructuring

Perhaps the most effective way of ensuring that we understand what we have read is to convey that information in another form. Children can restructure information from the work that they are doing in other curriculum areas. They might read or listen to the five-day weather forecast and draw pictures or symbols to accompany it. They might turn directions into a diagram, illustrate a menu, turn the symbols on a seed packet into sentences. Questions they might explore are how effectively is the information communicated in the various forms, bearing in mind the potential audiences.

Margaret Mackintosh, lecturer at the School of Education at the University of Plymouth, uses the term 'graphicacy' to describe the pictorial communication of spatial information. 'Graphicacy is a life skill that we, as adults, depend on every day as we read road signs and maps of all sorts, assemble flat pack furniture, interpret pictures in catalogues and brochures, and in many other contexts' (*The Primary English Magazine*, April 2006: 10).

In design and technology children can experience the transition from 2D to 3D by deciphering construction diagrams to build Lego, Meccano or Airfix models or drawing their own diagrams to demonstrate how they made a model. What are the advantages of diagrams over written instructions?

In geography the transition from 3D structures to 2D representations can be explored by providing children with the opportunity to construct a model of the playground, for example, and photograph it from a range of oblique and aerial views.

Reading electronic texts

Some of the electronic texts that children will encounter are very similar to the texts that they meet in books. Children need opportunities to practise reading on screen which may involve scrolling up and down the way they would turn pages. There may not be as much information on display at one time as there might be in a double page spread in a book, yet the reader can have more control over what they have on the screen through the use of the scrolling arrows or the font size. Some of the strategies for interacting with texts to assist understanding may be similar to those used with paper-based texts. For example, children can use the mouse to select a highlight colour to text mark just as they would use a highlighter pen on a photocopied page or a disposable text.

However, more commonly there are ICT texts that are programmed to encourage the reader to interact with text, such as Longman's Digitexts (www.longman.co.uk/digitexts), a series of interactive ICT texts for KS2. This interaction may work in a similar way to a traditional text in that there may be links to a glossary. There may be hyperlinks that allow you to move from one document to another in the way you would move between different information texts using an index. Different ways of presenting information on a CD-ROM such as letters, documents, diary entries, can provide different perspectives, just as can happen in an informative paper-based text. However, there may also be video clips, sound effects, animation. Ease of navigation may be an advantage with interactive ICT texts and enable children to develop multimedia reading skills more easily.

Because the information presented is likely to be non-linear, the skills of radial reading are important. Children have to know not only how to access information from any point on the screen, but a range of strategies that they might employ to decide what information will be useful to them in a particular context. Encouraging children to select and evaluate the material that is presented and to discriminate between fact and fiction is still crucial. Complex web pages such as the BBC website (www.bbc.co.uk) will also require the reader to move around the text in a non-linear way and gain access to pictures and video clips, but again the development of critical reading is central.

With the expansion and increased sophistication of interactive multimodal texts, children need to continually refine the skills they use to select and evaluate the material. These skills will be a combination of those higher-order reading skills that they apply to printed texts and visual image but increasingly they may need to operate in a number of dimensions simultaneously, as the boundaries between print, visual image and sound become less defined.

Bias

A creative approach to teaching non-fiction at KS2 must develop children's critical understanding of how books and other media present information so that they can become critical, discriminating readers and users. Issues of bias and manipulation in many of the texts that children are confronted with directly or indirectly are serious concerns and a creative approach to teaching must encourage children to question and challenge; make connections and see relationships; envisage what might be; explore ideas and keep options open and reflect critically on what is presented. Children need to ask the important questions of who is communicating the information, what their purpose is and who the intended audience is.

As far back as 1989 Cary Bazalgette reported on the need for media education in the primary school. 'Media education aims to create more active and critical media users' (p3). Although the curriculum statement encompassed the entertainment aspect of contemporary culture as well as the presentation of information, the questions it addressed should underpin how we teach children to read non-fiction texts in all their varied forms. Media education should also build on and extend the knowledge and understanding that children bring from outside of school.

In 2003 the Department for Education and Skills (DfES) commissioned a bfi Education publication entitled *Look Again*, a guide to using film and television with three- to eleven-year-olds. A Primary Education Working Group worked with bfi staff including Cary Bazalgette, Head of the Education Department. They point out that 'A major intellectual aspect of the Primary and Early Years curriculum involves unpicking the construction of texts, fact or fiction, as well as understanding genre rules and seeing where artists and writers have transformed genres' (DfES 2003b).

The teacher's role

The teacher has a significant role in choosing the texts that are presented to the children. We need to be aware that the texts that surround us are often value laden; they present a cultural view that may need to be questioned in terms of social practice and social justice. Texts that we come into contact within the real world will reflect the prevailing ideology, which may exclude certain sections of society. We need to teach children to challenge and interrogate the texts that are presented to them.

Teachers who have been concerned with developing critical literacy have always encouraged this close critical analysis of text. It has had various acronyms in the past: DARTS (Directed Activities Related to Texts); the EXIT model (Extending Interactions with Texts) mentioned earlier and has been covered in media education through looking at media agencies, categories, technologies, languages, audiences and representations. The difference today is the range, sophistication and volume of texts that form part of children's lives outside school and that are accessible to us in the classroom as a result of the advances in technology that sit alongside more traditional texts. It is essential that we teach children the critical skills to negotiate and make decisions on information in all its manifestations that will affect their lives and the lives of others. Only then will they be fully literate.

David Wray (2004) in his chapter 'Developing a critical approach to texts' in *Teaching Literacy: Using Texts to Enhance Literacy* (2004) cites the CARS checklist which, as he points out, was developed to evaluate websites. However, it can be applied to any text. The acronym refers to Credibility, Accuracy, Reasonableness, Support. A creative approach to using this test might involve the children in devising their own questions around each of the four areas and working with them to locate the evidence to answer their questions. The main consideration for children of this age is to know how to find out information about the author, to consider the purpose of the writing, and the potential audience.

Because many of the texts that we read are constructed to persuade rather than inform and, even if written to inform, are rarely neutral or context-free, it is important to provide children with strategies to help them distinguish fact from fiction. Sometimes the language provides an indication. Phrases such as 'It would seem' or 'This suggests that' are not problematic, but whether we spot them depends on how they are slotted into the text. An opinion may be hidden, intentionally or unintentionally, amidst mainly factual writing and go unnoticed. Although we might teach critical literacy skills in English, it is essential that children have the opportunity to apply them in other curriculum areas.

> To leave areas of fact unexplored is as much a sign of bias in a text as to use persuasive or emotional language in supporting an idea.
>
> (Wilson 1999)

Omission of crucial pieces of information from non-fiction texts is common. For example, a party political flyer for the local elections may list the positive initiatives they have carried out and leave out where they have failed. Historical accounts of a nation's achievements in war may omit the atrocities carried out. The creative teacher will not avoid such texts but remind the children to consider who the author is and their intention. Crucially children should reflect on how the material might be presented more fairly and accurately.

Activities to encourage critical awareness

The following activities are designed to help children challenge and interrogate the information that they encounter on a daily basis. I have focused on advertising and news reports as so much of the information we receive comes under these broad headings.

Advertising all around us

Carrier bags
Collect a range of carrier bags. Children can help with this. Select one of the carrier bags and ask children what message the shop or company is trying to put across. What can we learn from the colour, the words or slogan, the font, the logo? Children can look at the material it is made from in terms of durability, sustainability, cost. How has it been produced? What is the producer's intention? Who might the buyer (audience) be? Issues of stereotyping may arise. As a class devise a checklist of features including an 'any other information' category that will help them 'read' a carrier bag. Give each group of children a selection of carrier bags and ask them to use the checklist to read these 'texts'. Each group chooses one bag to report on to the rest of the class.

Children can design and make their own carrier bag in Design and Technology considering purpose and audience.

Packaging

As part of a topic on healthy eating children might consider not only the design but the ingredients on food packaging and the reluctance of producers and supermarkets to standardise how that information is presented. Ask children to work in pairs to restructure the information on, for example, cereal packets so that it is in a standardised form. Are there omissions? Compare the information across brands. Consider the relationship between image and design, product name and description and factual information on ingredients.

Children to write their research up for a school *Which?* magazine.

Different media

Television, radio, poster, magazine, newspaper and internet adverts can be examined in relation to the features of the different media and how they are received. The potential for exploration and critical reflection is enormous. Collect a selection of 'car' adverts saying where they came from. For example *The Observer*, Capital Radio, ITV, AOL. Give each group an example from two different media sources. What features do they notice about each advert? Use this information to formulate questions such as:

- How is a product sold on the radio as opposed to purely visual display?
- Why use jingles?
- What effect does music have?
- How does the television advert differ from radio?
- From online advertising?
- How much text is there, if any, on a poster?
- How is colour used?
- What font size is used, when and why?
- Which celebrities advertise which projects?
- How are people portrayed in terms of age, gender, ethnicity, disability, class?
- When are adverts shown?
- How frequently?
- What numbers do they reach?
- What are the similarities and the differences not only in terms of the product but also in the target audience?

As part of an extended project each group might focus on creating an advert for one of the media forms using the information that has been collected. The use of tapes, digital cameras and video camcorders, clip art programs as well as typed text will enable the children to produce adverts in a range of forms.

As part of their own self-assessment and peer assessment children can devise an evaluation form to assess how effective the advert is and who they think the target audience is.

News reports

News coverage can also be explored in a similar way to advertising as the issues are similar. An important difference is that children might expect the reporting of news to be reporting facts and free of bias. By collecting evidence on what is presented and what is omitted, the more difficult questions of how and why can be broken down.

Give out photocopies of a news story taken from two different papers. Discuss as a class how a news story is presented in a newspaper, looking at headlines, sentence structure, vocabulary and photographs. How is the same story reported in another newspaper?

For example:

THE FAT POLICE

or

4-YEAR-OLDS TO BE SCREENED FOR OBESITY

Ask children in pairs to highlight the similarities in one colour, the differences in another, additional information in another. Ask children to use the information to explore the following questions:

- How neutral is the additional information?
- What might constitute bias in terms of language and image? Record examples.

Compare how a story is reported on the radio stations, the television channels, online. What makes the headlines? Global and local issues can be explored.

Incorporating drama

In groups children role-play a newsworthy story (for example, the decision to ban chips from school lunches or new traffic restrictions near the school). Children should assume a character (MP, headteacher, parent, child, cook, lunchtime supervisor) and use action and speech to convey who they are and their feelings. As the teacher you might use drama techniques such as thought tracking to help the children get inside their character, or decision alley to illustrate the opposing factions. Children might be asked to freeze-frame a significant moment, perhaps waving a banner or signing a petition. This still image illustrates what might end up on the front page of the local newspaper. Each group acts out its improvised scene to the class. The rest of the class has the opportunity to act as reporters to interview the protestors. Alternatively individuals can be put in the 'hot seat' to present their viewpoint.

Children in groups present one of the news stories as a newspaper or radio/television report either positively or negatively from what they have seen and heard. They evaluate each other's reports in terms of bias.

Developing critical literacy skills through other curricular areas

The skills that children need to develop to read critically are transferable to the range of written and image-based texts, including moving image, that they use in all the curriculum areas. The creative teacher will provide activities that encourage children to not take things for granted, to question and challenge what they see and to be innovative and willing to experiment in communicating their own ideas.

Below are some suggestions for promoting these skills through different subject areas:

Art and Design

Use a magnifier to examine detail from a painting. What technique was the painter using? Analysis of technique can be related to overall effect of the picture, just as words can be looked at in isolation but need the broader context to be fully understood.

Geography, History, Citizenship

Using either an overhead projector, slide projector, video frozen frame, epidiascope or interactive whiteboard, show children a small detail from the still image. What do they think it is? Gradually reveal more of the image, stopping to discuss how and why their original predictions were confirmed or changed. This is a way for children to discover that we make more fully informed judgements the more information that we have.

Science

Children can examine or 'read' an insect, material or plant part using different levels of magnification to understand how the process of magnification changes appearance. They can use this knowledge to read more critically the pictures or photos that they see on websites or in information books. The use of soft and sharp focus and the intention behind it might be considered.

History

View archive material of the local area. Consider film, photography, drawings, text as evidence of the past and present. What was recorded and why? How have technological advances influenced what we record? Is it more or less reliable as a source of evidence?

Geography

Projects that have a geographical focus are an ideal context to introduce a range of different ways of representing our world such as photographs, maps, signs and symbols and film. There are close links with media education, as children's questions about the representations of a place, for example, must consider the notion of multiple perspectives and the purpose of the image.

PSHE, Citizenship, RE

Consider representations of disability, gender, ethnicity and social groups in a range of texts. Explore 'positive' and 'negative' images. Who produced the images and why?

The British Film Institute publishes a range of classroom resources. In 2003 they developed an educational resource pack exploring disability issues through moving-image media. Many of the principles underlying the suggestions for working with moving image apply to print and still image. For more details on bfi resources visit: www.bfi.org.uk/education/resources

Producing non-fiction material

Strategies for teaching and learning

Not only do children need opportunities to engage with non-fiction texts, they need to experiment with presenting information in different forms to make it accessible to the intended audience. David Wray (2004) uses the acronym IDES: Immersion, Deconstruction, Exemplification, Scaffolding in relation to the explicit teaching of writing. However, as we have discussed, not all of the information we receive is in a traditional, written form but is increasingly conveyed using a range of technologies. We have argued that children should be taught to be critical consumers, but it is also important that we provide them with the opportunities to use different media forms and technologies to communicate. How useful is IDES as a framework for teaching children to produce written non-fiction texts, and texts that are communicated using speech and sound and still and moving image?

Immersion and deconstruction

Immersion in and deconstruction of texts is essential to help children to write effectively, but only if we provide examples that reflect the reality of what they may encounter. Through whole-class shared or guided group reading we can explore the vocabulary and syntax, as well as the presentation, to see how a written text works, but we also need to discuss the differences and what makes a text effective. By focusing on generic features that relate to the purpose of the text, we can identify how other features may be incidental and reflect the decision of the writer and their understanding of the audience.

Children might explore written instructional text in this way. For example, a collection of recipes will include essential features, such as ingredients and what to do with them. However, they will not all use imperative verbs or bullet points or even temporal connectives. They may incorporate features of travel writing or historical or cultural information. Similarly, written instructions for playing board games will vary according to the complexity of the game and the intended age range of the audience.

Many children play computer games. How are instructions presented on screen? At what stage do you read them?

Immersion and deconstruction are valuable tools for examining how meaning is conveyed whatever the medium, as long as we avoid using only simplistic texts produced to exemplify rigid criteria. Understanding how language works and the power it conveys can motivate children to want to communicate, but only if there is an audience to receive it. The importance of providing 'real' audiences for children's work is as important for non-fiction, if not more so, as it is often about communicating information, as it is for fiction and poetry.

Exemplification and scaffolding

Exemplification and scaffolding are ways of supporting writers in their attempts to communicate. Teachers need to demonstrate all stages of the process which, with non-fiction material, might include decisions on where to research the information, what to include and what to omit, and how to present it. Throughout they need to emphasise the need for accuracy and awareness of audience and purpose. Teacher demonstration is important and can be used effectively with all the different means of communication, not just with writing. Another scaffolding strategy is collaborative working where groups or pairs support each other, possibly with the help of the teacher or learning support assistant.

Writing frames are another mechanism specifically designed to support writing. Wray and Lewis (1997) and Wray (2004) provide examples of writing frames, and planning frames known as 'skeleton' frameworks were used extensively in the NLS teaching materials on non-fiction writing. However, the writing frame is premised on the notion that text types have a list of common features and may lead us to ignore the complexity of many texts. The phrases that some writing frames supply to introduce new paragraphs often lead to formulaic writing that lacks invention and creativity. The frame for persuasive writing seems designed to assess children's ability to use causal connectives (on the one hand, furthermore, therefore) as a required learning objective rather than the ability to convey passion and enthusiasm to influence an audience. A more creative approach might be to produce skeleton frameworks with the children, using real texts to gain an overview of the writer's intention and consider how effective it is. Can children map out what they want their own text to look like?

Verbal communication

Providing children with the opportunity to listen to information being conveyed in a range of contexts and to hear the teacher modelling different types of talk is also important in developing children's spoken and written communication skills and awareness of audience. Sue Palmer (2003) reflects on the use of 'speaking' frames to introduce new forms of language to young children and at KS1. The Listen>Imitate>Innovate>Invent sequence that she describes recognises that we often expect children to 'invent' without them having 'internalise(d) language structures through the experiences of the earlier stages' (p. 19). It is important that the environment that we provide in KS2 classrooms and beyond recognises the importance of oral communication in today's society as well as written text and visual images. Our aim as teachers is to extend children's language repertoire so that they are able to experiment, to be creative and move beyond the formulaic.

Activities to promote spoken communication skills in a range of genres

Children are given opportunities to:

- use notes or headings to describe a visit or excursion they have experienced
- recount in role an episode from the life of an historical character or famous person that they have researched
- hot-seat a real character they have researched
- bring a freeze frame to life by articulating the thought process of one of the characters
- give verbal instructions to a partner to enable them to carry out a task
- present an item of news as a radio or television presenter
- provide information about an artefact
- interview a person to find out information about a proposed project, for example the introduction of healthy school meals
- argue a point of view to an audience
- use information to engage in a formal debate linked to a class project.

Cross-curricular projects

The creative class teacher at KS2 will provide opportunities for children to practise the skills that they need to read and write information texts through extended projects that capture and sustain their interest. By working on a topic for half a term, children have the opportunity to move beyond a superficial understanding of subject content and pursue and disseminate their own interests within the topic. There is time to research thoroughly, explore ideas in school and for home-work and produce an end product of which they can be proud. If children know that they are putting on a performance, producing a book, video or CD-ROM for an identified audience other than the teacher, they have more of an incentive to ensure the content as well as the presentation reflects their capabilities. A collabo-rative approach to working over an extended period of time enables children to draw on their own and others' skills and to engage in dynamic, creative activity.

The following extended projects exemplify how three different teachers pro-vided opportunities for creative practice, building on children's own interests and moving beyond short-term objectives to embed creativity into their interpretation of the curriculum.

Case study: Using drama

Living history museum

As part of Black History Month, a class of 11-year-old children in a Baltimore school I visited were researching Black African Americans. They had visited the recently opened 'Blacks in Wax' museum. After an initial trawl for famous figures, they researched a famous figure that they were interested in. Their choices included historical and contemporary figures. There were leaders, politicians, scientists, doctors, people from the entertainment world such as sports figures, singers, musicians, writers, poets. The children researched their information using information books including biography, diary, letters. They searched the Web, used video material, photos, visited a museum.

The project culminated in a 'living museum' that they put on for the other classes. They dressed up as their character and used still image or a simple mime to express their character. Each character was brought to life by being touched on the shoulder. In some instances this was through voicing an interior monologue, reading aloud a letter or giving a speech. For others the character was given life through song, music, dance or athletic skills. The children had to choose what they felt was the most appropriate method of conveying the significance of their character's life.

The project was successful because it began with the children's own interests. They identified with the character that they had chosen. They had to use a range of sources to gain as much information as they could before selecting a significant scene to present to the audience who were other classes within the school and some visiting teachers from another country. This involved looking at their own intentions in conveying selected information. They wanted to share their enthusiasm and pride. They used their literacy skills to collect information from a range of sources but had to present the information they gathered in a different form, through the spoken word and through actions.

The children had been asked whether they wanted the performances photographed and videoed and if so for what purpose. They had decided that they wanted a record of the hard work that they had put in and the fun that they had had. They wanted to see themselves. The teacher intended to use the material to engage children in self-assessment. One child suggested that the video and photo album with accompanying documentation might become a resource for the class or school.

Britain since 1930

The National Curriculum for History includes an optional study of Britain since 1930, which can include the impact of the Second World War on the lives of men, women and children from different sections of society. As part of this history topic a Y5/6 class in a north London school had been immersed in researching the experience of men, women and children during the Second World War. They explored the individual stories of the people caught up in a common experience and how their lives had changed. They looked at novels such as *Goodnight Mr Tom*, picture-books, a television series, memoirs, transcripts of interviews, excerpts from documentaries and photos. They also visited the Imperial War Museum in London.

As part of their work in language and literacy the children had been looking at the differences between spoken and written language and how language changes over time. As part of the history project they focused on how individuals' stories reflected the changes of the time.

In the corner of the classroom a 'park bench' was set up and a box of simple props (hats, scarves, a walking stick, bags, etc.). When the children came in from break, or as part of the lesson activities that they were engaged in, they were encouraged to role-play people who had lived through this time in history. They would sit on the bench and become a character reminiscing on their past life. The composite life histories were told in the first person narrative. The role-play extended their experience of recounting their news. They explored dialect and the impact of region, class, gender and generation on their character to create their individual story. They would incorporate phrases such as 'avin a few beers wiv me mates' and the standard English that they heard from the 'wireless' when the war broke out. Their experience of 'soaps' and 'sit-coms' provided a rich source of material as they discussed the loss or reunion with loved ones. They drew on the informal register that we use when we tell stories of what has happened to us. The only problem with this activity was persuading the children to come out of role!

As an extension of their work on knowledge about language which had arisen fom their history topic, the class had been considering how information is presented and had studied the different types of information books on the topic. They decided to write information texts for the parallel class to supplement the resources. Using the structure of the picture-book *Dear Daddy* by Philippe Dupasquier, which tells a story from two different perspectives using pictures and texts, the class produced their own parallel stories written from the perspective of women, children and men whose lives were affected by the events of the war.

The children worked in pairs and then fours to produce their illustrated parallel stories using the informal and formal language structures that they had been rehearsing in their role-play. One child recounted how as an evacuee she was left to last because of 'one mingy spot'; another how as a private soldier he had danced around the room with the General when the end of the war was broadcast, commenting that 'the General was not *generally* pleased.'

After examining book jackets the children went on to review the books as newspaper journalists and add sound-bite comments to the back covers. Through this project the children learnt about how information might be presented, what 'true life accounts' might look like and how information is received, judged and sometimes mediated through a third party. The children began to question the notion of 'truth'.

A question book on caterpillars

As part of their project on 'living things', a Y4 class in an Enfield school made a class *Big Book on Caterpillars* as a resource that other classes might use and that would be kept in the school library.

As part of the science lesson the children had observed caterpillars with and without magnifiers. They photographed them with digital cameras and video cameras. They looked at a selection of information texts that had diagrams and photos, as well as posters and postcards. In groups they used a KWFL grid to devise and select questions that they still wanted answering or that they felt other children might be interested in.

Table 6.1   KWFL grid

What do I know?	What do I want to find out?	Where will I find the information?	What did I learn?
They eat leaves	What sort of leaves do they eat?	On the internet	Caterpillars from the peacock butterfly like nettles

Each group chose two questions to go in the book. Each question was typed up and pasted on the left-hand side of a double page spread, with the right-hand section left for the information which was presented in different ways such as photos, writing, labelled diagrams. As a class they decided on the order of the pages and produced a contents page and a glossary explaining unfamiliar vocabulary. Each group put forward their idea for the title of the book and a vote was taken. The questions were written in speech bubbles and stuck on to form the cover of the book. One-line reviews were written on the back cover.

The research and completed book took three weeks to complete but the children had learnt to collaborate, to ask meaningful questions, to locate information and present it effectively, to understand why a contents page and glossary are helpful for the reader and evaluate the finished project.

A way of developing this way of working might be for groups or pairs to produce different books or electronic texts to compile a series of information texts on minibeasts, using the skills that they had practised in the scaffolded class project.

Writing and ICT

The National Curriculum (1999) states that 'pupils should have opportunities to plan and review their writing, assembling and developing their ideas on paper and on screen.' In some classes children regularly use word-processing to draft and revise the content of their work as well as editing and proofreading to correct transcriptional errors. Many more use the computer for presentational purposes. If children are working on extended projects, revising and editing work, whether on paper or screen, will be embedded in the organisation of the project. The creative teacher will plan for the effective use of resources and this may vary in different situations. Important teaching and learning strategies, such as the effective use of response partners when reviewing content, are applicable whatever the medium.

Hooper and Reiber (1995) identified five stages in which ICT is used effectively in teaching and learning. The last two stages have particular relevance for a creative approach to teaching and learning. These are *reorientation* – where learning and teaching are transformed by the use of ICT and *evolution* – where teachers and children start to become creative with the medium itself, rather than using it as an aid to creativity.

Desktop publishing packages are now common enabling children to produce newspapers and magazines for a wider more public audience than their own class. Pictures can be interspersed with text, reinforcing the message that still image may be as effective as written text in conveying information. Increasingly children are being encouraged to replicate new genres such as weblogs and to experiment with different media forms such as digital photo stories and short videos. However, a critical perspective on purpose and audience must underpin the use of technology for it to enhance children's effective communication skills.

E-mail and text messaging

As well as using ICT to support the more traditional print- and image-based literacy, teachers must acknowledge the changes in communication that e-mail and mobile phones have brought to our daily lives. Although e-mail and text messages are written they have some similarities with phone calls in that they are ways of communicating quickly with someone at a distance. However, there are significant differences. In a phone call facial expression and gesture may be absent but tone of voice and interjections by the recipient may influence the message and how it is received. Senders of e-mails and text messages have had to devise ways of overcoming these disadvantages. Phonetic spelling, exaggerated punctuation or none at all, abbreviations and emoticons (for example, smileys) enable the sender to write more quickly and establish tone. These devices have arisen out of the writer's need to communicate effectively with their audience.

Inevitably there are people who raise concerns about how new technology will affect children's ability to spell and punctuate in a conventional manner, despite the fact that many children in today's society write in different scripts and use different grammatical constructions. Having access to other ways of communicating is broadening one's repertoire, not supplanting other ways of communicating. Rather than seeing these new digital forms of communication as a threat, creative teachers can harness the experience that children bring to school and provide real purpose and audience for communication. In some instances the children may have more experience and expertise in using these literacies than their teacher and learn from each other rather than being explicitly taught. Discussion and understanding of digital literacies can enhance children's understanding of more traditional forms of literacy and enable them to make informed choices about the form and degree of formality their writing might take.

Developing your creative practice

In order to extend your creative practice in teaching about non-fiction texts at KS2, reflect on your current practice and use of resources and on what you have observed and experienced in school. The following are suggestions to help you develop a creative approach in the classroom:

- Explore and critically evaluate a range of paper-based and interactive ICT texts.
- Select a range of resources, including multimodal texts, to support the teaching of a cross-curricular topic of your choice.

- Become familiar with news websites and consider how they might be used in the classroom.
- Plan a range of activities to develop children's information retrieval skills drawing on some of the ideas in this chapter and from further reading and research.

Teaching non-fiction creatively at key stage 2: A summary

To conclude this chapter, we have summarised the key ideas that underpin a creative approach to teaching and extending children's understanding of non-fiction:

- The texts that we offer children should reflect the texts that they will encounter in their daily lives and should include multimodal texts.
- It is important to develop children's critical reading skills so that they are aware of bias and manipulation.
- Critical literacy skills can be developed through curricular areas other than English.
- New technologies extend children's repertoire rather than diminish it.

References

Bazalgette, C. (ed.) (1989) *Primary Media Education*. London: bfi.

DfEE (2000) *English in the National Curriculum*. London: HMSO.

DfEE (1998) *The National Literacy Strategy Framework for Teaching*. London: HMSO.

DfES (2003a) *Excellence and Enjoyment: A Strategy for Primary Schools*. London: HMSO.

DfES (2003b) *Look Again: A Teaching Guide to Using Film and Television with Three- to Eleven-Year-Olds*. London: bfi Education.

Hooper, S. and Reiber, L.P. (1995) 'Teaching with technology' in Orstein, A. C. (ed.) *Teaching: Theory into Practice*. Needham Heights, MA: Allyn and Bacon.

Palmer, S. (2003) *How To Teach Writing Across the Curriculum at Key Stage 1*. London: David Fulton Publishers.

Wilson, A. (1999) *Language Knowledge for Primary Teachers: A Guide to Textual, Grammatical and Lexical Study*. London: David Fulton Publishers.

Wray, D. (2004) *Teaching Literacy Using Texts to Enhance Learning*. London: David Fulton Publishers.

Wray, D. and Lewis, M. (1997) *Extending Literacy*. London: Routledge.

The Primary English Magazine (April 2006).

Useful websites

www.bfi.org.uk/education
is an invaluable site for teachers wishing to work creatively with moving image. It provides information on teaching-guides and resources, many of which are free. Material for the key stages is clearly signposted.

www.becta.org.uk
provides guidance on choosing ICT resources, as well as practical help with creating your own ICT resources.

www.teachingideas.co.uk/welcome
is a very accessible site. There are practical suggestions for teaching literacy, including higher order reading skills. Many of the activities are suggested by visitors to the site.

www.bbc.co.uk/education
is an excellent site with plenty of resources to support creative literacy teaching through topic-based work across the curriculum.

www.tes.co.uk/resources
enables teachers to be part of a network, evaluating and sharing resources. You have to register with the TES resource bank but the material is free.

www.standards.dfes.gov.uk/rosereview/finalreport/

www.longman.co.uk/digitexts/

Children's literature and other resources

Philippe Dupasquier's *Dear Daddy* (1986), Picture Puffin.

PART 3

Creativity and poetry: An overview

Central to poetry is play.

(Michael Rosen)

Poetry today has a higher public profile than it has enjoyed for some time. There is a Poetry Society, a National Poetry Day; there are poems on public transport, literary prizes, poetry events globally, nationally and locally. A poem for the day is published in some newspapers and on certain radio stations. Book titles include *The Nation's Favourite Poems* and *A Poem a Day* and there are CDs of poetry being read by poets and performers. There are websites devoted to poets, poetry resources, poetry reviews and sites where adults and children can publish their own poems. And yet for many people poetry is still seen as elitist and not relevant to their daily lives.

This chapter asks and tries to answer some important questions that relate to why we have decided to devote a third of this book to teaching poetry creatively in the early years and primary classroom.

Those questions are:

- What is poetry?
- What is poetry for?
- Why teach poetry?
- How do we teach poetry creatively?

What is poetry?

If you type 'definitions of poetry' into a search engine you will be overwhelmed by the results. Many of the definitions I browsed defined poetry by saying what it was not:

> *Poetry cannot be paraphrased. It loses its essence. Every word counts.*
>
> *Poems are not created by recipe or by pouring content into a currently acceptable mould.*

Others described what they considered to be the essential characteristics of poetry in comparison with prose:

> Poetry exploits the potential of words.
>
> Poetry is language pared down to its essentials.
>
> (Ezra Pound)
>
> Poetry is language at its most distilled and most powerful.
>
> (Rita Dove)

Some definitions stressed the power of the spoken word, the sound and rhythm of language:

> Speech framed . . . to be heard for its own sake and interest even over and above its interest of meaning.
>
> (Gerald Manley Hopkins)
>
> Genuine poetry can communicate before it is understood.
>
> (T. S. Eliot)

Some definitions referred specifically to oral poetry and stressed the primacy of the spoken word over the literary tradition, reminding us that some of the most famous literary works began as oral works:

> Once upon a time, all poetry was oral poetry. Before writing was invented – about 5000 years ago – the only way to express poetic language was through the human voice.
>
> (Asher and Martin Hoyles 2002: 10)

Today many performance poets value the vernacular, the speech of the people, as a counterbalance to what might be considered literary elitism:

> Performance poetry not only needs to be heard, it usually also has to be seen to be properly understood. It relies on rhythm, intonation, gesture, and sometimes music and song to gain its effect.
>
> (Asher and Martin Hoyles 2002: 5)

Although many of the statements were referring to poetry aimed at adults, for the most part they were equally applicable to the poems that we share with children. For example, children delight in the sound of words long before they attach meaning to them. They benefit from seeing and hearing poems performed, even when they are able to read them. When we encourage children to respond to poems we should not merely interrogate them on the meaning and when we encourage them to produce their own poems, we must inspire them to move beyond the formulaic and play with and enjoy language in all its variety.

Performance poet, Adisa, has written a poem entitled *What is Poetry?* that stresses the centrality of poetry to life. The first verse, printed below, summarises much of what we hope children will come to understand.

> Poetry is everywhere
>
> Poetry is music to your ear
>
> Poetry is a graceful dancer with elegance and flair
>
> Poetry has many shapes and forms, but poetry is not square
>
> Poetry is written on paper, but poetry doesn't live there
>
> For poetry is in your eyes, in your smile and even in your tears
>
> Poetry is your happiness, your anger and also your fear.

Genre: Different types of poetry

Throughout the chapters on poetry you will encounter a range of forms from nursery rhymes to sonnets. In fact the range is so wide that it is impossible for anyone, child or adult, to dislike all poetry, just as it would be to dislike all stories. We believe that children come with a love of the sounds and rhythms of language and that it is our responsibility to encourage and develop that fascination with words. As teachers we need to extend children's repertoire and potential for enjoying imaginative use of language. It is only by increasing our own experience and understanding that we can introduce them to a wide range of texts that will enable them to engage creatively and imaginatively, both as audiences for and producers of poetry.

What is poetry for?

This question is often raised, particularly by those who have a utilitarian approach to life and education. What use is poetry? What's its value? Poet, Michael Rosen, has attempted to answer the question. As he sees it, 'the value of poetry is that it should matter,' both to the writer and to the reader (http:news.bbc.couk/cbbcnews). He reminds us that 'language is a resource available to every single one of us to use and play with.' It is this centrality of 'play' to poetry that perhaps goes some way to answering our question as 'Play is the open-ended process of trial and error, without worry of failure or derision, that enables us all to grow and learn.' Poetry enables us to grow and learn and make sense of the world.

Why teach poetry?

Part of the answer to this question is embedded in the answer to the previous question. However, much of the language teaching that occurs in the English curriculum and through the other curriculum areas is concerned with functional literacy. It is often rule-bound, uses a standard form of grammar, punctuation and spelling. When we introduce poetry into the classroom we are introducing a form of language, spoken or written, that is inherently creative and therefore life-enhancing. There is or should be a continuum from babies babbling and playing with sounds through to children and adults playing with and experimenting with the limitless range of language resources at their disposal. Poetry is also part of our cultural heritage; it spans the spectrum of oral and literary traditions and communicates the lived experience of people across ages and cultures.

How do we teach poetry creatively?

The way we teach poetry must reflect our understanding and appreciation of its importance. Just as storytelling is a part of the human condition, so too is poetry. Our role as teachers is central. As black performance poet, Benjamin Zephaniah, states:

> *We want more teachers who are passionate about poetry, not just teachers who do poetry as an add on to English.*
>
> (Zephaniah 1992: 76)

If that passion fuels creative teaching, children's experience of poetry will be an enjoyable one.

There are lots of ideas of how to raise the profile of poetry in your classroom and how to teach it creatively in the age-phase chapters of this book. In this introductory overview we include some generic suggestions that are premised on encouraging and developing a whole-school commitment to ensuring poetry is at the heart of its curriculum.

A whole school approach

There needs to be a shared commitment to the value of adults and children engaging with poetry in all its wide manifestations. Using poetry creatively could be identified for staff development. This would help to establish a network of support among staff and support those who may feel less confident with this aspect of language and literacy. A whole school approach will enable better provision and sharing of resources, a recognition of the importance of sharing poems from a range of cultures, showing and publishing children's work both spoken and written, beyond the confines of the classroom.

- Reading a poem to the children in assembly will raise the status of poetry and develop a repertoire of poems that children and teachers can share and enjoy.
- Giving children the opportunity to choose a favourite poem to read to the school or in a year-group assembly values their choice and allows them to share what they enjoy with the school community.
- Providing a focus such as poet of the week/month in the entrance hall, the corridor or the library and making books, tapes and videos available for children to borrow helps to involve parents, carers and visitors from the wider community in the language experiences of the children. The choice of poets over the year should reflect the range of cultural/language backgrounds of the children.
- Use of resources can be maximised by using mobile poetry trolleys as an extra general resource that can be wheeled into the classroom to supplement classroom resources.
- Displays of poetry posters around the school including poems that are not specifically for children (for example, Poems on the Underground) reflect the importance of poetry for the wider community, rather than poetry being something 'you do in school' and leave behind when you leave.
- Poetry boards around the school where children's own poems are displayed provide a wider audience for their work.
- Collections of children's poetry writing can be kept in the school library for other children in the school to enjoy.
- Artwork around the school can be labelled with alliterative sentences, rhyming couplets or haiku making explicit links between these creative forms.

- A 'live poetry swap', where children read, perform and share their favourite poems or own writing with another class, can be timetabled across the school, promoting the value of spoken language and recognising its diversity.

Visiting poets

Many schools invite poets to come and perform their poems and do workshops with the children. A whole school approach ensures that visits are planned and budgeted for. Jamaican poet and teacher, Valerie Bloom, visits many schools in Britain and Ireland and feels that children's attitudes to poetry have changed for the better:

> there's so much more emphasis on enjoyment . . . There's much more interaction between the makers of poetry and the users of poetry these days. Also, there's a lot more travelling now and sharing of cultures. You get more performance poetry now, which we didn't have before. That gives children scope for taking part in the poetry, but also for making poetry – they get so much pleasure from making poems with the poets. When I first started going into schools and said we're going to write some poetry together, you'd hear a big groan go up! Nowadays, when I say we're going to write some poetry, the children actually go 'Yesss!'
>
> (Hoyles 2002: 84)

Performance poet, Cuban Redd, reports similar reactions:

> It's great to see (the children) come alive, writing about what they're feeling inside, catching the rhythm, realising that you can dance to poetry, that it is alive, that it can move you.
>
> (Hoyles 2002: 136)

As teachers we have found that we gain inspiration listening to and seeing poets perform their work and sitting in on workshops with children and student teachers. Some of the passion rubs off and encourages us to raise the profile of poetry in our classrooms and in our teaching.

Organising a poetry week

A 'poetry week' can raise the status of poetry within the school and community. It should celebrate poetry in a variety of cultures, languages and forms. Local libraries and bookshops are often helpful in suggesting local poets, writers and performers, who will visit to perform or read from their work, talk about their writing and run workshops. A poetry week can involve all the children from nursery to Y6 as well as including babies and older members from the community. However, one headteacher that I spoke to recently felt that her school had come so far in recognising the importance of story and poetry as part of a creative curriculum that poetry had a high profile throughout the year. It was embedded in other curriculum areas so that 'every week was a poetry week.' Nevertheless, for many schools a poetry week can be a focus for the school and the local community and raise the profile of creative, imaginative playing with language that is an essential aspect of a creative approach to learning and teaching.

Reading and responding to poetry

Reading and responding to poetry at whatever age is about engaging with the sounds and rhythms of language and often seeing and experiencing things in a way that you had not done before. It is about personal response, recognising the multiplicity of meanings that might reside in a single word or phrase or in the text as a whole, not about correct interpretation. It is not about spotting 'metaphors' or naming of parts. The opportunity to experience and enjoy the world of the poem is essential. How that world or atmosphere has been conjured up may then be of interest, but it is the enjoyment that must come first if we are to continue to read poetry in our adult lives. Throughout the age-phase chapters we provide practical suggestions for encouraging a creative response to poetry using other creative art forms. Throughout we emphasise that poetry should be heard as well as read, that it benefits from more than one reading or telling and that it has the power to fire the imagination and touch the emotions.

Writing and constructing poems

To produce or write a poem is a creative act and all children should be given the opportunity to experiment with ways of expressing themselves that are not constrained by rules of syntax and punctuation. Very young children may play with sounds, invent words and rhymes for the sheer enjoyment of hearing the sounds and may share them with other children or adults in their lives. At KS1 and 2 children begin to craft their writing, searching for the words that will capture the ideas within their heads. They may need support and encouragement to persevere in searching for precise words or phrases or figurative language to express complex ideas, feelings or experiences. Most importantly they need to want to communicate and know that the audience will be responsive to their attempts.

Inclusive practices

Rhymes, songs and poems can be incorporated into all curricular areas, not just literacy, and be shared and enjoyed in spare moments throughout the day, for example, when waiting to go to the dining hall for lunch. Because poetry comes in many forms and can be enjoyed and understood at different levels, because response does not necessarily entail writing but encompasses speech and drama, music, art and dance, all children are able to engage in creative activities. It is essential that all children are supported within the classroom so that they share the poems and are part of a class community.

In an inclusive classroom, children feel free to take risks. They know that they will be supported and that their work will be valued. Playing and experimenting with language is an important part of the creative process and is particularly applicable to poetry. Children can work on their writing and seek advice from others. They may work collaboratively in groups to gain inspiration; they may contribute a line to a class poem; they may write a poem as their response in another curriculum area. By sharing, discussing and explaining the language choices they make, all children's spoken language is extended.

Gender

Although there are concerns that boys are underperforming when writing fiction (Ofsted 2003), there is research to suggest that boys respond well to writing poetry, perhaps because of the shorter form and the immediacy of ideas (Maynard 2002). The use of shared writing for younger children is part of the success in this genre. It is often the secretarial aspects of writing that deter children. Throughout this book we emphasise the importance of collaborative writing and the oral rehearsal of ideas as a prelude to writing. We believe such practice supports all learners in their journey to find their own voice.

Bilingualism

The rhythms of language are appreciated before language can be understood and poetry is therefore particularly suitable for sharing with children who may be at different stages of learning English. For younger children, versions of lullabies, counting rhymes, action rhymes in their own language will provide an inclusive ethos and broaden the language experience of all children. Older children might enjoy tapes and hearing and seeing performance poets using music and dance to convey meaning.

SEN pedagogy

The practice described in the poetry chapters in this section subscribes to the philosophy that 'good teaching is good teaching for all'. We have focused on using a range of strategies that ensure children have the opportunity to access and respond to poetry in a variety of ways. Collaborative group work using a variety of groupings ensures that children's strengths in other areas are used and helps build confidence and self-esteem.

References

Hoyles, A. and Hoyles, M. (2002) *Moving Voices: Black Performance Poetry*. London: Hansib Publications.

Maynard, T. (2002) *Boys and Literacy: Exploring the Issues*. London: Routledge/Falmer.

Ofsted (2003) *Yes He Can: Schools Where Boys Write Well*. HMI 505.

Zephaniah, B. (1992) 'I have a scheme', in Hoyles, A. and Hoyles, M. (2002) *Moving Voices: Black Performance Poetry*. London: Hansib Publications.

Useful websites

http:news.bbc.co.uk/cbbcnews
This BBC site links to News Round and one of the features includes Michael Rosen giving advice on how to write poetry. There is also A Guide to Poetry on this page addressing many of the issues raised in the poetry chapters of this book.

CHAPTER 7

Teaching poetry creatively in the Early Years

Humpty Dumpty sat on a dog
Humpty Dumpty ate a log
All the king's cats and all the king's mice
Played with Humpty cos he was nice

(Dictated by Ola, aged 4)

Introduction

Poetry explores a fascination with words and sounds, rhythms and imagery. It is a creative and vibrant genre where children and adults are encouraged to innovate with language. For the young child, poetry should allow silliness, exploration and enjoyment. Poetry in the Early Years revolves predominantly around rhymes, rhythms and songs where music and text unite to create imaginative worlds and where, importantly, everything need not make sense.

In order to teach poetry creatively, the Early Years practitioner needs to build upon young children's instinctive relationship with oral language play and exploration of sounds and meanings. The creative teacher will understand that word play and the pleasure in hearing, reading and making sounds forms the basis of an early approach to reading and responding to poetry in its many forms.

Building on home literacy

In the earliest months of a baby's life, they begin to explore the possibility of using their voice for effect. They soon learn to play with the feeling different sounds make – the tickle on their lips as they blow 'raspberries' or the joyous repetitions of combining sounds babababababababa. The enjoyment of creating sounds and the effect these sounds have on others around them propel these early sounds to form the basis of spoken language and talking. Indeed the importance of this early oral exertion is well documented (Crystal 1998).

Babies and their carers often explore these new sounds and rhythms and words together throughout a child's infancy and children's enjoyment continues well into their more formal schooling. Playing with sounds, rhymes and songs forges our relationship between young babies and their carers through reciprocal mimicking, repeating and extending the sounds that will ultimately help the children to develop effective verbal communication. Indeed, many theorists believe that these early interactions have the power to teach babies and infants about their social and creative potential: 'The repertoire of songs developed between child and care giver allows the child to play at experiencing different emotions, almost at will. The young child's demands for repeat performances of favourite songs indicate the way in which they enjoy feeling over and over again the fear, happiness or anticipation that songs can engender' (Pound and Harrison 2003).

Poetry is often the mainstay of the warm and intimate relationship between babies and young children and their carers. Babies are reassured and aided to sleep by the melodic tones of the lullaby; the toddler is transported to squealing heaven through vigorous knee bouncing and tickling rhymes. Children are urged to dress by poetry: 'This is the way we put on our socks . . .' They travel to nursery with poetry: 'The wheels on the bus . . .' They eat their tea: 'Yummy, yummy in my tummy . . .' and have their bath: 'Five little ducks went swimming one day, over the hills and far away . . .' These poems are passed from generation to generation across cultures, class and languages. Poetry for children in these early forms has been in existence as long as language itself has been recorded and probably long before. These rhymes and poems exist in all cultures and across all languages. They are part of what makes us human.

Poetry and the Early Years curriculum frameworks

The *Curriculum Guidance for the Foundation Stage* reinforces the importance of poetry as a significant genre for young children to play with. By the end of the foundation stage, children should 'listen with enjoyment, and respond to stories, songs and other music, rhymes and poems and make up their own stories, songs, rhymes and poems' (DfEE 2000: 50). They should 'extend their vocabulary, exploring the meanings and sounds of new words' (DfEE 2000: 51) and 'explore and experiment with sounds, words and texts' (DfEE 2000: 62).

The *NLS Framework* for YR makes some explicit reference to poetry particularly in suggesting the range of texts to be used during the year including 'a wide variety of traditional, nursery and modern rhymes, chants, action verses, poetry . . . with predictable structures and patterned language'. The word level work is dominated with reference to rhyme and rime as part of a dedicated phonics programme and emphasises the importance of learning the alphabet through songs and rhymes. The guidance advocates that children should be taught to 're-read and recite stories and rhymes with predictable and repeated patterns and experiment with similar rhyming patterns' and 'to use experience of . . . poems . . . as a basis for independent writing, e.g. re-telling substitution, extension, and through shared composition with adults' (DfEE 1998: 18–19).

The *NLS Framework* for YR emphasises the use of poetry as a learning tool to reach another end (e.g. to learn the alphabet; to support phonemic awareness; to use as a model for children's own writing). While these are important areas of the Early Years curriculum, it is also important to see poetry as something enjoyable and creative in its own right.

Why teach poetry in the Early Years?

We discussed in the introduction to the poetry section of the book, how important poetry is to all ages before, during and long after school age. In addition to improving children's ability to read and write (see convincing research by Goswami and Bryant 1990), exploring rhymes, rhythms and a wide range of poetic forms has enormous benefits in developing a real community of tellers, readers, writers and composers. Poetry enables adults and children to have the opportunity to:

- come together to share familiar songs, rhymes and rich narratives demonstrating clear links between school and home
- share culturally significant texts from different linguistic and cultural and generational backgrounds and to consider similarities and differences between each other
- enjoy listening to and articulating the sound of our languages
- have opportunities to ponder on evocative descriptions and ideas that just can't be shared in any other way
- be creative – there is never a right or wrong answer when responding or when composing your own poems. Taking risks and having a go must be valued and respected.

Poetic forms for the Early Years

There is of course no exhaustive list of 'suitable' poems to be shared and enjoyed by children in the Early Years. What matters is that any new poem, rhyme, song or ditty is introduced to the class with enthusiasm and integrity. Poetry in the Early Years (or indeed in any year) need not reside only with the individual reading and deciphering of cerebral tomes by dead authors. Poetry in the Early Years creative classroom should have no boundaries of 'greatness'. A rich text with memorable language read or recited by enthusiastic children or adults is an excellent starting point. Immersing children into the language and structures of a wide variety of poetic forms by firstly reading to them and reciting with them will support them and you to find enjoyment in exploring the possibilities of poetic language.

Making poetry part of your everyday classroom routines will enable the children to be confident in their approach to using and applying poetry.

Some particular poetic forms are found commonly in the home and early years class. It is worth considering the richness of these forms without wanting to narrow the field. I have known teachers read lengthy narrative poems deemed for much older children to three- and four-year-olds with much enthusiasm and excitement. I have conversely seen children not interested when familiar nursery rhymes are chanted without enthusiasm or interest.

Lullabies

These are perhaps the first poems parents and carers share with their children. These soothing songs and rhythmic poems are often passed from parent to child over several generations and are rarely written down identically as they reside firmly within the oral tradition where each of us has control to alter, amend and adapt the words and phrases within the privacy of our own homes with our near-est and dearest. Lullabies are not something relegated to the distant past, however. Websites designed for new parents offer chat rooms for people to share lullabies from their own childhoods and ask for help remembering the words of a song or rhyme they once heard as children and now want to pass on to their own children, demonstrating the importance of these poems in forging links between genera-tions. My own twin baby girls learned to sleep to my strained version of *Hush, Little Baby* (anon) with additional verses developed when needed:

Hush, little baby, don't say a word.
Mama's (other versions use Papa's) gonna buy you a mockingbird

And if that mockingbird won't sing,
Mama's gonna buy you a diamond ring

And if that diamond ring turns to brass,
Mama's gonna buy you a looking glass

And if that looking glass gets broke,
Mama's gonna buy you a Billy goat

And if that Billy goat won't pull,
Mama's gonna buy you a cart and bull

And if that cart and bull turns over,
Mama's gonna buy you a dog named Rover

And if that dog named Rover don't bark,
Mama's gonna buy you a horse and cart

And if that horse and cart fall down,
You'll still be the sweetest little baby in town.

And one version (of many) with my additions developed in desperation for those occasions when sleep still eluded them:

Hush, little baby, don't say a peep.
Mama's gonna buy you a fluffy sheep

And if that fluffy sheep won't baa,
Mama's gonna buy you a pink sporty car

And if that pink sporty car goes slow,
Mama's gonna buy you a boat to row

And if that boat to row comes loose,
Mama's gonna buy you a golden goose

And if that golden goose won't lay,
Mama's gonna buy you a silver tray

And if that silver tray drops down,
You'll still be the sweetest little babies in town.

Asking children to share lullabies and sleeping songs from when they were babies is often a wonderful way to extend genuine links between home and school literacies. Build a class anthology with contributions from parents and carers and include songs and rhymes in all community languages. Tape the children or their families singing or saying these lullabies and display with the book in the reading area. Sending tapes and books home to share (photocopy and duplicate the anthology so several children can read the book together) will help to endorse the importance of these songs at home and at school. Include reference to some of the wonderful websites available with tunes and search engines to find those elusive lyrics to half-remembered poems and songs.

Nursery rhymes

Nursery rhymes are often described as children's first poems. The name 'nursery' refers to these rhymes as being designed and written primarily for children and yet if you consider the research of cultural theorists such as Iona and Peter Opie, many rhymes were originally told as cautionary or gossipy tales for adults with implicit reference to the society and politics of the time. Take for example the popular rhyme:

Seesaw, Margery Daw
Johnny shall have a new master
He shall earn but a penny a day
Because he can't work any faster.

Various histories of this rhyme can be found, including:

> The words of 'Seesaw Marjorie Daw' reflect children playing on a see-saw and singing this rhyme to accompany their game. There was no such person that we can identify who had the name Marjorie Daw and we therefore make the assumption that this was purely used to rhyme with the words 'seesaw', i.e. 'Seesaw Marjory Daw'. The last three lines of 'Seesaw Margery Daw' appear to reflect the use of child labour in work houses where those with nowhere else to live would be forced to work for a pittance (a penny a day) on piece work (because he can't work any faster). The words of 'Seesaw Margery Daw' might be used by a spiteful child to taunt another implying his family were destined for the workhouse.
>
> (www.rhymes.org.uk/seesaw_marjory_daw.htm)

and:

> It is possible that this rhyme . . . [was] originally sung by sawyers to keep the rhythm of the two-handled saw.
>
> (Opie and Opie 1951: 297)

Indeed in *The Oxford Dictionary of Nursery Rhymes,* Iona and Peter Opie share an additional and less well known example of this rhyme from the nineteenth century:

> See-saw, Margery Daw,
> Sold her bed and lay upon straw;
> Was not she a dirty slut
> To sell her bed and lie in the dirt.
>
> (anon cited in Opie and Opie 1951)

A fascinating glimpse of the history of these rhymes begins to illustrate the importance of these first poems as documents of social history as well as vital links between adults and children across generations.

Parents and carers now, as ever, routinely share nursery rhymes with young children in all areas of their lives: to calm them (*Rock-a-bye baby . . .*), warn them (*Humpty Dumpty . . .*), amuse (*Hey Diddle Diddle . . .*) and teach them (*10 Green Bottles . . .*).

As babies grow into infanthood and their relationships with adults become more physical and interactive, so nursery rhymes have developed to ensure there is a poem or song for every game:

Knee bouncers

This is the way the baby rides,
Baby rides, baby rides
This is the way the baby rides,
So early in the morning.

This is the way the lady rides . . .
This is the way the jockey rides . . .

Tickling rhymes

Round and round the garden
Like a teddy bear
One step, two step,
And tickly under there.

Sung while trailing a path around the baby's palm, up and under their arm.

This little piggy went to market
This little piggy stayed at home
This little piggy had roast beef
This little piggy had none
And this little piggy went
wee wee wee wee all the way home.

Spoken while wiggling little toes and then tickling the whole foot.

Action rhymes

Wind the bobbin up,
Wind the bobbin up,
Pull, pull, clap, clap, clap

Wind it back again,
Wind it back again,
Pull, pull clap, clap, clap

Point to the ceiling,
Point to the floor
Point to the window
Point to the door

Put your hands together
One, two, three,
Lay them gently upon your knee.

And then as infants grow and their parents and carers are keen for children to learn to read and write and count, so rhymes and songs have been developed to support the next stages:

Alphabet rhymes

A was an apple pie
B bit it
C cut it
D dealt it
E ate it
F fought for it
G got it
H had it
I inspected it
J jumped for it
K kept it
L longed for it
M mourned for it
N nodded at it
O opened it
P peeped in it
Q quartered it
R ran for it
S stole it
T took it
U upset it
V viewed it
W wanted it
X, Y, Z, and ampersand
All wished for a piece in hand.

Counting rhymes

One, two, three four five
Once I caught a fish alive
Six, seven, eight, nine, ten
Then I let it go again.

Nonsense rhymes and poems

The tradition of nonsense rhymes begins with the early play between parent and child ('Heidi beidi pudding and piedi') and continues throughout the poetry traditions to adulthood (football chants, advertising jingles, limericks). Poems written specifically for young children often celebrate the zaniness of our world through nonsense rhymes: Dr Seuss's *Green Eggs and Ham*, Edward Lear's *The Owl and the Pussy-cat*, Michael Rosen's limericks in *Book of Nonsense* and Quentin Blake's *All Join In* offer rich pickings to share and enjoy with young children.

Indeed many parents and carers will make up songs and rhymes and poems to amuse and engage babies and small children. Our tiny girls were too small for the smallest baby gro's and resembled young chickens with their legs tucked up inside when they were born so were temporarily rechristened as we sang:

> Captain Bantam and the Space chicken
> Flying through the air
> People laugh at our little legs
> But we really don't care
>
> Captain Bantam and the Space chicken
> Flying through New Cross
> We're going to move to the countryside
> So we can get a horss (!)

These songs amused us more than the babies in those twilight hours and yet it is this mutually satisfying and bonding experience that makes these early poems so vital.

Narrative poetry

This is perhaps the most familiar form in the Early Years classroom as many children's stories are told in rhyme and/or in poetic language – the brevity of the text often demanding the eloquence and vivid imagery possible with poetry. There are many wonderful stories told in predictive rhyme including *This is the Bear and the Scary Night* by Sara Hayes, *Where's My Teddy?* by Jez Alborough, and Janet and Allan Ahlberg's *Each Peach, Pear, Plum*. Reading and rereading these rhyming stories to children will support their ability to tune into the rhythms and sounds of poetry as well as offering them supportive, predictive texts to share.

Many other children's books offer a story in wonderfully vivid language with a frequent refrain that the children can join in with. *Where the Wild Things Are* by Maurice Sendak is a perfect example: . . . 'The night Max wore his wolf suit and made mischief of one kind . . . and another' with the memorable refrain 'they roared their terrible roars and gnashed their terrible teeth and rolled their terrible eyes . . .'.

Other stories use the descriptive language of alliteration, similes or metaphors to give simple and repetitive stories a depth and vigour to ensure the reader is taken on a vivid journey in only a few choice words. *Handa's Surprise* by Eileen

Browne demonstrates this in the description of her fruit: 'creamy, green avocado' and 'tangy purple passion fruit'.

Raps

Rap poems and rhymes engage and encourage participation with fast-paced tempo and repetitive lyrics with a distinct and strong rhythm. Some examples are suitable for classroom use including some poems by Benjamin Zephaniah and James Berry. The form is popularly used to retell familiar stories and can be used to encourage a participatory role for the children in singing and dancing and acting out the poem:

The Three Bears Rap (traditional) is a good example:

Once upon a time in a nursery rhyme there were three bears.
(click, click, click)
A Papa bear, a Mama bear and a wee bear.
(click, click, click)
One day, they went out walking and a-talking in the woods.
(click, click, click)
Along came a girl with long, curly hair.
(click, click, click)
'Someone's been sitting in my chair,' said the Papa bear.
'Someone's been sitting in my chair,' said the Mama bear.
'Hey, Mama Three Bear,' said the little wee bear,
'Someone has broken my chair.'
YEAH!!

'Someone's been tasting my porridge,' said the Papa bear.
'Someone's been tasting my porridge,' said the Mama bear.
'Hey, Mama Three Bear,' said the little wee bear,
'Someone has eaten my porridge.'
YEAH !!

'Someone's been sitting on my bed,' said the Papa bear.
'Someone's been sitting on my bed,' said the Mama bear.
'Hey, Mama Three Bear,' said the little wee bear,
'Someone is here in my bed.'
YEAH!!

Goldilocks woke up and broke up the party.
(click, click, click)
'Bye, bye, bye, bye, bye, bye, bye,' said the Papa bear.
(wave hand)
'Bye, bye, bye, bye, bye, bye, bye,' said the Mama bear.
(wave other hand)
'Hey, Mama Three Bear,' said the little wee bear,
'Bye, bye, bye, bye, bye, bye, bye.'
(wave both hands)
YEAH!!

Playground rhymes

In the Early Years an adult or older child in the setting often initiates these rhymes and songs. They usually revolve around group action songs and are frequently passed on through siblings – each group with their own slightly amended version. Popular traditional examples include:

The Farmer's In His Den (anon)

In And Out The Dusky Bluebells (anon)

The Okey-Cokey (anon)

A sailor went to sea, sea, sea to see what he could see, see, see . . . (anon)

More recent additions that I collected when teaching in Peckham, south London at the end of the 1990s, include:

My mummy is a baker
Yummy yummy fat tummy
My daddy is a dustman
Pooey ooey, pooey ooey
My sister is a show off
Curly wurly, curly wurly
My brother is a cowboy
Bang bang you're dead
Fifty bullets in your head
Singing aye aye yippy yippy aye
Singing aye aye yippy yippy aye
Singing aye aye yippy
Aye aye yippy
Aye aye yippy yippy aye.

And

Down, down baby
Down, down the roller coaster
Sweet, sweet baby
I will never let you go
Shimmy, shimmy wah
Shimmy, shimmy wah, wah, wah
Doctor, doctor please come quick
I need a doctor 'cos my baby's sick
She's got the rhythm in her feet: stamp stamp
She's got the rhythm in her hands: clap clap

She's got the rhythm in her head: ding dong
She's got the rhythm in her hot dog
Put 'em all together and what've you got?
Ding dong clap clap stamp stamp hot dog.

These poems were enthusiastically sung and danced in the playground. Older girls passing them down to younger brothers and sisters who would mis-hear the words and alter to make new words and meanings. The children would need to learn sophisticated actions, dances and etiquette which accompany many of these rhymes and songs. They need to be valued for their imaginative and vibrant use of language as well as their ability to unite a group.

Reading and reciting poetry

Poetry is usually written or composed to be heard. The words on the page come to life when spoken as the rhythms and sounds of the language are felt and heard by the reader and the listeners.

Reading and reciting poems to children

The role of the adult in reading or reciting rhymes and poems to individuals or groups in the Early Years setting cannot be underestimated. Reading or reciting your favourite poems is a wonderful place to start to ensure a creative and vibrant 'poetry friendly' classroom. It is helpful to practise reading or reciting poems before you share them in class to ensure that they are as engaging as you remember them. Reading or telling poems to the children will enable you to:

- engage the children with infectious excitement and enjoyment in the words and sounds of the language
- introduce new or unfamiliar poems as well as reinforcing old favourites and thereby creating a 'community' of poetry enjoyers
- develop a dialogue about the poem with the children (see activities below under responding to poetry).

Children and adults reading or reciting together

Shared recitations of poems and rhymes can be a wonderfully social and collegiate activity. It accentuates the importance of a community in the class and a growing sharing of commonality. It is also a time for children and adults (staff and parents and carers) to introduce rhymes, poems and songs important in their lives. There is no right way to share poems with groups of children but you may wish to consider:

- seating children in the round so that they can see you and the other children – many poems and rhymes use gestures and actions to support the telling
- using puppets and props to help you bring the poems to life (a green sock with long white teeth could support the telling of John Agard's thrilling *Don't Call Alligator Long Mouth Till You Cross the River*, for example: 'Call alligator long-mouth, Call alligator saw-mouth . . .')
- reproducing and enlarging the texts on flip-charts or whiteboards – interactive white-boards connected to the internet can be very helpful here and will enable the children to follow the text as they learn to join in
- taking turns to introduce new rhymes or songs from home – ensuring time for the children to plan and lead poetry-sharing sessions
- reciting popular poems regularly, which the children will soon learn through repetition (avoid formal teaching by rote as this will spoil any enjoyment – the children will learn poems through regular and meaningful group sharing). Poems with simple structures and predictive rhymes such as Evelyn Beyer's *Jump or Jiggle* work particularly well here with the memorable rhyming couplets: 'frogs jump, caterpillars hump/ worms wiggle, bugs jiggle . . .'.

Children reading or reciting poems independently

It is important to ensure that you plan opportunities for the children to read and recite poems and rhymes without necessarily having to perform to an audience. Ideas to support this independent work might include developing:

- **a box of favourite poems or rhymes** copied onto card or laminated which the children can take out and share with a friend or by themselves. Encourage them to take the poems home to read with parents, friends or siblings;
- **a tape recorder with taped poems** that the children can listen to on their own or with others. Try to include tapes made by you and the children as well as commercial tapes read by actors and poets. Ensure that you include poems read or recited in any community languages known by the children in your class (parents and carers will often help you with this);
- **opportunities to role-play** familiar nursery rhymes and poems with props to retell familiar works and to develop new ideas and verses (see below for more activities related to play).

Response to poetry

The importance of engaging children with the poems through intonation, gesture and even dance cannot be underestimated. If children are to engage creatively with poetry they need the opportunity to actively explore the meanings as well as the sounds and rhythms the poem offers.

Response through play

The key role of the Early Years educator is to build upon a child's early enthusiasm and love of language play and to recognise that their prior experience brings a wealth of knowledge about poetry. This understanding will support the practitioner in extending the child's repertoire of poetic forms and their understanding of the meaning in the texts.

Activities developed through play will allow children time and opportunity to reinforce their knowledge and to extend their repertoire by learning from each other in a non-threatening atmosphere. It is fine to make up rhymes and songs and poems (even rude ones) as part of your play without an adult asking you to perform. Although in the creative Early Years classroom, it is assumed that all activities will be based in children's play, we have taken some specific areas to consider:

Role-play areas

Imaginary worlds based on narrative nursery rhymes or poems can be developed to support the children's response by getting inside the poem – literally. Consider role-play areas such as:

- *Sing-a-song-of-sixpence* based in and around a castle complete with regal and blackbird costumes or hats for the main characters, a pie, money, bread and honey, a washing line and pegs. Encourage the children initially to retell the rhyme and then ensure time for the children to develop and extend the narrative through their own unique play. After some weeks of play, you may wish to consider introducing characters or props from other nursery rhymes to extend and develop their play.

- *The Owl and the Pussycat* – animal masks, a small island area with a rowing boat, a jar of honey and plenty of money will help to bring this narrative poem to life. Display the words of this wonderful rhyme with its well known nonsense words and encourage the children to make up new words for everyday items. Younger and less experienced readers will join in with the predictable rhyming patterns with great glee.

- *The nursery rhyme shop* where rhymes can be bought and performed for you: where outfits from characters can be hired and where toys, books and DVDs can be bought and exchanged.

Small-world play

Manipulating characters and props from familiar rhymes and poems will enable children to enjoy repeating old favourites in a variety of situations alone and with other children. They will have the opportunity to practise and enjoy the rhymes independently and without the need to perform in front of an adult. As the children grow in confidence and experience they will begin to use these characters to innovate and to extend the narratives:

- **Nursery rhyme 'story boxes'** building on the ideas developed by Helen Bromley, and discussed in some detail in 'KS1 fiction', it is a good idea to create a shoebox scene based around a popular nursery rhyme. Encourage the children to help you to plan the key ingredients as this will support them in developing their understanding and memory of the rhyme. *Humpty Dumpty* or *Little Miss Muffet* works well with their iconoclastic characters and scenes. Once the children are familiar with retelling the rhymes you could introduce a new character into the box or even combine rhymes – What would Humpty make of the spider? Could Miss Muffet put Humpty together again and save the day?

- **Puppets and props** to retell and repeat the rhymes and to teach each other new ones. Encourage the children to tell rhymes in their own languages – ask parents and carers to share their favourite rhymes. Simple puppets can be made by the children (finger bobs made from felt with wool and 'bits' stuck on; characters drawn and laminated and stuck on lolly sticks; characters photocopied and laminated with adhesive magnetic tape on the back for using on a magnetic whiteboard).

- **Display poems and anthologies and related props in all areas of learning** throughout the setting: five little ducks and a mother duck in the water tray; Jack, a sack of malt, a rat, a cat, a dog, a cow (with a crumpled horn), etc. in the construction area; 10 green bottles in the maths area, and so on.

Response through drama and film

Drama techniques and methods can be applied very successfully in the Early Years classroom with small groups of children with adult support. These ideas can be adapted to use with any text but can be particularly helpful when encouraging young children to think about the meaning behind many familiar poems and rhymes. These ideas can sometimes encourage them, and us, to look at an old favourite in quite a new light.

The aim of many of these ideas is to add to our enjoyment by letting us play alongside the characters – be careful not to interrogate the poems and rhymes too far and thereby spoil any spontaneity. These ideas should be applied sparingly but during the year can become useful tools to support children's understanding of any texts.

The following activities are designed for use with small groups of children and a supporting adult who will extend the children's experience by careful open-ended questioning.

- **Hot-seating** favourite characters – children can plan questions they would like to ask Humpty Dumpty as the adult takes the role of the doom-laden egg. 'Why did you sit on the wall?'; 'Are you really dead?'; 'Why are you so fat?'. Adults acting in role need to be prepared for challenging questions from curious three- and four-year-olds. By creating a discussion about a key character, we are enabling children to consider the text and to form opinions. Understanding that there may be more to a story than the text itself is a very important possibility to begin to consider.

- **Simple improvisation** where children work in pairs or small groups to act out a simple rhyme or poem as it is read or recited by an adult or confident child. 'How might Jack and Jill go up the hill?'; 'Can you think of another way?'; 'Show me your happy face.'

- **Mime** – by asking children to plan and act out the rhyme without saying the words, you will enable them to reread the text and decide what they think it means. It is important to note that as many rhymes and poems are open to interpretation and there is never just one 'right' way.

- **Freeze frame** – ask the children to choose a significant part of the rhyme and to freeze – just like a photo – a moment in time. Ask the other children to try to guess the rhyme from the freeze frame. This will need some careful intervention from the adult and several rereadings to help agree on one moment.

- **Thought tracking** – as the children are miming or involved in freeze frame or miming activities encourage them to think like the character or item they are portraying. As you touch them on their shoulder ask them to tell you what they are thinking: 'I don't have any food for the poor doggy,' the bare cupboard might muse; 'I need to go to Sainsbury's before it closes,' thinks Old Mother Hubbard.

These activities can be developed further by using film or video to record and to explore the poems. By filming a performance or a rhyme, you could fast-forward the tape or slow down the action. You could even play the sequence backwards. How does this affect the poem? Can you still recognise the nursery rhyme? Let's say it backwards to see if it fits with the pictures.

Response through music and dance

The links between poetry and music and dance are evident – the importance of rhythm and tempo; the illusions cast by words, music or forms; the creative and dynamic role of the listener or observer as well as the reader or performer. Activities to link these art forms might include:

Choral reading   This is a very useful classroom activity to ensure children participate and enjoy poetry in a secure group environment. Children and adults recite or read well-known poems together or in groups for enjoyment or for performance (there are no rules how to divide up the poem as long as all the voices have a chance to be heard alone or in unison). It is useful to choose a poem or rhyme that will 'come alive' when read and one where there is some repetition (e.g. *London's Burning* (anon), *Row, Row, Row the Boat* (anon), Michael Rosen's *I Don't Like Custard* are all great starting points).

Clapping and stomping   Clapping and stomping rhythms of rhymes and poems is a useful way of encouraging children to join in and feel the rhythm of the poem. Try clapping favourite rhymes without the words to see if the children can 'hear' the poem.

Percussion   Using instruments can help the children to feel and 'tune into' the beat and rhythm of a poem. Using instruments to support recitations or readings from different languages is helpful to place poems in their cultural environments.

Sound effects   Adding sound effects to poems when making poetry anthology tapes is another great way of bringing poems to life. Using vivid poems with onomatopoeic language works particularly well (e.g. *We're Going on a Bear Hunt*).

Poetry and dance   The strong rhythm and beat of many nursery rhymes and songs for young children instinctively demands babies and young children move and sway and bang and clap as the rhymes are shared. Many songs and rhymes for babies come to life only when the baby is jiggled on your knee (Davies 2003: 40). By combining poetry with dance in the Early Years classroom, we are building on a tradition of established action rhymes and songs. Many Early Years practitioners already use a range of songs and rhymes to encourage dancing and moving to the beat. Children in my reception class would scream with excitement as they jumped up and wiggled their bottoms for *Alice the Camel*: 'Alice the camel had five humps, Alice the camel had 5 humps, Alice the camel had five humps . . . so go Alice go boom, boom, boom.'

In addition to set pieces (*Oranges and Lemons* or *Teddy Bear, Teddy Bear*, for example) where the dance is known or taught and the moves handed down through the family or school generations, poetry lends itself very well to creating images and exploring meanings through the whole body in dance.

Starting points for developing the use of dance might include:

- Reading or singing a poem and rhyme to the children with their eyes closed. Children to use only their fingers to 'dance' to the rhythm. Extend movements to hands and then feet and then whole bodies.

- Children could work with a partner on a familiar rhyme or poem combining mime with music – choose your poem or song carefully with vivid imagery and a strong rhythm (*The Animals Went in Two by Two* works very well with wonderful images when 'The bear and the monkey played all sorts of tricks' and 'The stegosaurus got stuck in the door').

- Read a longer poem aloud to the children (e.g. Ogden Nash's *Adventures of Isabel*) as they join in at particular points, e.g. as the wind whistles or the lions roar.

Word play

Playing with the sounds of our language begins in the first weeks of life and enjoyment continues throughout our lives. Jokes and puns, rude rhymes and inappropriate noises continue to amuse and titillate into adulthood. A love of the feel and sound of language is at the root of enjoying listening to, reading and composing our own poems.

Developing children's ability to recognise, hear and segment sounds is central to the Primary National Strategy's current reading and writing programme for the early years (*NLS Progression in Phonics* (DfEE 2000), *PNS Playing with Sounds* (DfES 2004)). Much research on the teaching of reading and writing agrees that being able to hear and discriminate between sounds will form the basis of children's success in the encoding and decoding of texts (Wray 1994; Goswami and Bryant 1994). The debate between the most effective methods to teach phonemic awareness and phonics continues to rage into the 21st century and is beyond the scope of this book. What is important for this chapter is to consider how the imaginative use of language can support and extend children's access to, and enjoyment of, poetry and support their creativity in responding to and developing their own unique poems.

Alliteration

Repeating initial sounds or phonemes is a fundamental part of learning to talk. It is also a key feature of many poems and is importantly great fun to play with. Consider some of the following activities:

Alphabet rhymes and songs with reference to the letter sounds as well as the names. A favourite in my class was sung to the tune of *Skip to My Lou, My Darling*:

> Ants on the apples a a a,
> Ants on the apples a a a,
> Ants on the apples a a a,
> Skip to my Lou, my darling
>
> Balls are bouncing b b b . . .
>
> Caterpillars crawling c c c . . .
>
> Dolls are dancing d d d, etc.

The most effective and meaningful alphabet songs are ones developed by the children and staff themselves, preferably adapting a familiar song or current jingle. I observed one reception class in south London chanting their letter sounds to the, then popular, tune of *Who Let The Dogs Out?* by Baha Men: 'Who let the A out? A, a, a, a; Who let the B out? B, b, b, b', etc.

- *alphabet friezes*: as well as using commercially made friezes, try to develop your own with reference to the children's interests (e.g. food packaging: Alpen, BigMac, cornflakes, etc. or toys: Action Man, Barbie, Construct, etc.);
- *interactive computer programmes*, e.g. Animated Alphabet;
- *alliterative classroom notices and captions*: 'Find Freddie's Fish!'; 'Beautiful, Brilliant, Brainy Books';
- *Word games*: 'I-spy with my little eye something beginning with . . ./ I hear with my little ear something beginning with . . ./I smell with my nose as well something beginning with . . .' games and class books;
- *Tongue twisters*: use established traditional rhymes, e.g. 'Peter Piper picked a peck of pickled pepper' as well as making up new ones with the children: 'Lucy licks lemon lollies for lunch.'

Onomatopoeia

The first grasp of language for a child or baby is often to imitate the sounds or noises that animals make. These onomatopoeic words sound like their meaning, e.g. baa, woof, miaow. Children love to use evocative language – 'woooosh' or 'wheeeeee' as they run outside in the windy playground. It is therefore important to plan experiences for children to have feelings to describe and share. These experiences could include:

- touching the coldness of snow
- jumping in 'sploshy' puddles
- listening to the roar of aeroplanes
- feeling the excitement of a busy market
- smelling warm biscuits baking.

Encourage the children to develop new words for new sounds – 'plick' for the sound the DVD makes as it is switched on, for example. Collect and display these onomatopoeias to support the children's writing of poetry.

Rhymes

In addition to regularly reciting nursery rhymes with their highly predictive and familiar rhythmic word endings (Jill/hill), there are many enjoyable activities you could develop to extend children's experience of rhyme. Working from a rhyming text is a good way to start as this contextualises the word play. The following examples are taken from Lynley Dodd's *Hairy Maclary*:

- Read the text through to the children without stopping for text interrogation. Enjoy the text and invite the children to listen and hear the story as well as the sounds of the language. Talking with the children about their dogs will of course form an important part of this initial reading. It is vital to allow time to discuss the meaning of the story before homing in on the sounds of the words – which are meaningless out of context.
- Reread the text encouraging the children to join in with you – the predictive quality of the rhymes will support many children, as will the vivid illustrations.
- Use the predictive rhymes to encourage contributions – pause at the rhyme for suggestions and thereby returning to the meaning of the text.
- Cover key rhyming words with Post-it notes to invite predictions and compare the children's ideas with the author's and encourage innovations ('Bottomly Potts all covered in . . .' 'dit dots!' – 'what a great idea – this author thought of "spots" but I think your idea really describes his spots vividly.'). Begin to collect lists of rhyming words to display and look at later.
- Create a class book using the ideas to describe the children in the class – Dawn Maynard tries very hard; James Watson drives a Swatson; Sumita Singh wears a ring – making up rhyming words when you cannot find one. Of course it is important to create positive images with the children when using specific names.

Additional ideas to explore rhymes include:

- listening to rhyming poems and stories in a range of accents through a wide range of poetry tapes, to increase experience of rhymes and language sounds
- passing the rhyme – children sit in a circle following on with a rhyming word inspired by a toy or object: 'I went to the market and I bought a bin'; 'I went to the market and I bought a bin and a fin' . . . (It is important to encourage made-up words as long as they rhyme. Keep going if any rude words slip in – best not to fuss as long as the rhyme is followed!
- Rhyming boxes with collections of objects and pictures for children to add to. Include some objects that do not rhyme to encourage careful listening. Use these collections of words to help develop rhyming couplets.

Planning and composing poetry

Composing new poems in the Early Years does not need to begin, or indeed end, with writing. As discussed at some length at the beginning of this chapter, the first poems many children hear are from an oral tradition and as such rarely definitively recorded in print. Young children's first attempts at composing their own poems occur long before they begin school: 'dolly, Polly in the trolley, golly, golly Molly Bolly' (overheard on a bus as a little girl played and hummed to herself in her buggy).

Immersion

In order to encourage young children to extend this ability to compose nonsense rhymes as part of their early speech and play, it is important to ensure, first, that they are fully immersed in hearing and seeing poetry all around them (see the ideas under 'Classroom routines'). It is through hearing and reciting poems that the children will build up an individual as well as a class repertoire from which to draw upon when composing their own works.

Shared writing

Writing with small groups of children in the nursery or larger groups in Reception can enable a useful process of share thinking and pooling ideas. It is a time when adults can model the writing and thinking process and when children are free to focus on one aspect of the complex writing process. The NLS offers a useful overview of the possibilities of shared writing in YR in *Developing Early Writing* (DfES 2001). When writing poetry, it is essential to allow plenty of talking and thinking time. We need to hear the sounds of the words before putting them on paper.

Innovation

Young children instinctively alter and amend familiar rhymes as is expected of the nursery rhyme genre. Each generation has their own 'naughty' versions of well known songs and rhymes:

> We three kings of Leicester Square
> Selling ladies underwear
> How fantastic
> No elastic
> Only a penny a pair!

Or even the classic

> Happy Birthday to you
> Squashed tomatoes and stew
> Bread and butter in the gutter
> Happy birthday to you.

In the same spirit, encouraging children to adapt and alter well known rhymes and poems is a useful way into independent composition as by altering just one or two words, a whole new meaning can be had with great amusement (as well as developing phonological awareness).

By sharing a familiar rhyme on a whiteboard or large sheet of paper, the children can begin to spot the rhyme and rhythm:

> Hickory Dickory Dock
> The mouse ran up the clock
> The clock struck one
> The mouse ran down
> Hickory Dickory Dock.

The children can be supported through a kind of oral cloze procedure to develop a new rhyme. The children will join in enthusiastically as you pause and wait for the rhyming word:

> Hickory Dickery Din
> The mouse climbed into the—
> The clock struck four
> The mouse did—
> Hickory Dickery Din.

Once the pattern becomes familiar, so the rhyme can be extended by the children with less adult support:

> Hickory Dickery Do
> The mouse ran to the loo
> The clock struck three
> The mouse cried hee hee
> Hickory Dickery Do.

Inspirations for writing

In addition to the vital first-hand experiences discussed under 'Word play', you need to consider how to inspire and motivate the children to develop their own poems. Other stimuli might include:

- images – paintings, photographs, video, film
- objects – sculpture, natural objects, ordinary items placed in juxtaposing places (a hairbrush in a sand pit, for example)
- sounds – traffic, bird songs, chatting, market hubub
- tastes – fruit, sweets, spices
- visiting poets – to inspire and support different types of poetry writing.

Writing forms

Children in the Early Years will predominantly respond to poems verbally or through music and dance. Some shared writing of poetry with an adult scribe will enable the children to explore a range of simple forms:

Rhyming couplets
Many poets use rhyming couplets to structure their thoughts and ideas as seen in this opening to John Agard's *Who is de Girl?*:

> Who is de girl dat kick de ball
> Then jump for it over de wall?
>
> Sallyann is a girl so full-o zest
> Sallyann is a girl dat just can't rest.
>
> (Agard in Huth 1987)

This form is highly predictable and accessible for young children and closely resembles many familiar nursery rhymes. Adults can model the first line to support less experienced poets:

> La La stands up straight and tall
> She likes to play with her ball.
>
> Dipsy sits with his black and white hat
> He loves to play with a black and white cat.

List poems

Lists are powerful and simple ways of developing ideas, particularly as a group poem where each child can contribute:

> I walked to the park and I saw:
> A broken pot
> A yellow leaf
> A plastic toy
> An old bench
> A singing bird
> A big ice-cream
> I walked home again.

Magnetic poetry

Fridge poetry where individual words are magnetized and strewn across a fridge door ready to be turned into poetry can be easily replicated in the classroom. The children could help to choose some favourite words to be typed up, laminated with magnetic adhesive tape stuck on the back. The children can then move the words around (include some of the children's names to personalise their poems. You can photocopy the poems to keep a more permanent record.

Acrostic poems

> **A** simple form
> **C**onsisting of a line beginning with each letter
> **R**elating to the word if possible
> **O**r not!
> **S**o plenty of
> **T**alk about words starting with each letter before you begin
> **I**n a shared writing session
> **C**ould help develop some wonderful poems.

Words and pictures

Develop lists of favourite words, rhyming words, made-up words, words that begin with the same letter, funny words, sad words. Combine the words with pictures and photos and read aloud.

Publishing and performing poetry

As with all written work, it is essential that the children have a clear purpose and audience for their writing. These could include:

- making individual or anthology books by theme, author, groups of children
- poetry cards and posters
- poetry for captions
- poetry for cards
- publishing on the school's website
- poetry tapes or videos
- poetry for performance.

Using ICT to bring poetry to life

Poetry is well supported by a range of ICT tools:

- current popular **TV programmes** for young children often offer a range of songs and poems, often with related websites. At the time of writing you might consider exploring the BBC *Fimbles* website – songs and stories with words to print out, music and animations or singing and chanting along with the *Teletubbies* nursery rhymes (see websites at the end of this chapter);

- **websites**: there are many great and interactive sites offering poems and songs specifically designed for young children to access. See the examples listed at the end of this chapter as a starting point. It is essential that the teacher is familiar with the contents of these sites and that you regularly check them for suitability;

- **interactive whiteboards**: these are useful to sequence images from familiar rhymes – try ordering them in different ways to make new poems – do they still sound good? How could they be improved? This is particularly useful when composing or innovating upon established rhymes or poems;

- Use **digital video** or DVD to support children's retelling and performing of well known, and their own, poems – composition does not need to be written! Filming small-world play using nursery rhyme story boxes is a wonderful precursor to the children making their own animated films of longer poems (see wonderful case study in 'KS2 poetry' chapter);

- **poems and animation** using a simple multimedia programme such as 2create.

Classroom routines

It is important to develop poetry as part of the Early Years classroom routines in order to establish the genre as unthreatening and accessible for all and, most importantly, fun! Try to establish some of the following:

- photos of the children with alliterative name sentences displayed in a large class book or wall frieze with posed photographs: James juggles jellybeans; Princess plays with Pretty Polly; Ely elbows elephants;

- nursery rhyme or poetry story boxes with characters and settings to retell and rework familiar rhymes (older children or parents could help to make these);

- boxes of poetry books displayed in the reading area with clear labels developed with the children themselves: Nursery rhymes; Funny poems; Our favourite poems; Animal poems, etc.;

- tapes of poems and nursery rhymes in a range of voices (actors/parents/you/the children) in the book corner;

- poetry tapes and books kept in corresponding areas of the classroom (counting rhymes in maths area; alphabet rhymes in the writing area; watery poems next to the water play, etc.).

- have a range of nursery rhyme websites bookmarked as 'favourites' for the children to select from. Links to these sites could be stored on the setting's own website so they can be accessed from home too, where children have access to the internet;

- if you have space, consider planning a specific poetry area with books, posters, tapes and a board for poem of the week/half term. Children could tape their rhymes in the area and begin a collection of rhymes from around the world (ask children and carers to help with this);

- rhymes and poems duplicated onto laminated cards stored in a box for reading and sharing at any time of the day. These cards could be taken home with further suggested activities written on the back. (Suggested activities to do at home with Incey Wincey Spider might include: searching for a spider and watching it very closely – what can you notice?; develop different actions for each part of the rhyme; find as many words as you can to rhyme with sun);

- using rhymes, poems and songs to help demarcate specific classroom routines. If you complete a weather board, for example, you might include a relevant rhyme: 'rain, rain go away . . .'; 'the sun has got his hat on . . .'; 'the more it snows TIDDLY POM . . .'.

Opportunities for extending experience of poetry in outdoor provision

As with other classroom areas, the outside area should be exploited for its potential to share and enjoy poems. Consider some of the following:

- **writing rhyming words** in chalk on the ground or walls – encourage adults and children to change and add to weekly;

- **sound trails**: listening to environmental sounds is a good way of encouraging young children to be inspired by their own environment. Tape the sounds around the playground (children's voices, bell, bus, birds, skipping ropes) and create a sound trail that children can listen to and explore again in the classroom by playing matching games with laminated photos of the corresponding sounds;

- **poems in the playground** – a take on *Poems on the Underground* – display a poem for children, parents and carers to enjoy before and after school;

- **laminate and display poems and rhymes around the outdoor area**: consider displaying poems about trees on the trees, transport poems on the road fence, seaside poems near the sand pit, etc:

- **playground rhyme time** – plan a regular slot where children can come together to join in with ring games and songs – perhaps towards the beginning or end of each setting to encourage parental involvement. Consider the use of a suggestion box to broaden your repertoire and to encourage songs and games from different cultures and in different languages.

Poems making the curriculum whole

Table 7.1 demonstrates how just one nursery rhyme or poem can begin to generate a wealth of ideas to support children's learning across the Areas of Learning. This work could consist of a week's focus or could be developed to run for a half-term unit of work by introducing further nursery rhymes or extending the link to other thematically related texts involving eggs perhaps or accidents or links with royalty or . . . The creative teacher will, I hope, use these ideas as a springboard for their own ideas.

Table 7.1 Humpty Dumpty across the curriculum

Foundation Curriculum Area of Learning	Activities	Working towards related Early Learning Goal
Personal, social and emotional development	Learning rhyme in different languages	Developing awareness of views and feelings of others
Communication, language and literacy	Reciting rhyme	
	Cloze procedure on rhyme	Extend vocabulary, exploring the meaning and sounds of new words
	Rhyming couplets 'Humpty Dumpty sat on a dog/car/house/hat, Humpty Dumpty fell on a log/didn't go far/saw a big mouse/fell on the mat'	
	Compare with Little Lumpty – consider the true story using hot-seating	Use language to imagine and recreate roles and experiences and retell narratives
	Imaginary rhyming name alphabet book: Alice Palace/ Ben Hen/ Cherry Berry . . . Humpty Dumpty	Naming and sounding the letters of the alphabet
Mathematical development	Role-play area of nursery rhyme shop (to buy rhymes; toys; games; books and pictures connected to nursery rhymes)	Use developing mathematical ideas and methods to solve practical problems
	10 round Humpties sitting on the wall, 10 round Humpties sitting on the wall	Count reliably up to 10 everyday objects
	and if one of those Humpties did accidentally fall . . . There'd be 9 round Humpties sitting on the wall	Recognise numerals 1 to 9

Continued

Table 7.1 *continued*

Foundation Curriculum Area of Learning	Activities	Working towards related Early Learning Goal
Knowledge and understanding of the world	Exploring the properties of eggs (tapping, dropping breaking, cooking, tasting, etc.)	Investigate objects and materials by using all their senses as appropriate.
	Working together to plan how to fix a broken papier-mâché egg	Ask about why things happen and how things work
		Build and construct with a wide range of objects, selecting appropriate resources, and adapting their work where necessary
Physical development	Acting out the rhyme in small groups	Move with confidence, imagination and in safety
	Mime	
	Planning and performing a Humpty dance	
Creative development	Humpty small-world play	Use their imagination in imaginative role play and stories.
	Designing and making papier-mâché Humpties to sit on the wall	Express and communicate their ideas, thoughts and feelings by using a widening range of materials, suitable tools, imaginative and role play, movement, designing and making, and a variety of songs and musical instruments
	Rhyme and rhythm – clapping rhyme, choral chanting, performing the Humpty dance	

Case study: Composing jungle poems in nursery

Anna is a nursery teacher in a Brighton school nursery class. Her class are used to being immersed in a rich menu of rhymes and poems from around the world. Her classroom shows her own love of poetry and the children's confidence in using rhyme and rhythm in their daily routines: at lining up, the children often respond to rhyming couplets taken from popular rhymes: 'Rick, Rick sat on the wall'; 'Rick, Rick had a great fall' responds Rick confidently. The reading area has a box labelled *Poems we love to read again and again* with a range of nursery rhymes and short poems mounted on individual laminated cards – the dog-eared corners are testimony to their popularity.

A tape of the same poems read and recited by the older children in the nursery class was in prominent display alongside a range of poetry books from around the world.

As part of a class focus on the anthology *There's a Rumble in the Jungle*, Anna was keen that the children should combine their experiences of shared poetry writing with an introduction to simple musical annotation to produce a unique and child-led performance piece. The work continued over three afternoon sessions but was continued independently for many weeks after by the children.

1st session

The children were asked to think of their favourite wild animals from the book. The animals' names were written on the white board with the children helping with the sounds they could hear. Each animal was then recited 4 or 5 times with an emphasis on the syllables:

Ti ger   ti ger   ti ger . . .

The animals' names were then recited with claps stressing the syllables and forming a beat. An adult pointed to the words as they were chanted. Two animals' names were then chosen to chant together:

Crocodile   tiger   Crocodile   tiger   Crocodile   tiger
xxx   xx   xxx   xx   xxx   xx

The children clapped the beats as they chanted. These were performed quietly and loudly following a 'conductor' (initially Anna took this role but gradually the children took turns at this) using hand signals (hand low for quiet gradually getting louder as the hand moves up)

2nd session

Anna and the children looked at more animals' names and recorded the beats with dots underneath as before:

crocodile   snake
x x x   x

They then chanted different combinations of animals in the same way:

elephant   elephant   snake   hippopotamus
xxx   xxx   x   xxxxx

The children then thought of sounds the animals made. Pictorial symbols were added to the whiteboard to represent these sounds and actions:

crocodile snap   crocodile snap (jaw movement of a crocodile with arms)

snake ssss   snake ssss (slithering arms)

Finally the animals' names, beats and sound symbols were then written and drawn on individual cards and laminated for the children to combine and use as part of their free play (Figure 7.1)

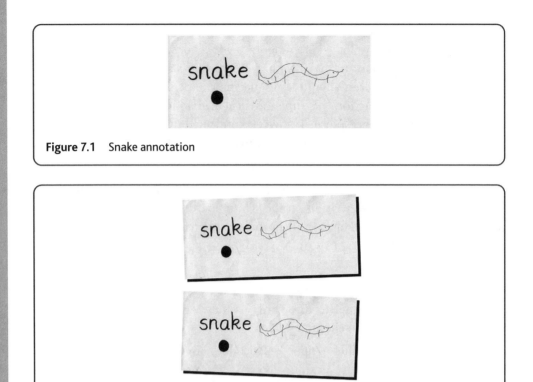

Figure 7.1 Snake annotation

Figure 7.2 Bea's chant

3rd session

The children revised each animal sound, beat and action playing the chant by reading the annotated cards. They then worked in small groups with an adult to order different animal cards to develop their own unique chant (Figure 7.2). When the children had perfected their chants, Anna introduced playing percussion instruments to stress the beat. Finally, each group performed and taped their performance to make a class jungle anthology.

Developing your creative practice

In order to extend your creativity in the teaching of poetry in the EY, reflect on your current practice and try to have a go at the following activities:

- Find a favourite poem and rhyme from your childhood and recite it to the children in your setting. Enhance your performance by the use of props or puppets, if relevant.
- Encourage the children to share their favourite poems and rhymes from home and build an anthology of these on tape for the children to listen to. Encourage rhymes, songs and poems in a range of languages.
- Develop a role-play area or small-world play themed on a popular poem or nursery rhyme. Ensure that the children are given the opportunity to contribute to the theme and include the necessary props to support their play.
- Begin a log of your favourite poems and rhymes you and your children enjoy. Begin to classify those that are useful to support other areas of learning.

Creative poetry in the Early Years – a summary

To conclude this chapter, it is helpful to summarise the key areas related to ensuring young children engage creatively with poetry:

- It is vital to value and build on young children's already wide experience and enjoyment of poems, songs and rhymes.
- Engaging with poetry in the Early Years should be predominantly oral and interactive and enjoyable.
- Poetry can bridge generations, cultures and languages.

- Innovation and deviation should be encouraged – the best poems break the rules!

- A creative and positive classroom environment can be enhanced by integrating poetry into everyday routines.

References

Barrs, M. and Ellis, S. (1995) *Hands on Poetry*. London: CLPE.

Clipson-Boyles, S. (2004) Chapter 3 in Marsh, J. and Hallet, E. (eds) *Desirable Literacies*. London: Paul Chapman Publishing.

Crystal, D. (1998) *Language Play*. Harmondsworth: Penguin.

Davies, M. (2003) *Movement and Dance in Early Childhood*. London: Paul Chapman Publishing.

DfEE (1998) *NLS Framework for Teaching from Reception to Year 6*. London: DfEE.

DfEE (2000) *NLS Progression in Phonics*. London: DfEE.

DfES (2001) *Developing Early Writing*. London: DfES.

DfES (2004) *PNS Playing with Sounds*. London: DfES.

Fisher, R. and Williams, M. (2000) *Unlocking Literacy*. London: David Fulton Publishers.

Goswami, U. and Bryant, P. (1990) *Phonological Skills and Learning to Read*. Hove: Lawrence Erlbaum.

Opie, I. and Opie, P. (eds) (1951) *The Oxford Dictionary of Nursery Rhymes*. London: Oxford University Press.

Pound, L. and Harrison, C. (2003) *Supporting Musical Development in the Early Years*. Buckingham: Open University Press.

Wray, D. (1994) *Language and Awareness*. London: Hodder & Stoughton.

Useful websites

Some wonderful examples of lullabies from around the world can be found at: www.harmonics.com/lucy/lsd/bedtime.html

A website designed to support new parents includes further examples of lullabies: www.babycentre.co.uk/baby/sleep/lullaby/

Nursery rhymes and some interesting stories behind them: www.zelo.com/family/nursery/index.asp

The Poetry Society offers a wealth of information on current poetry and events competitions for children. It also offers advice on contacting poets for work in schools and nursery settings. www.poetrysociety.org.uk/education/edindex.htm

The BBC CBeebies website offers a useful link to children's popular culture including some great songs and rhymes for the very young. www.bbc.co.uk/cbeebies/fimbles/

To explore the history of your favourite nursery rhymes look at this fun website: www.rhymes.org.uk/

Nursery rhymes and early poems are prevalent in all known languages. See these translated examples from China:
www.activityvillage.co.uk/chinese_nursery_rhymes.htm

A school's website sharing some lovely examples of poems and stories using a multi-media authoring programme:
http:web.dameellenpinsent.bham.sch.uk/penguins.htm

Children's literature and other resources

John Agard's *Don't Call Alligator Long Mouth Till You Cross the River* reproduced in *Animals in Poetry*, Poetry Society Education.

Jez Alborough's *Where's My Teddy?* (1992), Walker Books Ltd, London.

Janet and Allan Ahlberg's *Each Peach, Pear, Plum* (1981), Scholastic, Leamington Spa.

Giles Andreae and David Wojtowycz's *Rumble in the Jungle* (1996), Orchard Books, London.

Quentin Blake's *All Join In* (1990), Jonathan Cape, London.

Lynley Dodd's *Hairy Maclary from Donaldson's Dairy* (2002), Viking Kestrel Picture Books, London.

Sara Hayes' *This is the Bear and the Scary Night* (1991), Walker Books Ltd, London.

A. Huth (ed.) *Island of the Children: An Anthology of Poems* (1987), Orchard Books, London.

Miko Imai's *Little Lumpty* (1994), Walker Books Ltd, London.

Edward Lear's *The Owl and the Pussy-cat* (1871), London.

Iona Opie (ed.) *My Very First Mother Goose* (1996), Walker Books Ltd, London.

Jan Pienkowski's version of *The Animals went in Two by Two* (2003), Walker Books Ltd, London.

Michael Rosen's *Book of Nonsense* (1998), Hodder, London.

Maurice Sendak's *Where the Wild Things Are* (1967), The Bodley Head, London.

Dr Seuss's *ABC* (1991), HarperCollins, London.

Dr Seuss's *Green Eggs and Ham* (1962), HarperCollins, London.

CHAPTER 8

Teaching poetry creatively at key stage 1

I'm good at poems because I can do rhymes and my poems make people laugh.

(Jack, aged 6)

Introduction

Children in this age group enjoy playing with language. They are becoming increasingly sophisticated users of language and delight in jokes, riddles, puns, rhymes, chants and singing games. They enjoy 'funny words' and 'good rhythms'. Perhaps the most important consideration for us as teachers is to ensure that we introduce poetry in a way that that allows for an interactive response from the children and builds on the action rhymes and songs that are an essential feature of Early Years practice and the culture of the playground and the community.

The National Curriculum for English at key stage 1

Somewhat surprisingly, poetry does not have a high profile in the Speaking and Listening component of The National Curriculum for English at KS1. In fact, poetry is not specifically mentioned under EN1 Speaking and Listening.

EN2 Reading, however, does include poetry under the Literature headings.

The range should include:

a   stories and poems with familiar settings and those based on imaginary or fantasy worlds

b   stories, plays and poems by significant children's authors

d   stories and poems from a range of cultures

e   stories, plays and poems with patterned and predictable language

f   stories and poems that are challenging in terms of length or vocabulary.

Also under the heading **Literature** children are expected to:

c   express preferences, giving reasons

d   learn, recite and act out stories and poems

e   identify patterns of rhythm, rhyme and sounds in poems and their effects

f   respond imaginatively in different ways to what they read (for example, writing poems based on ones they read, showing their understanding through art or music).

EN3 Writing in the NC only mentions poems, the general term, under the range of different writing forms children should attempt.

The National Literacy Strategy

It is interesting to compare the statutory requirements of the National Curriculum with the range of poetry suggested for Years 1 and 2 in the National Literacy Strategy Framework which I set out below for ease of reference. Although the literacy hour is now part of the Primary Strategy and is still non-statutory, the NLS framework informs the content of the English curriculum in most primary classrooms.

Year 1 Term 1 Rhymes with predictable and repetitive patterns

Year 1 Term 2 Traditional rhymes; poems [in] familiar, predictable and patterned language from a range of cultures, including playground chants, action verses and rhymes

Year 1 Term 3 Poems with patterned and predictable structures; a variety of poems on similar themes

Year 2 Term 1 Poems with familiar settings

Year 2 Term 2 Poems from other cultures; poems with predictable and patterned language; poems by significant children's poets

Year 2 Term 3 Texts with language play, e.g. riddles, tongue twisters, humorous verse

A lot of the NLS text and word level work for Years 1 and 2 focuses on phonological awareness and patterned language with the emphasis on oral work.

Year 1 Term 1

Phonological awareness
Word level work includes exploring and playing with rhyming patterns and generating rhyming strings.

Reading comprehension

Text level work includes reciting rhymes with predictable and repeating patterns, extemporising on patterns orally by substituting words and phrases, extending patterns, inventing patterns and playing with rhyme.

Writing composition

Children should use rhymes and patterned stories for their writing.

Year 1 Term 2

Reading comprehension

Children should learn and recite simple poems and rhymes, with actions, and to reread them from the text.

Writing composition

Children should substitute and extend patterns from reading through language play, e.g. by using the same lines and introducing new words, extending rhyming or alliterative patterns, adding further rhyming words, lines.

Year 1 Term 3

Reading comprehension

Text level work focuses on reading poems on similar themes; comparing and contrasting preferences and common themes in poems; collecting class and individual favourite poems for class anthologies and participating in reading aloud.

Writing composition

Children should use poems or parts of poems as models for their own writing, e.g. by substituting words or elaborating on the text; compose own poetic sentences, using repetitive patterns, carefully selected sentences and imagery.

Year 2 Term 1

Reading comprehension

Children should learn, reread and recite favourite poems, taking account of punctuation; comment on aspects such as word combinations, sound patterns (such as rhyme rhythms, alliterative patterns) and forms of presentation; collect and categorise poems to build class anthologies.

Writing composition

Children should use simple poetry structures and substitute new ideas, write new lines.

Year 2 Term 2

Reading comprehension

Children should read own poems aloud; identify and discuss patterns of rhythm, rhyme and other features of sound in different poems; comment on when the reading aloud of a poem makes sense and is effective; identify and discuss favourite poems and poets, using appropriate terms (poet, poem, verse, rhyme, etc.) and refer to the language of the poems.

Writing composition

Children should use structures from poems as a basis for writing by extending or substituting elements, inventing own lines verses; make class collections, illustrate with captions; write own poems from initial jottings and words.

Year 2 Term 3

Reading comprehension

Children should read, respond imaginatively, recommend and collect examples of poems; discuss meanings of words and phrases that create humour, and sound effects in poetry, e.g. nonsense poems, tongue twisters, riddles; classify poems into simple types; make class anthologies.

Writing composition

Children should be taught to use humorous verse as a structure to write their own by adaptation, mimicry or substitution; to invent own riddles, language puzzles, jokes, nonsense sentences, etc. derived from reading; write tongue twisters or alliterative sentences; select words with care, rereading and listening to their effect.

Creative interpretation of the frameworks

When we consider the range of poetry and the expectations stipulated in the National Curriculum and the National Literacy Strategy at KS 1, there is a welcome emphasis on forms that play with language and reflect the experience that children bring from their home and cultural background and the playground. As teachers we may also wish to build on children's experience of popular culture: the rhymes and word play that often form part of the television programmes, videos and DVDs that children watch.

As well as humour and word play, there is provision within the documents for children to explore poems that deal with feelings such as anger, or fear of the unknown. Just as there are story and picture-books that we might use to enable children to confront their fears in a safe environment, there are many sensitively written poems that may be used in a similar way.

For example, a poem such as *First Day at School* by Roger McGough is close enough to children's experience of starting school and captures the gap between the adult's and child's perceptions of the world.

From the safety of two years in school, children enjoy recalling their own experience of starting nursery or school. They are sophisticated enough to enjoy the play on words.

Lessin
What does a lessin look like?
Sounds small and slimy.
They keep them in glassrooms.
Whole rooms made out of glass. Imagine.

and

'Tea-cher. The one who makes the tea,' but can also empathise with the young child's predicament:

I wish I could remember my name.
Mummy said it would come in useful.
Like wellies.

A poem such as this can be incorporated into PSHE or as part of a topic on 'Ourselves'.

Understanding and enjoyment

It is in the National Curriculum rather than the National Literacy Strategy that different ways of responding to poetry feature, as in the example quoted earlier that mentions 'showing understanding through art or music'. The National Literacy Strategy does include the phrase 'respond imaginatively', but not until Y2 Term 3! The only mention of 'enjoyment' comes in the National Curriculum where reading strategies include 'to read with fluency, accuracy, understanding and enjoyment'.

Perhaps the reason phrases such as 'enjoy', 'delight in', 'take pleasure in' do not feature in either document is that the documents are framed in such a way that teaching rather than learning is the central focus. Both documents preface the detailed provision they include with 'Pupils should be taught to.' Teachers can certainly provide opportunities for enjoyment, pleasure and delight, just as they can turn children against poetry through inappropriate teaching methods, but whether children's enjoyment can be measured and recorded and given a level in the way that the government wants is another matter. Enjoyment does not feature in the league tables, yet if we consider children's self-assessment of the activities that they engage in, 'enjoyment' as a category can be included quite easily.

Children can show their enthusiasm through simple 'thumbs up' at the end of listening to a poem or engaging creatively with the text. They can add a smiley or sad face to written or illustrated responses. Teachers' continuous assessment can also record children's motivation and enjoyment through observation, photographs, interviews and discussions.

Creating a poetry environment

In order to ensure that children see poetry as fun and enjoyable, listed below are some routines that are easy to implement in the KS1 classroom:

- Read a poem to the children every day just for them to enjoy.
- Give each child the opportunity to choose a favourite poem to read or for the teacher to read to the class over the term.
- Ask children to select a favourite action rhyme, poem, jingle or playground rhyme to teach to the rest of the class.
- Teach the children rhymes to accompany their games while on playground supervision or during PE.
- Implement a poetry browse time.
- Bookmark favourite poems for browse time.
- Provide a focus such as poet of the week/ month. Ensure related books, tapes and videos are available for children to browse and borrow.
- Take the opportunity to read poems and rhymes and sing songs in spare moments during the day, for example, when waiting to go to assembly.
- Have tapes of poems that reflect and extend the range of cultural/language backgrounds of the children. Include action rhymes and songs.
- Ensure there is a range of poetry books, including modern and classic verse, illustrated versions, and from a range of cultures in your classroom.
- Suggest that your school has a poetry trolley as an extra general resource, which can be wheeled into the classroom to supplement classroom resources.
- Display poetry posters.
- Provide a poetry board where children's own poems and favourites are displayed.
- Encourage children to label their artwork with alliterative sentences.
- Display wordplay games, puns, riddles and jokes to extend children's fascination with language.

Listening and responding

It is important for children to have the opportunity to listen to, share, interact with and enjoy rhymes, songs and poems. Graves (1983) describes a teacher of seven-year-olds who surrounded them with poetry including lots of choral speaking. The teacher's approach was to 'stress the sounds of the language with increased attention to meaning. The children heard, spoke, tasted and thought their way into poetry.' This practice predates the NC and the NLS but there are several important lessons that we might reflect upon. The teacher shared poems with the children that were part of her; she did not pass out worksheets or engage in extensive discussion. The children joined in with what they remembered, just as children join in shared reading today. The benefits of this practice apart from the shared enjoyment were twofold: 'Because (the children) were able to recite the poems they carried the language with them . . . And the language became part of their writing' (Graves 1983: 72). Additionally 'many of the children literally learned to read through poems they could already recite' (p. 70).

Playground rhymes

The playground is a good place to start to find out how children use rhymes in their play and how many traditional rhymes have been subverted to take account of popular culture. The Opies' (1959) comprehensive account of playground rhymes, *The Lore and Language of Schoolchildren*, is a useful resource for teachers, as it provides a comprehensive historical collection of street and playground rhymes throughout the ages, including contemporary versions. It was reprinted in 2001, with an introduction by Marina Warner. Warner wonders whether the sense of crisis around children's culture is well-founded. Are computer games, television and DVD, fear of letting children play out eroding the traditions of the past? There have been examples cited in the media of adults being drafted into schools to pass on the games and rhymes they used to play and chant. However, children's culture may be far more robust than we give it credit for. The rhymes and rituals and language play may reflect the increased commercialisation and advertising targeted at children, but as Warner states, the current crazes also inspire the language play that children spontaneously engage in.

Playground rhymes differ from the nursery rhymes that children become familiar with from home and nursery. As discussed in more detail in the preceding chapter on poetry in the Early Years, nursery rhymes are passed from adult to small child and not passed on until the next generation. Many nursery rhymes were originally adult rhymes and more significantly they are adult approved. In sharp contrast, school and playground rhymes are passed from child to child. They are often rude and subversive and not intended for adult ears. They are passed on quickly and adapted through constant retelling. As children experiment with language, they adapt and change traditional rhymes, creating their own clever, funny, subversive versions.

The Opies divide these oral rhymes into two classes. One set is related to the regulation of children's games and their relationship with each other. They are a means of communication, tried and tested rituals when language is still being learnt. The others are 'expressions of exuberance' such as jingles, nonsense verses, tongue twisters, joke rhymes.

The most common category of rhyme is *counting out* rhymes for starting a game, for example, 'One potato, two potato, three potato, four, five potato, six potato, seven potato more.' The Opies provide a new rude version which has probably already been superseded many times. There are rhymes to accompany *chasing, catching* and *racing* games, some of which feature at children's parties, for example, 'I sent a letter to my love and on the way I dropped it.' There are also rhymes to accompany *exerting, daring* and *duelling* games, some of which may be seasonal, such as rhymes to accompany conker fights. Rhymes for *clapping, skipping* and *ball* games usually have a strong rhythm and provide the pace for the actions that accompany them.

Children of this age love playing with words, are fascinated with tongue twisters, enjoy jokes and riddles and delight in never-ending songs such as 'There was an old man called Michael Finnigan' with the refrain at the end of 'begin again'. Whereas at four and five they enjoyed the familiarity of nursery rhymes, as they move through KS1 and into KS2 they love to parody the childish rhymes they have outgrown. Children spontaneously adapt, augment and amalgamate the rhymes they encounter, rather than invent new rhymes, and as teachers we can build on this fascination with words in the classroom.

There are many published resources to give you ideas, some of which are included at the end of this chapter, and the children and their families may supply their own versions of traditional favourites. There is an excellent website www.woodlands-junior.kent.sch.uk/ where the pupils themselves have posted skipping rhymes, clapping rhymes and playground rhymes with instructions for the accompanying actions. This is a useful site for teachers and pupils across the Primary age range to access current versions of the rhymes that children have traditionally used. Children can compile their own versions or adaptations and include rhymes from different countries.

Other useful sources for rhymes include: *Inky, Pinky, Ponky: Children's Playground Rhymes* (Rosen and Steele); *Muslim Nursery Rhymes* (Mustapha McDermott); *A Caribbean Dozen: Poems from Caribbean Poets* (Agard and Nichols).

Developing children's love of rhyme in the KS1 classroom

As well as building on the spontaneity of children's playground rhymes, as KS1 teachers we can also extend the experience that children have had in nursery and reception, before coming in to Y1. Action counting rhymes such as

Oliver Twist, Oliver Twist
Bet you a penny, you can't do this
Number One
Touch your tongue
Number Two
Touch your shoe
etc.

and

There were ten in a bed
And the little one said
Roll over
They all rolled over
And one fell out

There were nine in a bed
etc.

link literacy and numeracy.

Rhymes with predictive language may also be used to familiarise children with particular language structures. For example,

What's your name?
Mary Jane

Where do you live?
Down the lane
etc.

might be a fun way to reinforce questions! Children can substitute their own name in place of Mary Jane and think of their own questions and answers, for example,

What do you like?
Riding my bike/ Singing on the mike/ Going for a hike.

By building on the children's enjoyment of rhythm and rhyme in their playground games and their Early Years experience, we can encourage children to interact with poems and through that interaction gain a greater understanding of both the spoken and the written word. As teachers we can be instrumental in passing on the oral cultural heritage that precedes the literary tradition throughout the countries of the world. We can also recognise and value the language practices associated with popular culture.

Reading and responding

As discussed in the general introduction to this book, a creative approach to teaching English does not mean coming up with completely new ideas. For poetry it entails seeing the creative potential in the range of books and Web-based resources available for teachers, trying out some of the activities and using the successful ones as a springboard to inform your selection of resources and ways of working creatively with them.

In the following section, we will share some of poems and ideas from published resources that we have used successfully, adaptations of some of those activities and examples of creative practice that we have observed.

Activities to encourage a creative response to poetry

Recitation

A poem such as *On the Ning Nang Nong* by Spike Milligan is a perennial favourite with six- and seven-year-olds. It has talking animals, nonsense words, rhyme, strong rhythm, words that are difficult to get their tongues around and, perhaps most importantly, captures their imagination. Children will happily learn two or three lines

> On the Ning Nang Nong
> Where the cows go Bong!
> And the monkeys all say Boo!

to contribute to a class or group recitation and are quite likely to learn it all!

Recitation and mime

A particular favourite taken from *Exploring Poetry 5–8* is *Hands* by Peter Young, which can be performed by children without them even leaving their desks. It exploits the potential of mime as a strategy for developing understanding as well as being a creative exercise in itself.

> *Hands*
>
> Hands
> Handling
> Dangling in water
> Making and shaking
> Slapping and clapping

Warming and warning
Hitting and fitting
Grabbing and rubbing
Taking and breaking
Helping and giving
Lifting
Sifting sand
Hand holding
Hand.

The idea is that children have copies of the poem to explore in their groups in order to perform it to the rest of the class through use of voice and actions only. They decide as a group whether there is choral speaking, individual voices or a mixture of both. They need to consider how their mimed actions, using only their hands, bring out the meaning of the poem.

We have used this poem with student teachers, some of whom have been apprehensive about introducing movement and drama, either because of their own lack of confidence or because the children have had little experience of working in this way. Without exception they found it worked successfully. Each group's interpretation was different and the experience inspired them to search for poems that could be used creatively to support and extend children's understanding and enjoyment of language. Miming is a useful strategy for including bilingual learners and for extending children's vocabulary in a meaningful way. This way of working introduces a creative response in a classroom setting and can be adapted to fit in with a structured literacy hour. Children might wish to make a class anthology of hand poems written on hand shapes using close observation of their own, babies' or old people's hands.

One of the suggested extension activities is for children to use the structure of the poem to compose and mime their own group poems based on other body parts. The activity allows for flexibility and creativity as the group can follow the structure closely or play around and adapt the form. There are opportunities to make links with work in science, art and PSHE. We have found this poem works equally well with KS2 children.

Dialogue and characterisation

Use a rhyme that children are familiar with, perhaps a skipping rhyme, and practise reciting it as a class. Break into groups and challenge the children to recite it in a different way, perhaps dramatising it by alternating who speaks the lines and adding mime or actions. There is an example of Y3 children working in this way on the skipping rhyme 'Oliver Hyde' on the CLPE video (1992) *Story Matters*.

One of the students worked on the nursery rhyme, *Sing a Song of Sixpence*, with her Y2 class after watching the video. This familiar rhyme was split up into single lines which children spoke in the form of people gossiping in the palace. Sometimes the lines were repeated. By varying the intonation to deliver the lines as statements, questions or exclamations accompanied by actions and facial expressions, the rhyme became a small dramatic performance.

A. A. Milne's classic poem *The King's Breakfast* can be used in a similar way. Children love the repetition and rhythm of the verses, the first of which is printed below.

The King's Breakfast

The King asked
The Queen, and
The Queen asked
The Dairymaid:
'Could we have some butter for
The Royal slice of bread?'
The Queen asked
The Dairymaid,
The Dairymaid
Said, 'Certainly
I'll go and tell
The cow
Now
Before she goes to bed.'

The poem can be performed with the teacher as narrator and individuals taking the part of the characters. Simple props and actions help the children to bring the characters to life.

Music and movement

Build up a collection of noisy poems with a strong rhythm that children can move to.

Children love being the train in Clive Sansom's *The Train* with its refrain of 'Jickety Can Jickety Can'. If space is a problem, children can sit in a line in their seats and mime the action of the wheels with their arms and nominate a guard to blow the whistle. *From a Railway Carriage* by Robert Louis Stevenson has a similar fast rhythm and the rhyme also appeals to children. Other favourites are *The Tin Can Band* by Margaret Mahy and *Steel Band Jump Up* by Faustin Charles.

Music and dance

With the introduction of the Primary Strategy, there is plenty of encouragement to find creative ways of linking subjects and to consider the different ways that a child may learn. Angela Pickard in an article for *The Primary English Magazine*

(*PEM* April 2004) describes how she has linked dance and poetry using a patterned poem, *Patterns on the Beach* by Linda Hammond (Y1 T3, Y2 T2).

Patterns on the Beach

Look behind you!
Look behind you!
Patterns on the beach.
Running footsteps
walking footsteps,
all within your reach.
Wiggles with your fingers,
Squiggles with your toes–
As the tide comes in and out
All the pattern goes.

Look behind you!
Look behind you!
Patterns on the sand.
There are big marks
and little marks,
made by foot or hand.
Faces with your fingers,
letters with your toes–
as the tide comes in and out
all the pattern goes.

The simple structure of the poem, its strong rhythm and repetition, the end-stopped lines enable the children to interpret the words line by line and create a dance using simple movement patterns. There is scope for them to repeat lines or rearrange the sequence. Children can decide whether to work individually, in pairs or groups and show and evaluate their work informally in a plenary or perform it to another class. The PoS for dance at KS1 are an excellent vehicle for children 'to identify and discuss patterns of rhythm, rhyme and other features in poems' (Y2 T2 T9).

There are plenty of poems that might be used in a similar way depending on the topic the class is working on. A useful Web-based resource for finding suitable poems is www.poemhunter.com. Children can be encouraged to use dance and movement to convey their understanding of a poem and to extend their vocabulary as they find suitable words to describe their actions and the actions of others. They might use that vocabulary to write and perform a class or group poem.

Art

Many classic poems are published as illustrated texts. Edward Lear's *The Owl and the Pussy-cat* is an example. Sometimes a poem is made more accessible through the illustrations; at other times children need the opportunity to imagine the pictures. Just as children enjoy stories that are illustrated, an illustrated narrative poem may add to the pleasure of listening. If children see a poem such as Edward Lear's *The Owl and the Pussy-cat, The Jumblies, The Quangle Wangle's Hat* written up as part of a large frieze that they have created, they experience and appreciate the narrative structure of the poem and will often memorise some of the verses.

Art and Design

Children enjoy using their imagination at this age. *The Marrog* by R. C. Scriven was a starting point for practical work in Art and Design (NC 5a) with a mixed Y2/3 class. The children created a huge alien from boxes after listening to the poem, an excerpt from which is printed below:

The Marrog

My desk's at the back of the class
And nobody nobody knows
I'm a marrog from Mars
With a body of brass
And seventeen fingers and toes.
Wouldn't they shriek if they knew
I've three eyes at the back of my head
And my hair is bright purple
My nose is deep blue
And my teeth are half yellow half red?
My five arms are silver with knives on them sharper than spears.
I could go back right now if I liked—
And return in a million light years
I could gobble them all for
I'm seven foot tall
And I'm breathing green flames from my ears.

The children worked in groups to design and construct the different sections of the alien using the lines of the poem for guidance. They collaborated with others and worked on a project in two and three dimensions and on different scales and used a range of materials (NC5b). The alien was finally put together and spent a half-term sitting at the back of the class! Needless to say the poem became a firm favourite.

ICT

Alison Ball in PEM December 2005 provides some interesting suggestions for looking at poets and their work using ICT with young children. For example, the teacher can cut and paste a photo of a poet, perhaps poet of the week, into a document and children can add visuals using a photo or paint program showing how they feel about the poet. They might draw their thoughts on the computer using a paint program, as an alternative to hand-drawing or painting a response to a poem that they have listened to.

Drama

Children can benefit from exploring a poem in depth over several weeks through a range of drama activities as the following case study illustrates.

Case study: Exploring poems in depth

The following basic drama activities were carried out with a mixed Y2/3 class using the poem *Alone in the Grange* by Gregory Harrison. The poem was read over three days with the children being encouraged to join in with the repetitive lines.

Alone in the Grange

Strange,
Strange,
Is the little old man
Who lives in the Grange.
Old,
Old;
And they say that he keeps
A box full of gold.
Bowed, Bowed,
Is his thin little back
That once was so proud.
Soft,
Soft,
Are his steps as he climbs
The stairs to the loft.
Black,
Black,
Is the old shuttered house.
Does he sleep on a sack?

They say he does magic,
That he can cast spells,
That he prowls round the garden
Listening for bells;

That he watches for strangers,
Hates every soul,
And peers with his dark eye
Through the keyhole.

I wonder, I wonder,
As I lie in my bed,
Whether he sleeps with his hat
on his head?
Is he really magician
With altar of stone,
Or a lonely old gentleman
Left on his own?

Role on the wall

A life-sized silhouette of the little old man was pasted on the classroom wall. The children were asked to write words around the outside of the silhouette describing what the man looked like. Some of the words were taken directly from the poem such as 'little', 'old', 'thin little back', 'bowed'. Others such as 'bent over', 'black eyes' and 'skinny' showed their understanding of the poem.

The children were then encouraged to write inside the silhouette how the man might be feeling. There were very different responses, with some children seeing the man as 'lonely', 'sad' and 'tired' and others as 'mysterious', 'hating everyone'.

Hot-seating

Because of the children's mixed reactions to the little old man the teacher adopted the role of the character and the children asked questions to try to discover more about him. The student teacher in the class modelled some questioning and the children soon joined in. They wanted to know where the box of gold had come from, why the man was prowling round the garden and whether he could really make up spells.

Role-play

In the hall the children moved as the little old man while the teacher read the poem.

Freeze frame or still image

The children thought about the different scenes in the poem: climbing the stairs and going to bed; doing magic and casting spells; prowling round the garden listening for bells; looking out for strangers and peering through the keyhole. They acted out one of the scenes and at a signal from the teacher they froze leaving the teacher to guess which action they were performing.

Decision or Conscience Alley

The teacher took one of the children's suggestions that the old man had stolen gold from rich strangers that he had met and was hiding it in a box in his loft. The children made two lines to form a path for the teacher in role as the little old man to walk through. As the teacher passed along, the children acted as the man's conscience with one side giving reasons why the man should return the money to the owners, the other side giving reasons why he should keep it. The teacher made the decision on the evidence that was presented.

Thought tracking

The children took on the role of the man doing various jobs in his house and garden. When the teacher touched a child on the shoulder they had to speak aloud the thoughts in their head. One child was lonely, but was frightened to invite anyone into the Grange in case they discovered his secret store of gold.

The ambiguity of this poem with its focus on a central character lends itself to creative interpretation. The drama activities enable children to explore the mystery. The question that the poet leaves us with may be answered differently by individuals or may remain unanswerable.

Writing poetry at key stage 1

As we have already illustrated, writing poetry at KS1 does not have as high a profile as reading and responding, either in the National Curriculum or in the NLS. The programmes of study are concerned with children's ability to write in sentences and focus on transcriptional features such as spelling and handwriting. Poetry often breaks the rules and plays with language.

The NLS suggests that children are able to adapt and augment existing forms rather than create new ones. However, this does not rule out creativity. We have seen how creative children are in their use of playground rhymes and their ability to subvert nursery rhymes orally and they should be given the opportunity to record and publish their attempts for other children to enjoy.

Collaborative composition

Teachers can involve children in deciding which traditional rhymes they wish to subvert. By showing a nursery rhyme on the interactive whiteboard and removing the end rhymes, they can engage children in supplying alternative words and phrases. For example, in the following version of *Humpty Dumpty*, the teacher supplied the words in black and the children came up with the words in italics.

> Humpty Dumpty sat on the chair
> *Humpty Dumpty turned into a bear*
> All class one
> And all class two
> *Couldn't decide what they should do.*

The children illustrated the new rhyme and put it in a book of alternative nursery rhymes. Children then worked in guided writing to compose and illustrate group rhymes in a similar way. Some children composed individual rhymes in independent writing time. The book had pride of place in the book corner and children enjoyed not only reading the rhymes but also acting them.

Children can also learn from each other about composing when they write in groups or as a class. Initially, the focus should be on composing (thinking what to say) using the children's ideas and impressions. Moving the ideas and words around on an interactive whiteboard can suggest how the ideas might be shaped into a poem.

Gaining inspiration from creative texts

In the Foundation stage children are immersed in stories that draw on repetition and rhyme for effect and at KS2 narrative verse is a popular genre. However, there are also many stories written in verse suitable for KS1 children to enjoy. Some of these stories might provide inspiration for encouraging children to be creative in their use of language as illustrated below.

> *The Rascally Cake* by Jeanne Willis and Korky Paul is a story in rhyme and is perfect for reading aloud. It is the story of Rufus Skumskins O'Parsley, who
>
> Wouldn't eat supper unless it was ghastly.
> Wormcast butties, tubes of glue,
> Pans of slugs in slimey stew,
> Bogey burgers, brown rat roast,
> Fat black tadpoles squashed on toast
>
> When Rufus decides to make a Christmas cake he uses
>
> Ten pounds of flour, six rotten eggs,
> One hundred hairy spiders' legs,
> Some muck, some moths, some mouldy leaves
> And several snotty handkerchieves,
> A jug of spit, some garden snails,
> The clippings from his fingernails.
>
> Children love to help Rufus make his cake and come up with equally revolting ingredients, which can be left as a list.

An extension of this is to compile a writing frame by asking children to come up with rhyming words focusing on nouns that will form the last words in a rhyming couplet, for example, *bats, cats, cowpats, gnats, hats, rats.* Children can choose which two ingredients they wish to include and describe them.

The Witches' Chant in *Macbeth* could be another source of inspiration, or Roald Dahl's *The Centipede's Song.* The compilation of spells and unusual recipes allow children to use their imagination and draws on the subversive humour of the playground.

Working with visual images

Film as well as illustrations, photographs or paintings can provide a stimulus for young children's writing and address some of the NLS objectives in a creative way, whether it is collecting new words (Y1 Term 3 W8) or through language play (Y1 Term 3 T16).

The British Film Institute (*bfi*) has developed a resource called Story Shorts, which consists of short films of between five and ten minutes' duration. Repeated viewings of a short film can encourage children to see things afresh, in different ways, one of the features of poetic writing. The short film *Laughing Moon* does not tell a whole story but is a series of images and small scenes. Not only does film target the visual senses by using, for example, colour to communicate, but sound too. Sound may be an intrinsic part of the film generated by characters or objects or extraneous to the film in terms of a musical score. Sound and visual effects help to create atmosphere and evoke feelings and this can be explored with young children who are often less trammelled than adults in their responses. The language children use to explore and interpret the moving image can contribute to children's ability to use language creatively.

Redrafting and editing

The use of response partners where children respond to each other's work can work effectively at KS1 if children are given guidance and have the opportunity to see the teacher modelling the process. It is important that this is done orally. When the child has read their poem aloud, their partner can point out all the things they like about the poem and perhaps work with their partner to develop one aspect. The final decision should rest with the author.

Poems are particularly suitable for redrafting and presenting, because they are comparatively short. If children know that their poem is going to be published in a book, as part of a display or on a website, they will have the incentive to make it look good so that the meaning is communicated effectively. They may wish to try out different fonts on the computer or colour particular words or letters.

Audiences for children's poems

It is important that children publish their work so that others can enjoy what they have written. Children need to see themselves as poets. Their creative expressions can be incorporated into displays within the classroom and school environment. Their poetry should be read out in class, in assembly, performed, made into books or tapes and become part of the class or school library.

www.poetryzone.ndirect.co.uk is a very accessible website where even young children can send their poems to be published. There is a category First Words where they publish the work of children up to and including age seven. Children can also send in reviews of poetry books that they have enjoyed and have them published on the Reviews page.

Poems might be attached to balloons and released on a poetic journey to celebrate National Poetry Day, a child's birthday or a festival.

Developing your creative practice

In order to extend your creativity in introducing poetry at KS1, reflect on your current practice and on what you have observed in school. The following are suggestions for moving your practice forward in a creative way.

- Explore and critically evaluate poetry websites for creative ideas and resources.
- Include poems from a range of genres and cultures that you or the children have enjoyed as part of your children's literature log to support your teaching.
- Develop a poetry corner as part of a speaking and listening area where poetry tapes and books are available.
- Choose a poem and plan a range of cross-curricular activities drawing on some of the ideas in this chapter and from further reading and research.

Teaching poetry creatively at key stage 1: A summary

To conclude this chapter, we have summarised the key factors in ensuring that KS1 children enjoy and engage creatively with poetry song and rhyme:

- It is important to acknowledge the experience and delight in language that children bring with them from their community, home, the playground and Early Years settings.
- As in the Early Years, engaging with poetry should be primarily oral and interactive.

- Poetry should be an integral part of the whole curriculum and the Frameworks interpreted creatively
- Playing with language, collaborative composition and providing an audience for children's early creative writing provides the foundation for enjoyment and experimentation at KS2 and beyond.

References

Balaam, J. and Merrick, B. (1989) *Exploring Poetry: 5–8*. London: National Association for Teachers of English.

Graves, D. (1983) *Writing: Teachers and Children at Work*. Exeter, NH: Heinemann.

Opie, I. and Opie, P. (2001) *The Lore and Language of Schoolchildren* (revised edition with introduction by Warner, M.). New York Review of Books.

Useful websites

www.poetryzone.ndirect.co.uk/
is a very accessible website where young children can send their poems to be published. There is a category First Words where they publish the work of children up to and including age seven. Children can also send in reviews of poetry books that they have enjoyed and have them published on the Reviews page.

www.poemhunter.com/
is a useful web-based resource for finding suitable poems, old favourites and new, to share with the children, use in the literacy sessions on in other curriculum areas and to incorporate into topic or themed work.

www.woodlands-junior.kent.sch.uk/
is an excellent website where the pupils themselves have posted their own skipping rhymes, clapping rhymes and playground rhymes with instructions for the accompanying actions. This is a useful site for teachers and pupils across the Primary age range to access current versions of the rhymes that children have traditionally used. It might also inspire schools to create or develop their own website, incorporating a poetry section to support creative literacy.

www.virtualteacher.com/aupoetry.html
has links to a variety of poetry sites

Children's literature and other resources

John Agard and Grace Nichols (eds) *A Caribbean Dozen: Poems from Caribbean Poets* (1994) London: Walker Books Ltd.

Jan Balaam and Brian Merrick's *Exploring Poetry: 5–8* (1989) Sheffield: National Association for the Teaching of English.

Greg Harrison's *Alone in the Grange*, Oxford: Oxford University Press.

Peter Young's *Hands* Edinburgh: Oliver & Boyd.

Joanna Cole (ed.) *New Treasury of Children's Poetry* (1984) New York: Doubleday and Co.

James Reeves's, *Cows.*

L. Hammond's 'Patterns on the beach' (1990) in *Five Furry Teddy Bears*. London: Puffin.

G. R. Jones' (comp.) *The Nation's Favourite Comic Poems* (1998) London: BBC.

Spike Milligan's *On the Ning Nang Nong.*

A. A. Milne's *The King's Breakfast.*

M. McDermott's *Muslim Nursery Rhymes* (1981) Leicester: Islamic Foundation. http:islamicbookstore.com/b2027.html

Roger McGough's *Lessin* (2003) in McGough, R. *All the Best: the Selected Poems of Roger McGough.* London: Puffin.

M. Rosen and S. Steele's *Inky Pinky Ponky: Children's Playground Rhymes* (1996) London: Granada.

S. Taplin (ed.) *The Usborne Book of Poems for Young Children* (2004) London: Usborne Publishing Ltd.

Edward Lear's *The Quangle Wangle's Hat.*

Edward Lear's *The Owl and the Pussy-cat, The Jumblies.*

The Witches' Chant in Shakespeare's *Macbeth.*

R. L. Stevenson's *From a Railway Carriage.*

K. Webb (ed.) *I Like This Poem* (1979) London: Puffin.

R. C. Scriven's *The Marrog.*

J. Willis and K. Paul's *The Rascally Cake* (1995) London: Puffin Books.

British Film Institute's *Starting Stories*, DVD/T Pack.

Video (1992) *Story Matters*. London: Centre for Language in Primary Education.

Primary English Magazine, December 2005.

CHAPTER 9

Teaching poetry creatively at key stage 2

I enjoy poems that are funny and poems that are sad.
  Poems don't make me feel bad, they make me feel glad.
  And I know they don't *have* to rhyme.

(Jessica, aged 9)

Introduction

In this chapter we will look at children's experience of poetry within the KS2 curriculum. Does the love of rhyme and rhythm evident in the enjoyment of nursery and playground rhymes in Early Years settings and the fascination with word play in KS1 classrooms continue at KS2? Or does the fear and non-identification with an unfamiliar form that many of us have experienced in our secondary schooling start much earlier in our Primary schools?

At London South Bank University when we prepare students to teach poetry on their school placements and as future teachers, we ask them to recall the experiences of poetry that they had at school. Many recall being turned against poetry at secondary school, where enjoyment and response were sacrificed to deconstructing and analysing the written form.

Here are some sample responses from PGCE students

> The language was so obscure we spent half the time trying to decipher the meaning
>
> I never really got to grips with iambic pentameter
>
> It was all about spotting similes and metaphors
>
> One teacher would show us a poem and we had to decide whether it was any good without knowing who the poet was. You felt so foolish if you criticised Shakespeare!
>
> I didn't relate to many of the poets on the syllabus.

Many students recall having had to learn difficult poems by heart at Primary school or copying poems out as handwriting practice. Is it any wonder that many adults do not choose to read poetry as adults and even fewer choose to write poetry?

To discover how the National Curriculum (1999) and the National Literacy Strategy (1998) are addressing some of the issues identified with past practice of teaching of poetry requires us to consider the range and requirements set out in these documents. I have listed the main points below for ease of reference.

The National Curriculum for English at key stage 2

En1 Speaking and listening   There is no explicit reference to poetry under speaking and listening.

En2 Reading   Under the heading *Literature 4 a and f and i*

To develop understanding and appreciation of literary texts, pupils should be taught to

> **a** recognise the choice, use and effect of figurative language, vocabulary and patterns of language
>
> **f** consider poetic forms and their effects
>
> **i** read stories, poems and plays aloud.

The range should include

> **c** a range of good quality modern poetry
>
> **d** classic poetry

En3 Writing   Explicit reference is limited to 'poems' as one of the range of forms.

The National Literacy Strategy

The National Literacy Strategy, on the other hand, is overly prescriptive in its range:

> *Y3 Term 1* Poems based on observation and the senses
>
> *Y3 Term 2* Oral and performance poetry from different cultures
>
> *Y3 Term 3* Humorous poetry, poetry that plays with language
>
> *Y4 Term 1* Poems based on common themes

Y4 Term 2 Classic and modern poetry including poems from different cultures and times

Y4 Term 3 Range of poems in different forms [14 examples given!]

Y5 Term 1 Concrete poetry

Y5 Term 2 Longer classic poetry including narrative poetry

Y5 Term 3 Choral and performance poetry

Y6 Term 1 Classic poetry by long-established poets

Y6 Term 2 Study and compare a range of poetic forms [9 examples supplied]

Y6 Term 3 Comparison of work by significant children's poets.

An examination of the text level objectives from Y3 to Y6 under Reading Comprehension reveals a list of verbs: to read aloud, to recite, to describe, discuss, evaluate, understand, understand terms, select, locate, compare and contrast, distinguish, respond, give preferences, comment. The verb 'enjoy' is missing from all years.

However, in Y3 Term 2 children are allowed to choose and prepare poems for performance and in Y5 Term 2 to perform poems, maybe signalling an element of enjoyment. Perhaps the heading 'Reading Comprehension' in The National Literacy Strategy should include or be changed to Reading Response.

There is less detail under 'Writing composition' but there are several references to writing poetry based on the structure and style of the poems read.

The absence of poetry under the Speaking and Listening strand of the National Curriculum at KS2 and the over-prescriptive list of poetic forms under Writing in the National Literacy Strategy do not reflect the welcome emphasis on forms that play with language, nor reflect the experience that children bring from their home and cultural background and the playground that underpin the Foundation Stage and KS1 documents.

Creative interpretation of the Frameworks

Poetry is fun

As creative teachers it is important that we ensure that the children in our class have a positive experience of poetry through opportunities to listen, recite and respond to poetry in a variety of exciting, challenging ways, as well as having opportunities to experiment with language and form themselves. If we are faced with a class that is dismissive of poetry it is usually because they have been faced with poems that they have been unable to relate to, or they have had to emulate a form for no apparent reason. It is impossible to dislike all poetry just as it is impossible to dislike all stories, as the range is so wide. Creative teachers will need to read widely themselves to broaden their own repertoire to enable them to introduce poems that delight and challenge. Even if the NLS is being imple-mented, the categories are very broad and poems may fit into more than one category, thus allowing teachers and children more choice than they might realise. Creative teachers have an important role in the selection of resources and in planning activities that encourage children to interact with poetry in imaginative ways.

Peer pressure may put some children off poetry, especially boys, and there are many poetry books written to target particular groups. Roger McGough reflects on this in his tongue-in-cheek poem entitled *A Good Poem*, which begins:

I like a good poem
one with lots of fighting
in it. Blood, and the
clanging of armour.

However, it is important for us as teachers to explore and challenge stereotypical views and gender expectations and there are plenty of poems that we can use to help us.

Understanding and enjoyment

It is interesting that in the National Curriculum under En2 Reading at KS2, read-ing strategies include 'to read with fluency, accuracy, understanding' but omit 'and enjoyment', which is included at KS1. The absence of 'enjoyment' in the National Curriculum and in the National Literacy Strategy is a glaring omission, but as men-tioned in the previous chapter the documents are framed in such a way that teach-ing rather than learning is the central focus.

The responsibility for teachers to provide opportunities for enjoyment, pleasure and delight in poetry are just as important at KS2 and at KS3 and 4, if we want chil-dren to grow up with not only a wide knowledge and understanding of poetry but a love of poetry that will continue when they are adults. As potential parents they can then provide children with enjoyable and rich experiences of poetry and rhyme that schools can build on and extend.

Although the government may not require us to assess 'enjoyment' in a formal way, teachers' continuous assessment can and should record children's motivation and enjoyment through observation, photographs, interviews and discussions and convey this information to other teachers, parents and carers. Equally children's self-assessment of the activities that they engage in can include 'enjoyment' as a category quite easily, thus giving status to this important aspect of learning.

Creating a poetry environment

In order to ensure that poetry is recognised as an oral form as well as a written one we need to raise the profile of listening to and enjoying a range of poems, regardless of whether they are specified forms for a particular term. I have listed below some routines, many of which incorporate speaking and listening, that are easy to implement in the primary classroom.

- Read a poem to the children every day just for them to enjoy.
- Give each child the opportunity to choose a favourite poem to read or to be read to the class over the term.
- Bookmark favourite poems for browse time.
- Read a poem several times withholding the title. Ask children to choose a title to capture the essence of the poem.
- Read a long narrative poem instead of a story.
- Play music to set the scene for an atmospheric poem such as Alfred Noyes' *The Highwayman* and ask children to visualise the scenes as they listen to the poem.
- Provide a focus such as poet of the week/month. Make books, tapes and videos available for children to browse and borrow.
- Use opportunities to read poems at odd times during the day. For example, Alan Ahlberg's *Scissors* can be used at clearing-up time.
- Have tapes of performance poets that reflect and extend the range of cultural/language backgrounds of the children. Include raps and song lyrics.
- Ensure there is a range of poetry books including modern and classic verse and from a range of cultures in your classroom.
- Suggest that your school has a poetry trolley as an extra, general resource, which can be wheeled into the classroom to supplement classroom resources.
- Implement a poetry browse time.
- Display poetry posters including poems that are not specifically for children (for example, Poems on the Underground).
- Provide a poetry board where children's own poems and favourites are displayed.
- Encourage children to label their artwork with alliterative sentences, rhyming couplets or haiku.

- Display wordplay games, riddles to extend children's fascination with language.
- Implement a 'live poetry swap' where children read, perform and share their favourite poems with another class.

Listening, reading and responding

If we believe that it is important for children to have the opportunity to continue to enjoy a range of poetic forms and respond to them in creative and imaginative ways then it is important to move beyond merely asking them to write in a similar format as response. There are many ways of responding creatively to poems using other art forms. Many of the ideas suggested below extend the ideas developed in the previous chapter where we recognised the importance of listening and responding as well as reading and responding. Again we provide examples of poems and ideas from published resources that we have used successfully, adaptations of some of those activities, and examples of creative practice that we have observed.

Performance as response

Dialogue and characterisation

Choose a poem that has a dialogue and characterisation and ask the children in twos or threes to bring it to life. Simple props may help. I have used the poem *The Visitor* by Ian Serraillier very successfully with Y5 children. It is a very dramatic tale of a man stealing a ring from the finger of a skeleton and taking it home to give to his wife, without revealing where it came from. It is told in nine short stanzas, the atmospheric scene is set in the first three lines and the suspense builds up slowly as the following extract (stanzas 5, 6 and 7) illustrates:

> At midnight they woke. In the dark outside,
> 'Give me my ring!' a chill voice cried.
>
> 'What as that, William? What did it say?'
> 'Don't worry, my dear. It'll soon go away.'
>
> 'I'm reaching you now! I'm climbing the bed.'
> The wife pulled the sheet right over her head.

In groups of four the children decide who the speakers are and who the narrator is. They highlight in different colours the lines that the three characters say. This involves close reading of the whole poem and requires children to consider the motivation of the characters. The children then practise reading the poem as a mini-performance, bringing the characters to life through voice, facial expression and gesture. By bringing the poem to life in this way, the children engage with the meaning at a deeper level than if they had to answer questions about it. Each group presents their version to another group and discusses the differences in interpretation. The fact that there is no correct version allows for a creative response.

Some poems to try: *The Three Witches' Chant*, William Shakespeare; *The Sea Nymph*, Harold Monro; *O What is That Sound*, W. H. Auden.

Music and voice

- Children to bring in copies of favourite raps and pop songs to perform. Provide tapes and videos of poets performing their own poems, raps or songs in dialect, to inspire them. Poets such as John Agard and Benjamin Zephaniah are popular.

- *Dialect*   Children to recite/sing poems and lyrics from their own regions in dialect if appropriate.

- *Songs*   Children to listen to ballads, folk songs and to experiment turning a written ballad, shanty, love poem, lullaby into song.

- *Sound collage*   Children to add sound effects to a poem to convey atmosphere.

- Give children a copy of a poem that conjures up sounds, for example, Robert Louis Stevenson's *Windy Nights*. In groups the children add sound effects using only their voices or everyday objects to suggest the wind and the galloping hooves. The children decide whether to have sound in the background to the verse being spoken or interspersed between lines or verses. They will need to discuss the atmosphere that they want to convey and the effect on the audience. Children can record their poems on tape for the rest of the class to enjoy and keep as a resource for their class.

Some poems to try: *The House* by Ted Hughes; *The Listeners* by Walter de la Mare.

Musical interpretation

An alternative to sound collage is to ask children to interpret a poem using musical instruments to reflect the rhythm and patterns of sound suggested by a poem. This requires paying attention to detail as well as considering the overall mood or moods of the poem.

Poem to try: *The Cataract of Lodore* by Robert Southey, which conveys the growing strength of the cascading waterfall through a seemingly endless list of powerful verbs.

Music and movement or dance

- Children to build on work on noisy poems suggested in KS1 chapter.
- Children to interpret a poem through movement.
- What music might be used?
- Are the words of the poem going to be used?
- Groups would need to consider the use of space, timing, levels, pace, heavy and light movements.
- Are they going to work in unison, in groups, in pairs or as individuals?
- Children need to explore and discuss their ideas to produce a physical response to language.

The Pow-wow Drum (Campbell 1994) the first verse and chorus of which are produced below, is an example of a poem that children can choreograph in a variety of ways:

Long black braids and silken shawls
Moving side by side where the eagle calls,
Answering the beat of the pow-wow drum
we come again
to dance again

Hey-a, He-ya, Hey-a, He-ya!
Hey-a, He-ya, Hey-a, He-ya!

The repetition of the last two lines of each stanza and the chorus provide a structure to work with, while the first three lines of each verse enable the children to interpret the meaning creatively.

Thirteen Bony Skeletons by Jack Prelutsky is a much longer poem that lends itself to performance as skeletons dance 'in their bare, bare bones' in the 'mist enshrouded grave yard'.

A longer poem such as this can be worked on by the whole class. There are many ways of organising a performance and it will depend on the size and experience of the class. Groups can work on one or two stanzas with a group responsible for the chorus. Children may interpret their verses using voices, simple percussion instruments and movement. Alternatively some children may speak the lines, others provide the sound effects and others dance. It is important to involve the children in the decisions if they are to create their own performance. They will need to experiment and work collaboratively. As the teacher you will have to decide when to intervene, guide or support. Again it is important that there is an audience for the children's work. They may video it for themselves or perform to a parallel class.

A poem to try: *Sensemaya: A Chant for Killing a Snake* by Nicolas Guillen, translated by G. R. Coulthard, which can be found in *Exploring Poetry 8–13*.

Art and Design as response

- Children respond in drawing or painting to descriptive verse such as Tennyson's *Lady of Shalott*. They can compare their interpretation of a scene from the poem with Charles Keeping's illustrations. It is important to encourage the children to go beyond the referential to convey atmosphere and mood.

- Children illustrate selected verses from a poem such as *The Visitor* discussed earlier in this chapter. The first verse sets the scene and requires a panoramic view, whereas the second verse requires a close-up to bring out the horror of 'the ring on a bony finger'. Links with photography, including still image and film, might be explored.

- Children illustrate limericks through line drawings. These can be collected into a book as an alternative version to illustrators such as Edward Lear, Quentin Blake or Spike Milligan.

- Children design and make a monster such as James Reeves' luminous *Snitterjipe* and decide how to make 'his whiskers tremble' and produce eyeballs 'shining and shifting in their sockets'. Can they make his parts move, especially:

> His tapering teeth, his jutting jaws,
> His tongue, his tail, his twenty claws.

Animation or filmmaking as response

In the following case study, Paul a Y6 teacher in a South London Junior school, describes how he used verse speaking, plasticene model making and animation with the children to encourage a creative interpretation of Lewis Carroll's classic verse *Jabberwocky*.

Case Study: Building the Bandersnatch

General

I have used animation to develop and enhance a unit of literacy lessons based around Lewis Carroll – *Jabberwocky*, which can be found on many websites, such www.jabberwocky.com as well as in hardcopy. Since becoming a teacher I have used visual representation, such as animation, to support my teaching because I am a visual learner myself and have previously studied film semiotics and animation to degree level.

> Seeing comes before words . . . it is seeing which establishes our place in the surrounding world.
>
> *Ways of Seeing*, John Berger
>
> Our representation of the situation is the resultant of the two processes, that of internalising and that of externalising.
>
> *Language and Learning*, James Britton

I teach in a primary junior school and currently teach Year Six.

For literacy the year group is set into four ability groups (from three classes) based on their reading and writing levels.

Profile

This study was carried out on group three out of four. The average reading level of this group was 3a and their writing level averaged out at 3c, which is expected at Year 6. The group find the literacy conventions of grammar and punctuation quite difficult but engage well at text level and generally enjoy the work.

Although their practical reading and comprehension levels were at the national average, the group found *Jabberwocky* extremely difficult to comprehend. None of them were comfortable when we first read it, even though they had been encouraged to research it prior to the lesson. The idea that they would be able to comprehend something from the nonsense was untenable to them.

Lesson objective

- To understand the poem *Jabberwocky* and to seek clues in language to aid comprehension.

To make them feel more comfortable with nonsense I went through the process of deconstructing another nonsense text that made sense in grammatical terms. This helped them grasp the concept that some nonsense can make sense, but at this point the essence of the Jabberwock still eluded them. I have included the first two verses for those not familiar with the text or who need to be reminded of the language so that my description of the work we did is accessible without looking up the poem.

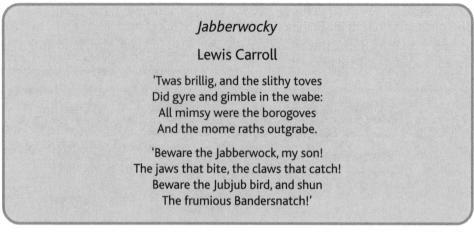

Lesson Practice

Because of the difficulty the children were having responding to the text, I decided to get them to build the characters. It was important that they did *not* build the Jabberwock. Having previously been asked to research the poem, many had brought in copies and each was illustrated in a very similar fashion. I knew it would not help the children's understanding of the poem to build (or draw) a simple representation of the illustrator's vision.

Each child was given a single colour blob of modelling clay. Each character in the poem was allocated to a colour.

Blue = Jubjub bird
Yellow = Bandersnatch
Pink = toves
Etc.

Each child was then asked to build the character according to the colour blob of clay they had. Before they began, however, we had a whole-class discussion about what each of the characters looked like.

From this I was able to encourage the children to draw out from the poem adjectives that described their character such as 'slithy', 'frumious', etc. Other words children began to use to help them explore their characters were 'outgrabe' and 'beware'.

At this point they started to see some meaning in the text and began using it to guide their design and building process. Children spent just ten minutes building their own model of each of these creatures. A brief discussion afterwards centred on the actual size, sound and smell of each character.

From here the process was extended to consider what each word in the poem might represent and what each line might mean. Sounds, smells, the environment and the time were all explored.

This then became the parameter as to how each line would be read as a narration to a moving picture. On reading back the poem, children were asked to visualise the actions of the characters, the environment (e.g. the Tumtum tree) and the overall feel of the poem. Comprehension was no longer an issue, reciting was now key.

I recorded the group reading the poem and decided (with a fair bit of encouragement from the children) to continue and make the animated film. From here we chose the characters that would be in the film. This was done as a whole class with reference to the poem at every stage in the decision making process. Children began to say 'her model looks best suited to the forest', and so on.

To make the film, the children volunteered to give up their lunchtime (as did I) to shoot the animation process. I chose a style of animation that would just see their characters morph from blobs to creatures to keep it as simple as possible.

Alternatively:

Another idea would be to simply take a digital still photo of a scene (one per paragraph) and input the photos in sequence using a simple program like 'Windows Movie Maker' onto a narration, making a simple moving storyboard (known as an animatic).

By the end of the week (a pretty intensive week), we produced a small film where pupil input had been on visual images of characters, how to cut from one scene to another, what sound fix would be used and how the narration would be read. The latter discussion gave many children additional confidence on how to recite their lines when recording their voices and developed their ability to speak audibly and clearly.

Assessment process

I asked the group to fill in the 'blob tree' chart (Figure 9.1) as a form of self-assessment.

Although my particular reference may be small, the data that can be extrapolated for the people in my group indicated that they had all climbed the tree to the top two spots. Two-thirds had moved to the top of the tree; the remaining third moved to the guy just below him. Twenty-four children had participated.

Quotes from children who participated:

The animation we did helped me have a running picture in my mind.

If you couldn't imagine what mome rath meant – it gave you an example of someone else's imagination.

I understood it better after building the models. I could see it clearly.

I thought the film was really good because I could picture what was going on.

Name_____

Activity_____

Colour in the 'blob person' which represents your thoughts
and feelings about the activity you are carrying out.

Before ☐   After ☐

Figure 9.1   The 'blob tree' chart

Ultimately the filmmaking process is multifaceted and gives children the opportunity to explore the many different aspects of their multiple intelligence elements. Using film and media in literacy can enhance a child's engagement with literacy. When asked to revisit *Jabberwocky*, the group were able to visualise it. By using the words 'playback', 'pause', etc. as tools to manage their writing, the children wrote more fluently and carefully. I believe that presenting children with alternative visual representation ignites their imagination so they can express their own views through written text.

ICT and interactive websites

The BBC website www.bbc.co.uk provides the opportunity for children to listen to poets reading their work aloud. There is also a section entitled 'Visual Poetry' where children can interact with poems on screen. At the time of writing there was a poem of 14 short stanzas by Mary Ann Sullivan called *Shaking the Spiders Out* where the reader had to click the stanza that they wished to view. Each stanza contained animation and words. The reader could play around with the order and choose how to read it. In this type of activity children are encouraged to become active participants rather than passive recipients of the poet's work.

Other poems on this site are accompanied by animation. *Today I Taste Lemonade* by Ingrid M. Ankerson evokes memories of summer with simple animation and moving font illustrating the words and exemplifying the meaning. Similarly *Gone Fishing* by Paul Seymour and illustrated by Noya Miller leads the reader through an animated story poem with moving text and provokes the question 'Why is the fisherman unsuccessful despite casting his line again and again?' The animated film pans out to the fisherman sitting on the moon and the solution 'There are no fish in the Sea of Tranquility.'

Interactive sites, as well as enhancing the reader's understanding and engagement with the text, have an important role in assisting the creative process, as we discuss at the end of the following section on composition.

Creative composition

Beyond formulaic writing

> Writing by formula is no more art than is painting by numbers, although it does have the advantage of being fairly straightforward to assess.
>
> Ashley (2005 : 16)

The prescriptive nature of the NLS sits uneasily with a creative approach to writing poetry. The numerous poetic forms children are meant to emulate to structure their own poems has led to more and more books being published providing writing frames and ideas for teaching children to write their own poems. As a result, all too often poetry writing becomes formulaic, with the form becoming more important than the creative development of ideas. It is important to explore the balance of structure and creativity but in ways that do not constrain or prevent experimentation. By sharing examples of poems written in different formats and considering how the form reinforces what the poet is saying, children can experiment with different forms or work loosely within them. By ensuring that language choice, word order, visual layout and oral performance are seen as important and often complementary elements in the creative process, we can encourage children to begin to make informed choices about what they write and how to present it. It is important that we recognise that sometimes it may be difficult for a child to produce a poem in the narrow time-slots of the literacy hour. If children research poets' interviews on the Web they will find examples of poets confirming that poetry cannot be written under timed conditions. Although the poems that the children write may be comparatively short when compared with other forms of writing that they do, they may want to make revisions before they are satisfied with the final version. If they are engaged with the writing they may want to work on their poems at home.

Research suggests that boys often respond well to writing poetry, enjoying the highly structured approaches it can demand and the immediacy of ideas (Maynard 2002). This may be due to the shorter form, as some KS2 boys find writing physically tiring (Higgins 2002). Boys also dislike timed conditions, a major factor in practising for SATs (Maynard 2002; Higgins 2002). These considerations may apply to some girls' experience too.

Figurative language

Poetic devices

In order to experiment with poetic devices in their own writing, children need to have read, listened to and enjoyed poets writing on a range of topics that they can relate to. Our role as teachers is to explore with the children why a way of describing something makes us as readers consider the image or event afresh. In the following section I will consider some of the figures of speech that lend themselves to creative interpretation and how children might experiment with using them in their own writing.

Kennings

A kenning is a compound word or phrase that signifies an object without naming it directly. Old English poets used this device not only to signify an object, but also to express their feelings towards it. John Updike, a more contemporary poet, describes the ocean through a series of kennings in his short poem *Winter Ocean*. Although perhaps intended for an adult audience, kennings such as 'portly pusher of waves, wind-slave' might equally appeal to children.

Children, if they are encouraged to reflect on their own experiences, will have little problem creating their own kennings such as 'slayer of sand-castles', 'toe-number', as well as more positive examples.

Simile and metaphor

Simile and metaphor are closely related in that the first is the explicit comparison of two unlike things using 'like' or 'as', and metaphor compares one thing to another by saying that one thing *is* another. When we search for examples of poems containing effective similes or metaphors for children to enjoy we need not confine our search to poems written specifically for children. Perhaps the most well known simile is Wordsworth's 'I wandered lonely as a cloud', which has unfortunately become stale for many adults because of its familiarity.

Children have the power to look at things afresh and should be given the freedom to use their powers of observation and imagination. When I was looking at the website www.childrenspoetrybookshelf.co.uk where children are able to publish their poems, there was a poem from a child who lives in the London Borough of Southwark. In the poem, the child used a simile that was drawn from their own experience to describe the London Eye:

> London Eye looks like people in transparent eggs,
> Looking out ready to be hatched.

An idea that is effective with KS2 children, but can also be used at KS1, is to provide an image such as 'the spiky hedgehog' and ask them what it reminds them of. Some examples collected from a Y3 class were:

> The spiky hedgehog is like my nan's pin cushion
>
> The spiky hedgehog is like my brother's haircut
>
> The spiky hedgehog is like a conker case
>
> The spiky hedgehog is like my hairbrush.
>
> The spiky hedgehog is like my grandad's chin when he needs a shave.

Similes such as these might be accompanied by illustrations. They can also be published as a split book where the top part of the book stays the same and the bottom part flips over to provide a different comparison.

The short poem *Fog*, written by Carl Sandburg (1897–1967), uses metaphor, likening the silent arrival of the fog to that of a cat:

> The fog comes
> on little cat feet.

It merely needs close reading and a little external help for the children to picture the scene and feel the atmosphere:

By asking children to illustrate or mime the arrival and departure of the fog/cat we can provide all children with the opportunity to make the poem their own. However, the children might also be encouraged to use the poem as a stimulus for their own extended metaphors. Does the fog remind them of another creature?

> The fog comes
> on a slithery belly
> It coils around
> the trees in my garden
> swallowing them whole
> and goes to sleep.
> (Y5 child)

Alternatively they can compose their own extended metaphor on a different aspect of the weather.

Personification

Personification is where an abstract idea, inanimate object or aspect of nature is given human attributes. The following examples that I have chosen relate to the weather, as children are required to explore poems on similar themes. Also, with a more thematic approach to learning being advocated in the Primary Strategy the examples illustrate how poetry might be linked with geography, art, science or dance.

The Wind by James Stephens (1882–1950) is a short poem that children can easily relate to and lends itself to movement or illustration. The poet uses the third person to convey the wind's power, 'The wind stood up and gave a shout', whereas Trinidadian poet Dionne Brand uses the first person rather than the third person pronoun in her poem *Wind*:

> I pulled a humming bird out of the sky one day
> but let it go.

This poem also lends itself to movement or illustration. The simple structure of the poem, which consists of a series of actions, is a form that the children might use as a model without forfeiting their creativity.

'There are many poems relating to the natural world that use personification as an extended metaphor. Another accessible example is *Sun is Laughing* by Grace Nichols, which can also be found in *A Caribbean Dozen*. Children can picture the sun pulling back 'the grey sky-curtains' and poking her head 'through the blue window of heaven', before changing her mood to slam 'the sky window close'. It is essential that children be exposed to examples of the poetic device that they might try out, but it is equally important that we provide examples that are creative in their use of language.

Children may have had experience of stories such as *The Wind and the Sun*, where these aspects of nature battle to make a man remove his coat. Children might compose their own poems to create very different moods, for example, the wind after his anger has been spent or the sun scorching the earth.

Alliteration, consonance and onomatopoeia

In the chapters on poetry in the Early Years and at KS1 we discussed alliteration, the repetition of consonant sounds at the beginnings of words, in relation to the pleasure that children take in tongue twisters and the often extensive phonics programme that accompanies the teaching of reading. At KS2 children can begin to appreciate the difference between hard and soft consonants and the different effects alliteration and consonance, the repetition of consonant sounds not confined to alliteration, may produce. The difference between 'a silent sea' and 'a cataract crashing' is enhanced by the sound of the words. Young children are often interested in onomatopoeia, words that imitate the sounds they describe, and at KS1 and KS2 will enjoy composing phrases that use a mixture of sound patterns, for example, 'bees buzzing busily'. The important thing to remember is that children should be encouraged to play with language and not be drilled in the naming of parts!

Word order

Poets often change word order to draw the reader's attention to important words. Sometimes the position of a word makes us stress the word if we read the poem aloud. A poet may choose to invert word order for suspense or mystery: sometimes to make us simply look at things afresh or in more detail. Upper KS2 children can consider why a poet chooses to experiment with the expected word order, just as they might explore complex sentence structure in prose, before trying a new construction out. The idea of poems for a particular age group should be considered carefully; teachers know their own class and the experience they have had. A poem such as *Niagara Seen on a Night in November* By Adelaide Crapsey (1878–1914) plays around with word order to create a striking image that children as well as adults can respond to:

Niagara
Seen on a Night in November

How frail
Above the bulk
Of crashing water hangs
Autumnal, evanescent, wan,
The moon.

Rhyme

We have discussed the importance of rhyme in some detail in the two other chapters on poetry where we consider the experience of children in the Foundation Stage and in KS1. As we have discussed, children grow up with nursery rhymes and playground rhymes and enjoy listening to and reciting rhymes. Rhymes are easy to remember and give pleasure through their sounds. Rhyme helps bind ideas together. Children may think that to write a good poem it has to rhyme, and concentrate on rhyme at the expense of meaning. It is worth discussing with children the types of poetry that use rhyme and why. Ballads and songs use rhyme as they were often sung rather than written down and rhyme made them more easily remembered. Humorous poems and nonsense verse such as limericks rhyme and are enjoyed by most children. However, they are quite difficult to write although fun to illustrate. This limerick came from one of our students but its origin was unknown:

A limerick's cleverly versed
The second line rhymes with the first
The third one is short
The fourth's the same sort
And the last line is often the worst.

Rhythm

Although rhyme and repetition of particular sounds can enhance our enjoyment of poetry, they are not essential elements of poetry, whereas rhythm is. In previous chapters we have seen how children respond to the beat in the playground rhymes and chants they engage in and the regular rhythms of much early verse. Responding to the rhythm of various poetic forms underpins our enjoyment of the genre and is an important reason that we ensure that poetry is seen a spoken medium as well as a written one. When children compose their own poems they need encouragement to read their drafts aloud as well as playing with words on paper or screen. They may enjoy listening to and composing raps where the regular stressed syllables contribute to the meaning. The BBC website www.bbc.co.uk/arts/poetry has a section called Out Loud, which can be accessed through Real

Player, where poets such as Benjamin Zephaniah and Roger McGough read their work out loud. There are more examples of the creative potential of ICT in the sections on Listening, Reading and Responding and Cross-curricular Links.

Using poetic forms creatively

> The other day my youngest grandson asked me what a metaphor was. I was pleased with the question, until he told me he'd asked it because his teacher said if they put some metaphors into their SATs writing test they'd get extra marks.
>
> Ashley (2005: 17)

As already mentioned, the National Literacy Strategy lists a range of poetic forms that children should be familiar with. There is a danger that by teaching particular forms children are encouraged to use the form at the expense of meaning. However, some forms allow children to consider the content of what they are saying more than others. For example, although children often enjoy rhyme, in their own search for a rhyme the image may be sacrificed. *This Poem Doesn't Rhyme*, edited by Gerard Benson, is a useful resource for teachers and children. It includes lots of examples of poetic forms children will enjoy that do not rely on rhyme. In the following pages I consider a selection of forms and how they might free children's imaginations rather than constrain them.

Haiku

Some forms such as the Japanese haiku can encourage children to use close observation and express their feelings about an image in one or possibly two short sentences. A haiku poem consists of seventeen unrhymed syllables organised into three lines:

Line 1 – five syllables

Line 2 – seven syllables

Line 3 – five syllables

Eric Finney's poem 'Haiku' in *This Poem Doesn't Rhyme* defines the form using the form and might appeal to children.

Many haiku poems refer to some element of nature. The following are some translations from the work of the Japanese poet, Basho. The syllable count varies in translation:

A caterpillar
this deep in fall—
still not a butterfly.

Awake at night
the sound of the water jar
cracking in the cold.

Some children may find it difficult to manage the strict syllable count but can express the essential elements of an image in a short sentence format. It may be helpful to provide a simple structure to help them become familiar with the form such as Where? What? When?

Child's poem Y4

Where?	On my window ledge
What?	The hungry sparrows squabble
When?	At the break of day.

Alternatively the final line might suggest 'why?' For example,

Why?	Over hard white bread.

The most important thing to convey to children is that it is the thought/observation that is most important and adjusting the syllable count may or may not improve the poem. It is helpful to remind the children that a haiku may be seen as a word picture and they could choose to label their artwork in this way.

Cinquain

The cinquain is another patterned structure of five lines and 22 syllables, building up two, four, six, eight, and back to two.

Children may choose to adapt the form and use word count, one, two, three, four, one, if this allows them more freedom to convey their thoughts. Again a writing frame may be helpful for some children, such as title, description, action, feeling, reference back to title, but it should not become a constraint.

Child's poem Y5

Title	Blackbird
Description	Yellow beak
Action	Searching for worms
Feeling	Afraid of cats
Reference back to title?	Hungry

Shape poems

Children enjoy playing with words and setting out a poem so that the shape enhances the meaning may encourage children to consider the words that they use and the order that they are read in. If a poem is in the shape of a spider's web, where is the beginning? Do the words reflect the strength and fragility of the web?

If children draw the shape they might overlay with tracing paper to experiment with where they want the words to go before transferring to a final copy.

Calligrams

Shape poems do not have to be lots of words, they might be just a single word with the letters arranged to show what the word means, such as

Thin or F A T

3D shape poems

Words and phrases might be attached to 3D models that the children produce in other subject areas. For example, a model of a volcano may be spewing out molten letters attached to the lava describing the sights, sounds and smell of the eruption.

Everyday poems

Despite the range of poetic forms on offer, we may find ourselves confronted by a class or individuals who have had a negative experience of poetry and insist that they do not like it. In an interview with Brian Merril, poet Charles Causley, who was once a Primary school teacher, had this to say: 'Poetry is an enormous forest or garden.' He also recalled how in some situations he did not use the word poem but spoke of the story or elements of the writing.

When encouraging writing, Causley stressed the importance of children writing about what they had experience of. Michael Rosen touches on similar issues in poems such as *My Dad's Thumb, I've Had This Shirt* and *My Brother is Making a Protest about Bread*, all of which are guaranteed to persuade children to reconsider what poems are about.

Children might consider Roger McGough's *A Good Poem*, mentioned earlier, in order to write their own version of what makes a good poem and compare their versions with others in the class.

Cross-curricular links

Art and Design

As well as children painting, drawing or modelling to show their response to a poem, there are opportunities for children to write creatively in response to paintings or sculptures. In a three-year educational project, Visual Paths to Literacy 1999–2002, sponsored by Morgan Stanley, over 2000 children from London Primary schools took part in a Literacy through Art project at the Tate. One of the strands of the project was for children to tell the story behind the painting or sculpture and a poem was often the preferred response.

Just as a visual work of art exists in time and space and has no one meaning, so too poetry may convey different ways of seeing the world. Both forms should engage the audience in a dialogue. Both need more than a surface read. To produce a poem in response to a painting requires a longer look and children need to be encouraged to explore what they see and realise that there is no right response. Michael Morpurgo in his in-service work with teachers (2000) at the Tate asked them to jot down three or four lines in response to three artworks to produce seeds for a story, a strategy he has used with children too. Some children might choose to produce a poem as an alternative.

In response to the Henri Rousseau exhibition at Tate Modern, London, poet Kathleen Jamie wrote a poem for *Tate etc* magazine inspired by *The Merry Jesters*. The monkeys in the picture are anthropomorphic and pose questions for the viewer. The Tate produces poster packs for teachers with ideas for classroom activities. One activity in the Rousseau pack asked children what they thought was happening in *The Merry Jesters* and to write down words to describe the colours, shapes and animals in the picture in order to create their own poem about the picture. Their interpretations could be compared with Kathleen Jamie's poem, which could be found on the Tate website.

There is also the scope when visiting an art gallery to use personal response or interpretation of a picture or sculpture to compose images that might be worked on at a later stage. By providing children with the opportunity to experiment with materials that may be reworked, children begin to understand that an artist works and reworks a sculpture, sketch or painting and that a poet may work in a similar way with words. Children on a visit to Tate Modern used a rubber with graphite paste as a response to sculptures changing and reworking the image. Back at school the teacher reminded them of how they had changed and developed their image at the gallery in preparation for the drafting that would accompany their poetry writing. Children understood that they were drafting and redrafting their poems and stories as an attempt to communicate their ideas in the most effective way that they could.

There are many opportunities to link visual image and language in innovative ways. A poem may be short but express depth of feeling or an alternative way of seeing things. *Voices in the Gallery, Poems and Pictures* chosen by Daniel and Joan Abse (1986) takes familiar works of art and provides a poem to accompany each picture. Sometimes the poem is written from the imagined perspective of a character within the painting or the painting is described from a modern perspective.

Although this book is designed for adults, a teacher can use it as inspiration to work in a similar way with children. Children can be encouraged to move beyond the literal and be creative in their response to and interpretation of the world around them. Things are not always what they seem!

For further information and ideas visit Tate Online at www.tate.org.uk

- *Self-portraits* Children compose their own poems based on their self-portraits using simile or metaphor. Out of all the information that they have on themselves, which details make them unique?
- *Contrasts inside/outside* Compare outward appearance to inner feelings (people) or atmosphere (buildings).
- *Colour association* Colour means different things to different cultures and individuals; it is a very personal thing.
- *Word pictures* The three-line, seventeen-syllable haiku is an appropriate form to describe an image in a different, creative and personal way.
- *Descriptions of everyday non-poetic objects*, considering properties and function, for example, a bath plug.
- *Comparisons using visual image* The old widow knitting is like a spider spinning her web.
- *Descriptions of natural and made objects* from a range of cultures or different historical times, focusing on what the material or artefact looks like, feels like.
- In response to surreal paintings, one-line *surreal poems* using random association from a selection of different parts of speech that work at a grammatical level, for example.

Table 9.1 Surreal poems

determiner	adjective	noun	verb	adverb	preposition	determiner	adjective	noun
The		screaming	table	trickles	gloomily	by	the		ferocious	trees

History

I watched a student teacher give an inspiring lesson in which children orally composed a class poem as part of the topic, 'Britain since the 1930s'. The children had looked at a television programme, archive film, photographs and paintings and listened to poems and memoirs from both the first and second world wars. The student had broadened the topic to look at the impact of wars on ordinary people, whatever their role, making links with PSHE.

The children had to produce just one or two lines that conveyed what it was like to be affected by war. They shared these images and feelings with the rest of the class. The session developed with the children being asked to file past an audiotape recorder and read their line aloud.

The class then listened and commented on the first oral draft of their class poem. In the next lesson the student teacher had transcribed the draft poem on to an interactive whiteboard for possible revisions. One child with learning difficulties had produced a line 'Oh the pity of it' which the children wanted to use as a refrain at the end of each verse when they redrafted the work to produce both a taped and written final version. He was so proud at its inclusion.

Local history

Children might use the work they do on local history to inspire their creative writing. When researching their local environment or the history of their school, they might present their findings in the form of a poem. Printed below is an extract from a poem written by a child in Southwark and published on the website www.childrenspoetrybookshelf.co.uk

---

My Home Friend to a River

Special, the name Southwark is;
People never heard it,
Cannot say the word,
Making it sound like South Wark.

Southwark or South Wark
By the South of the Thames
Making a place I call home
Friend to a river.

Geoffrey Chaucer School takes me to
Geoffrey Chaucer and Canterbury Tales;
All starts in Southwark, Centuries ago making me
Proud of my home.

Science

The topics that are covered in this subject are both within and beyond the children's experience. For example, life processes and living things; materials and their properties and physical processes. When we ask children to think creatively about how things work and make detailed observations we are combining imagination and first-hand experience, both of which are essential elements of creative writing. Some of these ideas and experiences might be recorded through poetry. Children may describe one thing in terms of another using simile or metaphor for their supposition or prediction and a more detailed precise description as a result of the evidence that they collect.

A class poem might include alternating metaphors and facts:

> *The moon is green cheese*
> The moon is a satellite
> *The man in the moon smiles down on me*
> The moon is a reflector of light
> *The moon goddess looks after the stars*
> Etc.

Jon Scieszka and Lane Smith whose book *The Stinky Cheeseman* is discussed in Part 1, Chapter 3, 'Fiction at KS2', have collaborated on another subversive text, *Science Verse*, published in 2004, in which all the verses are based on well-known poems. It also contains a CD. There is wonderful parody of *Jabberwocky* entitled *Gobblegooky*, which Y6, having worked on the original, would appreciate as they learn about healthy eating. It begins:

> 'Twas fructose, and the vitamins
> Did zinc and dye (red#8)
> All poly were the thiamins,
> And the carbohydrate.

This is a novel way to explore unfamiliar vocabulary related to the topic.

The authors also subvert nursery rhymes for science in the same book and KS2 children might attempt their own scientific nursery rhymes, after enjoying the examples.

Geography

When we teach geographical enquiry we ask children to pose questions. The examples given for the KS2 National Curriculum for Geography 1a are 'What is this landscape like? What do I think about it?' Again, this suggests a creative response that may be developed through various art forms, of which poetry may be one example. Providing children with an observation sheet (see example below, Table 9.2) to note their initial and considered responses enables them to collect information that they may work on over time and through different forms.

Table 9.2 Observation sheet

Things I can see
Description
What are they like?
Movements
Sounds
Smells
Touch
Taste
How do you feel?

ICT

Researching poets

As teachers we are now fortunate that there are a huge number of websites available for us to find not only poems that we want to use with our classes but information on the poets themselves. The website www.poemhunter.com is a site that is easy to navigate and KS2 children can research individual poets as part of their work in ICT (2C and 6D). Children might work in groups to present the life and work of a poet whose poems they have enjoyed. They can copy and print a photo, cut and paste relevant information for their peers, print poems, provide illustrations and record some of the poems. Presentations may be a display, an oral presentation, a bibliography or an illustrated anthology with a preface. It is important to give children some autonomy in how they present their material if we are encouraging a creative approach to learning. There is opportunity for peer- and self-assessment of how successfully the information is conveyed. Children can devise their own questionnaires on the computer for evaluation purposes.

Interactive poetry websites

We have already considered the potential of interactive websites such as www.bbc.co.uk/arts/poetry/display for developing a response to poetry. They can also be used to promote or support a creative approach to writing and provide teachers with ideas for presentation. The BBC site had a Poetree display of acrostic poems where every line starts with the first letter of a word. The acrostic poems were for the word 'leaf'

L	ovely
E	ven
A	fter
F	alling

and the poems were written on leaf shapes that formed part of a tree. This idea is easily transferable to a display board and can provide the inspiration for working with children to provide creative ways of displaying their work.

DIY Poetry on the same site enabled children to choose a background on which to write and to select words and phrases and arrange them to compose their own poems.

Redrafting

The National Curriculum states that children should have the opportunity to redraft on paper and on screen. Poetry can often provide this opportunity. Many of the poems children write are short. Their success often depends on finding the right word to convey meaning and so there is the opportunity to experiment with different words, maybe make up words or experiment with sound, font or layout. There are lots of copies of published poets' drafts for children to see how even established writers experiment. Because the writing is often condensed, a response partner can focus on the content quite quickly and discuss with the writer their intentions and the challenges. They may be used as another resource if the writer is stuck.

Many published poets prefer to work with pencil and paper: the reason often given is that word-processing makes the poem seem finished before it is. Because a poem relies on having exactly the right words in the right order, there are often many revisions; words are discarded and reclaimed and crossings out on paper retain ideas and choices.

Children can experiment with different ways of working. However, once finished, the word-processor enables children to present their work in a professional manner.

Editing　If children's poems are to be published, there is an incentive for them to revise spelling. Decisions on how punctuation is to be used, for example, whether new lines are to have capital letters, can be discussed in relation to children's experience and understanding of different poetic forms.

Presentation　How a poem is set out on the page informs how we read it. Children can use the computer to experiment with different fonts, size of print, colour, spacing, layout, background, illustrations and borders so that presentation becomes part of the creative process. Examples from interactive websites are useful as models, as is whole-class shared writing using the interactive whiteboard.

Children publishing poetry

An understanding of purpose and audience is essential for encouraging many aspects of spoken and written language and underpins a creative approach to speaking, reading and writing across the curriculum. One way of giving status to children's poetry writing is to publish it. The following suggestions include a range of audiences for children's creative work:

Books

- A ring binder where the children publish poems they are pleased with to be kept in the reading area. This is a flexible resource as it can be added to at any time. Poems can be removed or rearranged and might include printed copies of published poems that are favourites or inspired children's own creative attempts.
- Books of poems on particular themes composed by the class as a resource for the school library.
- Books of illustrated poems for younger children using alliteration or onomatopoeia to encourage their love of word play and support their phonological awareness.

Tapes

- Children record their own and published poems on to audio tape or video tape as resource for the class.

Online publishing

- There are plenty of opportunities for children to have their poems published online and to see the work of other children. One of my favourite sites is www.poetryzone.ndirect. This is a very easy site for children to navigate and children are shown how to submit their work. Under *Your Poems* there are different categories and age ranges and a new challenge each month. The poems remain for 2 to 3 weeks before being sent to *The Old Poems' Rest Home.* Favourite poems from the 7–11 age range are kept in *The Treasure Chest.*

Developing your creative practice

In order to extend your creativity in introducing poetry at KS2, reflect on your current practice and on what you have observed in school. The following are suggestions for moving your practice forward in a creative way:

- Explore and critically evaluate poetry websites for interactive creative ideas and resources and as a means of publishing children's work.

- Include poems from a range of genres and cultures that you or the children have enjoyed as part of your Children's Literature Log to support your teaching across the curriculum.

- Develop a poetry corner as part of a Speaking and Listening area where poetry tapes and books are available.

- Choose a poem and plan a range of cross-curricular activities drawing on some of the ideas in this chapter and from further reading and research.

Teaching poetry creatively at key stage 2: A summary

To conclude this chapter, we have summarised the key factors in ensuring that KS2 children continue to enjoy and engage creatively with poetry through reading, responding and composing:

- It is important to build on the experience and delight in language, rhyme and poetry that children bring with them from their community, home, the playground, Foundation Stage and KS1.

- Engaging with poetry should include and value the range of oral and written forms, both in terms of response and composition.

- Poetry should be an integral part of the whole curriculum and the Frameworks interpreted creatively.

- Children should be encouraged to enjoy and experiment with language and move beyond formulaic writing.

- Publishing children's poetry in books, on tape and online gives it status.

References

Abse D. and Abse, J. (1986) *Voices in the Gallery: Poems and Pictures.* London: Tate Gallery.

Ashley, B. (2005) in *Waiting for a Jamie Oliver: Beyond Bog-standard Literacy.* Reading: National Centre for Language and Literacy.

Higgins, C. (2002) 'Using film text to support reluctant writers', *English in Education,* 36 (1).

Maynard, T. (2002) *Boys and Literacy: Exploring the Issues.* London: Routledge/Falmer.

Useful websites

www.bbc.co.uk/arts/poetry/display is a truly interactive website. There is an excellent creative section entitled 'Visual Poetry' where children can interact with poems on screen. It also has a section called Out Loud, which can be accessed through Real Player, where poets such as Benjamin Zephaniah and Roger McGough read their work out loud. It can also be used to promote or support a creative approach to writing and provide teachers with ideas for presentation.

www.poemhunter.com
This website is easy to navigate and KS2 children can research individual poets as part of their work in ICT. It is also a useful resource for teachers trying to locate a poem.

www.poetryzone.ndirect
This is a very easy site for children to navigate and children are shown how to submit their work. Under *Your Poems* there are different categories and age ranges and a new challenge each month. The poems remain for 2 to 3 weeks before being sent to *The Old Poems' Rest Home*. Favourite poems from the 7–11 age range are kept in *The Treasure Chest*

www.tate.org.uk/learning/schools/poetry
The Tate website provides creative examples of linking art with other curriculum areas and there are links with both literacy and poetry. There are resources for teachers as well as information on conferences and inservice work.

www.childrenspoetrybookshelf.co.uk
is another useful site where children are able to publish their poems and see themselves as poets sharing their work with a wider audience.

www.englishandmedia.co.uk/publications/pubs/KS2.html
offers some interesting teaching material on poetry.

Literature and other resources

Brand, D. *Wind* in Agard, J. and Nichols, G. (eds) (1994) *A Caribbean Dozen: Poems from Caribbean Poets*. London: Walker Books Ltd.

Campbell, D. *The Pow-wow Drum* in Agard, J. and Nichols, G. (eds) (1994) *A Caribbean Dozen: Poems from Caribbean Poets*. London: Walker Books Ltd.

Carroll, L. *Jabberwocky* www.jabberwocky.com

Crapsey, A. (1878–1914) *Niagara Seen on a Night in November* in Miller, R. and Greenberg, R. (1988) *Poetry: An Introduction*. London: Macmillan Education.

Finney, E. *Haiku* (1990) in Benson, G. (ed.) *This Poem Doesn't Rhyme*. London: Puffin.

Guillen, N. (trans. G. R. Coulthard) *Sensemaya: A Chant for Killing a Snake* (www.vsoeducation.org/teacher/lesson_plans/2001/revuelta.pdf)

McGough, R. *A Good Poem* in McGough, R. (2003) *All the Best: The Selected Poems of Roger McGough.* London: Puffin.

Nichols, G. *Sun is Laughing* in Agard, J. and Nichols, G. (eds) (1994) *A Caribbean Dozen: Poems from Caribbean Poets.* London: Walker Books Ltd.

Prelvtsky, J. *The Dance of the Thirteen Skeletons* (www.masconomet.org/teachers/trevenen/prelvtsk.html)

Reeves, J. *The Snitterjipe* in Webb, K. (ed.) (1979) *I Like This Poem.* London: Puffin.

Sandburg, C. (1878–1967) *Fog* in Miller, R. and Greenberg, A. (eds) (1988) *Poetry: An Introduction.* London: Macmillan Education.

Scieszka, J. and Smith, L. (2004) *Science Verse.* New York: Viking Books.

Serrailier, I. *The Visitor* in Wilson R. (ed.) (1988) *Every Poem Tells a Story: A Collection of Stories in Verse.* London: Viking Kestrel Books.

Southey, R. *The Cataract of Lodore* www.cs.rice.edu/-ssiyer/minstrels/poems/652.html

Stephens, J. *The Wind* in Cole, W. (ed.) (1969) *Book of Nature Poems.* New York: Viking Books.

Stevenson, R. L. *Windy Nights.*

Tennyson, Alfred (1989) *The Lady of Shalott* (illus. Charles Keeping). Oxford: Oxford University Press.

Updike, J. *Winter Ocean* in Kennedy, X. J. (ed.) (1986) *Introduction to Poetry.* New York: Little, Brown and Co.

Index